# China's Local Councils

*HARVARD EAST ASIAN MONOGRAPH*

*161*

# CHINA'S LOCAL COUNCILS

## IN THE AGE OF CONSTITUTIONAL

## REFORM

## 1898–1911

Roger R. Thompson

Published by the COUNCIL ON EAST ASIAN STUDIES, HARVARD
UNIVERSITY, and distributed by HARVARD UNIVERSITY PRESS,
Cambridge (Massachusetts) and London                    1995

The Council on East Asian Studies at Harvard University publishes a monograph series and, through the Fairbank Center for East Asian Research and the Reischauer Institute of Japanese Studies, administers research projects designed to further scholarly understanding of China, Japan, Korea, Vietnam, Inner Asia, and adjacent areas.

Library of Congress Cataloging-in-Publication Data

Thompson, Roger R.
    China's local councils in the age of constitutional reform,
1898–1911 / Roger R. Thompson.
        p.   cm.—(Harvard East Asian monographs ; 161)
    Includes bibliographical references and index.
    ISBN 0-674-11973-8
    1. Local government—Law and legislation—China—History.
    I. Title.  II.  Series.
    KNQ2920.T49   1995
    342.51'09—dc20
    [345.1029]                                                94-49385
                                                              CIP

Index by Roger R. Thompson

*To Melissa Walt Thompson*

# Preface

Among the stewards of memory for China's 1911 Revolution are the political and intellectual descendants of Sun Yat-sen, the revolutionary whose imprint on Chinese history is still preserved by the branch that was headed by his protégé Chiang Kai-shek when it was transplanted to Taiwan in 1949. Chiang, once he had the reins of state power firmly in hand, had called an end to the revolution back in 1927. Some of his allies were stopped short just as they began to smash the social and economic structures of power that had survived the 1911 Revolution and the turmoil of subsequent years. When Chiang's Nationalist Party purged from its ranks persons who were also members of the Chinese Communist Party, the second branch of Sun Yat-sen's heirs diverged and reached, finally, to Beijing in 1949. At the time of Sun's death in 1925, however, both branches had been united in the battle to save China from foes foreign and domestic. With that measure of loathing reserved for allies-turned-enemies, both sides have been contesting Sun's legacy for most of the twentieth century.

These state makers have always agreed, however, on the symbolism of the Qing dynasty and the revolution that toppled it. By magnifying the failings of the imperial regime, much as any conquering dynasty in the past had explained its triumph over vanquished foes, Sun's descendants ignored their debt to state makers in Qing robes who had been searching for national wealth and international power at the turn of the twentieth century. The historical straitjacket imposed in Sun's memory began to loosen in the 1960s as a generation of American scholars led by Mary Wright joined colleagues from Taiwan, Japan, India, and Europe in challenging the orthodoxy about Sun Yat-sen and the 1911 Revolution. Their interpretations irrevocably decentered Sun as different players swirled in from both wings.

These revisionist views were challenged, in turn, as familiar sources were used to address new questions and as documents locked up in imperial archives and in libraries in the People's Republic of China became available to foreign scholars in the 1980s. The sources controlled by the Beijing branch of Sun's line were opened to researchers from abroad who already had access to less comprehensive archives and libraries in Taibei. New research agendas could be formed. The internal record of the government's actions, previously glimpsed only in published papers of Qing officials and a few documentary collections; in those Chinese newspapers, journals, and in government gazettes available outside China; and in foreign diplomatic records, could now be reconstructed from vast caches of sources. Although assiduous editorial work and extensive publication programs organized by Chinese archivists made some material available to scholars around the world, the full extant record could be consulted only in Asia.

Two members of my dissertation committee inspired me to undertake my exploration of these archival resources in 1982–1983. Jonathan Spence, who mined the Public Records Office in London for Mary Wright as she wrote her still-influential introduction to the conference volume *China in Revolution: The First Phase 1900–1913,* was among the first graduate students to use one portion of the Qing archives that became available in Taiwan in the 1960s. Beatrice Bartlett studied these imperial archives at the National Palace Museum in Taibei in the 1970s and continued her quest in Beijing after the No. 1 Historical Achives of China were opened. In 1981 she reported the first of her findings on the Qing archives held in Beijing.

Materials for a monograph on my topic, the late-Qing local self-government movement, were difficult to locate outside Asia. The publication in 1979 of *Qingmo choubei lixian dang'an shiliao* (Historical archival documents on preparations for constitutional government in the late Qing), besides presenting hundreds of pages of newly published documents, promised much more for anyone fortunate enough to be given permission to use the Qing archives in Beijing. Published accounts from China about the archives described files from the Qing Ministry of Interior, the official papers of the peripatetic and reform-minded provincial governor Zhao Erxun, and the archives of the Constitutional Commission. All of these were known and powerful attractions; unknown, prior to my arrival in Asia, was the extent of library holdings of late-Qing reports and gazettes that had been published by metropolitan, provincial, and county officials to both document and publicize their reform efforts. Libraries in Beijing, Taibei, and Tokyo proved to be rich repositories of this category of sources, only a few examples of which are available outside Asia.

This combination of both published and archival materials produced in or near the Forbidden City, provincial capitals, and county yamen made possible a study of the imperial communication network that crisscrossed China in the late Qing and the content of the messages that flowed to and from Beijing about the accomplishments and controversies associated with the planning for, and the establishing of, China's local councils. Center, province, and locality came into focus in new and stimulating ways as their interaction became apparent.

These discoveries contribute new facets to our understanding of state making and social mobilization in the late Qing that can be found in work by scholars like Mary Rankin, Keith Schoppa, and Prasenjit Duara. Together their studies draw attention to the social continuities and structural foundations that bridge the divide of 1911. Most provocative among this trio is Duara, who insists that from the perspective of villagers on the north China plain, the "state," whether it was staffed by officials of the Qing, the Republic of China, or the Japanese Imperial Army, had significant elements in common. Rankin and Schoppa emphasize social continuities in their studies of Zhejiang elites over the six decades between the suppression of the Taiping Rebellion in 1864 and the establishment of Chiang Kai-shek's regime in 1927. All three studies describe the state as it appeared from the perspective of society at local and provincial levels.

This study of the late-Qing local self-government movement, in contrast, views local society through the eyes of the state, a perspective made possible in part through the opening of the Qing archives in Beijing. These newly available sources, when complemented by rarely used library holdings of published Qing government records, provide a much fuller picture of government decision-making and actions in the years before the 1911 Revolution than the portrait drawn in previous decades when documentation on the government's role was fragmentary, widely scattered, or produced by the state's enemies.

Without the help, advice, and encouragement of many persons this study would still be buried in archival recesses. My advisor, Jonathan Spence, encouraged me to ask unanswered questions and never seemed to doubt my ability to subdue a legion of facts and place them in a coherent and significant pattern. I am especially grateful for his understanding when a short truce I called in order to work on my first book, *Report from Xunwu*, lasted much longer than expected. I also thank my archival mentor, Beatrice Bartlett, and Yü Ying-shih, both of whom served on my dissertation committee. My graduate work was enriched by studying Japanese history with John Hall and exploring the Chinese statecraft tradition and the structure of local society with Jerry Dennerline. I save for last special thanks to Parker Po-fei Huang, under whose vigilant and patient eyes I was guided through many a document of late-Qing history.

I cannot leave graduate school days behind without acknowledging my appreciation of the camaraderie provided by a genial group of fellow students in Chinese history who were at Yale when I arrived in 1979. These include Pamela Crossley, Kang Le, Richard von Glahn, and John Withers. Coming to New Haven that same year was Kandice Hauf. One could not hope for a better *tongnian* (literally, same-year), to borrow that label given to Chinese students who received their imperial civil-service examination degrees in the same year. I now know why *tongnian* ties, forged in the shared crucible of intense study and examinations, could last a lifetime.

Institutions that helped make my research years in Asia so memorable and productive include the Institute of Modern History, Academia Sinica, in Taiwan where I spent many illuminating hours talking with Chang P'eng-yüan (Zhang Pengyuan). His research on the late-Qing provincial assemblies established a template for my own work. In Beijing my unit was the Qing History Institute at People's University where I was shepherded intellectually and actually by Kong Xiangji. As we headed to the archives every weekday morning we often held a mobile seminar for two on late-Qing history while bicycling the ten miles from Beijing's northwestern suburbs to the gates of the Forbidden City. Prof. Kong also did much to buoy my spirits during the hard labor of archival study that he already knew so well.

Few scholars arrive at this point without harboring deep admiration for the curators, archivists, and staff members of many libraries and archives. The vistas these engineers of scholarly endeavor maintain provide such moments of excitement; it is a pleasure to recognize their institutions. At Yale, the Sterling Memorial Library; at Harvard, Widener Library and the Harvard-Yenching Library; at Columbia, the East Asian Library; at Princeton, the Gest Library; and at Stanford, the Chinese Collection at the Hoover Institution. In Asia I was privileged to use library resources in Taiwan at the National Palace Museum and the Institute of Modern History at Academia Sinica; in Beijing, at People's University, Beijing University, Beijing National Library, the Institute of Modern History at the Chinese Academy of Social Sciences, and the Qing History Institute; and in Tokyo at Toyo Bunko. The Qing archives granted such prominence above are held by the National Palace Museum in Taibei and the No. 1 Historical Archives of China in Beijing.

Other scholars have influenced this project in ways large and small. Mary Rankin and Philip Kuhn read and commented on drafts of this work written in the mid-1980s. Prof. Kuhn, whose research brought attention to the Qing local self-government movement, has been a steadfast supporter and much-sought-after critic. Dr. Rankin first contributed to this project in 1981 with her detailed critique on my first paper on this topic. She too has been very patient, especially so with a stubborn colleague who insisted on paying more attention to the state than to local society. I also thank Dr. Rankin, Helen Chauncey, Prasenjit Duara, and William Rowe for an invitation to join their reading group in 1988. Our sharp debates on modern Chinese history provided welcome and stimulating diversion from the rigors of teaching and the challenges of beginning a career in a new city. Finally, I thank Mark Allee, who shared with me findings from his own research that bolstered my conviction that important secrets about late imperial China remained to be discovered at the intersection of the state and local society.

Readers of *Late Imperial China, Modern China,* and *Republican China* may recognize facts and ideas first presented in essays published in 1987, 1988, and 1990. My thanks to the editors, James Lee and Charlotte Furth, Philip Huang and Richard Gunde, Roger Jeans, and their anonymous referees, all of whom influenced a work-in-progress.

I thank my colleague in the Department of History at the University of Maryland at College Park, Clifford Foust, who provided years of advice on the manuscript and helped me negotiate the path to publication. The following members of the Department were kind enough to read and respond to selected passages of the manuscript in 1991: Herman Belz, Marvin Breslow, James Gilbert, James Harris, and George Yaney. I also thank the General Research Board of the Graduate School at the University of Maryland for providing summer research stipends in 1989 and 1991.

A trio of institutions provided much-needed and appreciated space and research facilities for a wandering scholar. At the John King Fairbank Center for East Asian Research at Harvard University, which awarded me a postdoctoral fellowship in 1986–1987, I completed a revision of my doctoral dissertation. Roderick MacFarquhar, the center's director, was a gracious host who helped me foster new ties in a spirited intellectual community. Nearby at the Massachusetts Institute of Technology, one member of this community, Peter Perdue, opened doors in the summer of 1991. Finally, I thank Nicholas Lardy, Director of the Henry M. Jackson School of International Studies at the University of Washington, for providing an office in which I finished this work in 1993.

I acknowledge many funding agencies for their support. Dissertation research in Asia accomplished in 1982–1984 was made possible by a grant from the International Doctoral Research Fellowship Program for China of the Social Science Research Council and the American Council of Learned Societies. Funds for the Program were provided by the Ford Foundation, the National Endowment for the Humanities, and the Andrew W. Mellon Foundation. The financial and administrative support provided by the Committee on Scholarly Communication with the People's Republic of China for doctoral research carried out in China in 1983 was indispensable. The dissertation was written at Yale in 1984–1985 with support from a Mrs. Giles Whiting Foundation Fellowship in the Humanities. Additional research was assisted by a grant from the Joint Committee on Chinese Studies of the American Council of Learned Societies and the Social Science Research Council, with funds provided by the Andrew W. Mellon Foundation, in 1985–1986.

I am indebted to my editor at Harvard's Council on East Asian Studies, Katherine Keenum, for her contributions of editorial acumen and intellectual energy. Dr. Keenum's challenge, outlined in September 1992, framed the final revision of the manuscript. I also thank my copyeditor, Nancy Hearst, and Darlene King, who converted the entire manuscript from one word-processing program to another and also deciphered my longhand while typing new material for me at the University of Maryland in 1990–1991.

I dedicate this book to my wife, Melissa, who endured with grace my seemingly endless quest to shape this material into a book. I shall always be grateful for the unspoken banishment of "local self-government" after it had stayed too long, for that allowed to blossom instead many absorbing topics that Melissa brought home from her world of Chinese art. Welcome too were Melissa's gentle reminders of the joys, mysteries, and wonders of life that will always remain beyond the realm of history.

# Contents

# Contents

# Table

# Author's Note on Conventions for Romanizations and Characters

In order to reduce the number of Chinese characters needed in the Character List or Select Bibliography, I have observed the following conventions. In the text, I have given only the English translation for law schools *(fazheng xuetang)* and self-government bureaus *(zizhi ju)*, preparation offices *(choubanchu)*, and schools *(yanjiusuo)* that were established in accordance with directions from Beijing. Other institutions have been glossed in pinyin; characters for these are provided in the character list. Manuscripts that are cited in either the text or endnotes appear in the character list but are not listed in the bibliography. Published works in Chinese or Japanese that are cited in the notes only once are omitted from the bibliography, but a translation and full bibliographical data are supplied in the notes on the assumption that this information will allow readers to locate the items.

# China's Local Councils

INTRODUCTION

# The Idea of Local Self-Government in the Age of Revolution

As the twentieth century began, the Chinese government, through administrative, political, and educational reforms, tried to transform the emperor's subjects into a constitutional monarch's citizens. Among its many programs, the one styled local self-government *(difang zizhi)* affected the most people. It included plans for schools where select gentrymen and degree-holders learned about prescriptions for new roles in administration and provisions for local council elections that were outlined in regulations promulgated in 1909–1910. Beijing had scheduled elections for 1912–1914 in all subprovincial jurisdictions, but impatient local elites and tense provincial officials refused to wait. By October 1911, when a successful army mutiny in central China sparked a series of declarations of independence from most provincial capitals, government agencies had reported the establishment of about five thousand councils throughout China.

China's last emperor abdicated in February 1912, but two years passed before Yuan Shikai, president of the Republic of China, finally decided, in league with his provincial governors, that the councils were dispensable. This administrative centralizer, who desperately wanted China to be a powerful presence in Asia, abandoned the plan he helped create. In February 1914 Yuan dropped the curtains on the Qing dynasty's local self-government program. He was cheered by provincial officials who were nettled by local councillors controlling their own jurisdictions, and, more important, scarce tax revenues. A new set of regulations that was promulgated in December 1914 was no more successful in achieving a strong connection between the central government and local society.[1]

What was the promise of local self-government and why had it failed? Why had Qing officials severed the link between self-government policy and constitutional reform? Why were influential rural elites barred from voting? Why did the familiar practices of local corporatism, when influenced by new Western-style central-government ministries, factionalize urban elites? To what extent did the council election process exacerbate and institutionalize this trend? Who was the audience for the reform? How local is local self-government when planned by metropolitan bureaucrats?

Some answers are to be found in a study of the late-Qing local self-government movement. To turn subjects into citizens has daunted many reformers, but China's challenge could easily overwhelm. In a country of 400,000,000 people buffeted by waves of domestic and international crises, the reformers' task was complicated by the chasm between the handful of rulers and those they ruled, especially the vast majority of Chinese who lived in the countryside. How does a relatively small government communicate its vision in such a country without the aid of mass media? How can local initiatives be encouraged without jeopardizing the center's influence? How should conflicts between state activism and elite activism be mediated?

The imperial regulations promulgated in January 1909 inspired elites in many regions of China, but activists elsewhere had been trying new approaches, especially after 1905, to organizing and managing local affairs. A battle was joined. At issue was the definition of a locality. How should it be connected to the center? Who should discuss public issues? Who drafts regulations? Dozens of groups of elite activists answered these questions at the turn of the twentieth century, but Beijing delayed its definitive response until 1909. The contenders were often motivated by a common cause and like inspirations, but propinquity to provincial offices as well as to Beijing ministries influenced how authoritarians and democrats in and out of government thought and acted.

Urban China, typified by cities like Suzhou, Beijing, and Jilin city, was the scene for many of the first elite-led initiatives. The Beijing efforts spoke to municipal concerns, but those in the other two cities were conceived as the foundation for constitutional government. Returned students from Japan planned ways to unite rural and urban elites. The records of the Suzhou and Jilin city self-government societies were written by men reaching beyond city walls into the countryside. These urban-based elite activists used the word *local* to emphasize their autonomy from provincial administration, but this appropriation was challenged in turn by leaders in market towns and villages. At first the word was used simply to distinguish national *(guojia)* from local *(difang;* i.e., taxes for provincial use); but the struggle to control this label was significant, for imperial rhetoric proclaimed local self-government to be the foundation of a constitutional government that would move China out of an autocratic and anachronistic age.[2]

The term *local self-government* soon was burdened with a surfeit of definitions. The imperial formulation reflected the influence of returned students who drew on their Japan experience while playing important roles in the Qing bureaucracy in national, provincial, and local offices. For them "local self-government" signified the first few levels in a pyramid of elected assemblies whose topmost reaches included a parliament to whom a "responsible cabinet" would answer. This cabinet, in turn, would share executive power with a constitutional monarch. But the distance between top and bottom was great and even among returned students, or among people conversant with these new ideas, there were those who distrusted local leaders and disdained their politics as much as did Yamagata Aritomo, one architect of the Japanese structure of local self-government. Sometimes this prejudice was justified, especially when "local self-government" was snatched by men who were unaware of its Japanese origins but still used the new vocabulary. They might simply insert "self-government" *(zizhi)* in the titles of their old organizations. This manuever by a rural militia in Manchuria, for example, shocked a returned student who was the local prefect. Influential men sometimes just borrowed titles of institutions described in imperial regulations in order to add cachet to their gangs of local bullies. Reports from south China told of a local despot with overseas experience who faked a local council by selling seats to friends. Old cliques could slyly slip into new clothes.

But ignorance and corruption did not always blight the reforms. Imperially mandated local councils were as evanescent as a night-blooming cereus, to use a popular Chinese expression applied to the reforms, but the preparations for and establishment of these councils contributed to new Chinese definitions of the polity and the meaning of citizenship and democracy. Many returned students and their colleagues had prepared messages for rural audiences and some had explained to county and rural elites as well as ordinary peasants what a citizen was, what voting and representation meant in a constitutional monarchy, and what local councils should do. Their message could be appropriated and reduced to familiar terms, debased, or ignored, but it still heralded the new.

Propagandists like Liang Qichao and Kang Youwei and many of the students they influenced insisted that China needed "new citizens" who participated in the political life of the country. This vision began to be realized in 1909. The individual person was enfranchised in order to participate as a citizen in a revitalized political order. But the inspiring vision only fitfully became substantial, for interpretations varied and threatened interests dug in. One of the most respected reform-minded officials in the late Qing, Zhang Zhidong, sharply criticized the young men drafting electoral regulations in 1908, especially the returned students who had borrowed the Japanese neologism *kōmin* (Ch.: *gongmin*) to designate those with the right to vote. Zhang, who headed this government drafting committee, insisted that *xuanmin* (selector), a compound that resonated in the minds of the millions of men who had participated in the state-run civil-service examination system, be used.[3] Zhang rejected outright the Japanese loanword, but his point was more subtle: Now the Chinese regulations would avert using "public" *(gong)* in describing the enfranchised.

The debate had only begun. The contested meaning of words to cover concepts like "the people," "citizens," "rights," and "freedom" fuelled discussions that never ended. The meanings for such words are especially numerous during unsettled and dangerous passages for a country. China's own was influenced by many histories: England in the time of Cromwell, revolutionary tribulations in the United States and France in the eighteenth century, and the creation of Germany and Japan a century later. China's turn came after decades of humiliations capped by the trauma of a losing war with Japan in 1894–1895.

The consequences of this latest defeat were grave as China was forced to cede control of the island province of Taiwan and Japan almost wrested away the strategic Liaodong peninsula on the mainland in Manchuria. Western powers started to scramble for concessions, mark spheres of influence, and sign contracts to dig mines and build railroads. By 1897 histrionic Chinese were crying out that their country was in danger of being carved up like a melon while fretful and gleeful Westerners alike might have missed the irony Lord Beresford intended in entitling his topical survey, published in 1899, *The Break-up of China*. In the midst of this crisis the Hunan reform movement in central China took root. Its origins can be traced to the treaty port of Canton in the southern province of Guangdong, where rising stars like Kang Youwei and Liang Qichao, influenced in part by Western commercial and missionary interests long associated with this gateway, tried to blend the best of East and West. Their zealousness was encouraged by Hunan governor Chen Baozhen. Some of the patriotic Hunanese who had become convinced that Beijing was neither able nor willing to defend their province from foreign encroachers were heartened when Chen invited Liang and Huang Zunxian, another Guangdong native, to come to Changsha in 1897. They soon began to establish schools with a Sino-Western curriculum, give lectures to elite groups, help form government bureaus, publish a journal, and create a network of local study societies.

Huang Zunxian, unlike Liang Qichao and most reformers in late-nineteenth-century China, was able to convey to his students in

Changsha firsthand knowledge of the foreigners who threatened Hunan. He could have lectured from his recently-published book, the extensive (500,000 characters), pathbreaking, and influential *Riben guozhi* (A history of Japan) that he had begun writing midway through his tenure at the Chinese legation in Tokyo in 1877–1882. Drawing on a wide range of primary and secondary sources, Huang had completed a draft in 1882, when he was posted to the consulate in San Francisco. Upon Huang's return to China in August 1885, he turned down several official posts in order to continue working on his manuscript, which he finished two years later. Copies were sent to the Chinese Foreign Office (Zongli yamen), Yuan Shikai's mentor Li Hongzhang, and Zhang Zhidong. But *A History of Japan* remained unpublished until Japan's shocking military victories over China had created a crisis of confidence. A Canton edition appeared in 1895. And in 1898, besides Huang's presence and influence in Hunan, his book's influence reached the Forbidden City when it was presented to the Guangxu Emperor by a close advisor, Weng Tonghe, on 14 February 1898.[4]

A week later Huang himself took his message to an elite audience of three hundred people at the opening session of the Nanxue hui (lit., Southern Study Society) in Changsha. Although his speech included terms such as *zizhi* that associates like Liang might gloss as "self-government," Huang's rhetorical stance was Confucian. He told his listeners to both "cultivate themselves" *(zizhi qishen)* and to "attend *(zizhi)* to local affairs *(xiang)*."[5] Huang's usages echoed descriptions of elite activism that had appeared in the Shanghai press in the 1870s as well as venerable Neo-Confucian philosophy dating to at least the Ming dynasty.[6] He did not mention Japanese-style "self-government," although he had described it in his book.

But Huang's listeners were interested in far more than self-cultivation and local activism. The organizers of the Nanxue hui thought their "study" was preparing them for new political and administrative responsibilities. Participants argued that "every Western nation has a senate and a house of representatives which discuss political matters publicly. Under our political system, people dare not interfere with political matters. However, as our meetings at the prefecture, county, city, and village level elect members, our study society already emulates the Western system."[7]

The Hunan Spring proved to be shortlived. The description of Western institutions and values by Huang Zunxian and the iconoclastic reinterpretation of Confucian texts by Liang Qichao soon alarmed some members of the Hunanese gentry. Liang and his associates were attacked on intellectual, moral, and pedagogical grounds by Hunanese gentrymen vexed by ideas like democracy *(minzhu)*, people's rights *(minquan)*, and equality *(pingdeng)*.[8] The center of reform consequently shifted to Beijing as Liang and Hunanese students like Tan Sitong left for the capital, where they were joined by Kang Youwei. The Guangxu Emperor, who had been presented Huang's book earlier in the year and had heard murmurings of reform when key advisors like Weng Tonghe and Sun Jianai were nearby, was primed. Together, these disparate voices persuaded the young emperor to authorize a new social and administrative blueprint for China.[9] But the summertime reforms of 1898 were soon overturned by the emperor's aunt, the strong-willed Empress Dowager, Cixi, whose coup in September 1898 curbed her nephew and sent Kang and Liang fleeing to Japan. Others were not so lucky; six associates (including Kang's brother and Tan Sitong) were captured by government authorities and executed at month's end.

Nevertheless, the ideas bandied about in Changsha and Beijing in 1898 were not so easily extinguished. Even exile failed to prevent Kang Youwei and Liang Qichao from publicizing their cause. Liang's record of the events of 1897–1898, *Wuxu zhengbian ji* (An account of the coup in 1898), was soon published and was available in China.[10] Readers throughout China could learn, for example, what Huang Zunxian had told the Nanxue hui back in 1898.

The meanings attached to words like *zizhi* began to multiply. Huang Zunxian had meant self-cultivation or local activism and Kang Youwei had told the emperor how Western powers had jurisdiction *(zizhi)* over their own people in China because of their extraterritorial rights,[11] but in 1902 the term more often referred to the kind of local administrative reforms implemented by the Japanese in the 1870s and 1880s. Kang Youwei helped fix this new meaning with his assessment of these programs in "Gongmin zizhi" (Citizen self-government), one of a series of essays on reform he published in *Xinmin congbao* (New people's miscellany) in 1902–1903.[12]

Many propagandists at the beginning of the twentieth century stressed this latter definition. For example, in the student journal *Jiangsu*, published in Tokyo, an article appearing in 1903 by one Nai Xuan explained self-government. Nai argued that it was needed in places beyond the reach of central authority, where it formed a part, but not an independent part, of national administration. Nai emphasized the difference between autonomy *(zizhu)* and self-government *(zizhi)* and used the English words in his article: autonomy is related to feudal political systems; self-government is part of a system of centralized rule. Another essayist, whose work appeared in the Japan-based journal *Zhejiang chao* (Zhejiang tide) traced the development and significance of the ideas in a discussion about the influence of the Prussian scholar Rudolf Gneist, the Japanese reforms, the situation in China, and the role of the gentry.[13]

Ominously, however, other Chinese in Japan preferred agitation to explication, especially those who had been forced to leave Changsha after the crackdown in 1898. Young Hunanese students in Japan began to dream of a province that would be more than self-governing. Yang Dusheng's famous tract *Xin Hunan* (New Hunan), published in Japan in 1903, called for Hunanese patriots to take over the provincial government and declare independence from Beijing. After seceding from China, Yang urged, young Hunanese should establish an independent base from which would emerge a new China. Not all of Yang's classmates at Waseda University in Tokyo were so radical, but his voice was one of the loudest.[14]

The student journals published in Japan were distributed, often clandestinely, in China. But by 1905 the mainland press began explaining terms like *independence* and *self-government*. For example, in the Shanghai newspaper *Nanfang ribao* an author called for local self-government to be established in China as the foundation for constitutional government. Elections, public discussion *(gongyi)*, and national parliaments were central topics.[15]

But even though *zizhi* was becoming associated with new forms of government, it could still refer to familiar ideas and institutions. The provincial governor Zhao Erxun, for example, had described his modest reforms in local administration as an example of encouraging people to practice "self-government" in a memorial he submitted in November 1902. Zhao's memorial was quoted in *Zhengyi tongbao*, a journal of current affairs published in Shanghai that was distributed throughout the empire.[16] A similar use can be found in drafts of essays, probably written in 1903, by the Changsha native Zeng Qingbang for publication in the trimonthly vernacular gazette *Hunan tongsu yanshuobao*. In one essay Zeng used examples from Europe as he portrayed local self-government as a fundamental attribute of a strong and respected country. Zeng said that the rural communities that attracted Zhao Erxun's attention were a form of local self-government. In another essay, Zeng encouraged these communities to organize local militias *(tuanlian)*. Political reform was less important than revitalizing local militias to defend China against foreign attacks.[17]

The use of familiar institutions like local militias and mutual security groups *(baojia)* to explain the meaning of self-government was related to the similar use of statecraft ideas by Zhao Erxun when describing his Shanxi reforms. Like Huang Zunxian, Zhao emphasized the importance and legitimacy of local initiatives and pointed to thoughtful justifications provided by early-Qing thinkers like Gu Yanwu and late-Qing essayists such as Feng Guifen, whose posthumous collection of statecraft essays had been printed for distribution and comment to high officials by the command of the Guangxu Emperor on 17 July 1898.[18] Both Gu and Feng emphasized the need for local leaders to attend to local affairs.[19] These ideas, which were part of the so-called statecraft *(jingshi)* tradition, were seized by advocates of constitutionalism who were pressing for local self-government. They claimed precedents could be found in Chinese history as well as in classical texts from the age of Confucius. For example, in an article in the national digest *Dongfang zazhi*, published in 1906, ideas about local self-government were explained in terms of an essay Gu Yanwu had written over two hundred years earlier. Gu, in this plea for reform, had himself drawn on ancient texts like the

*Zhouli* (Rites of Zhou).[20] This obsession with antecedents led to portrayals of familiar theories of local administrative reform as well as of extant institutions for local security as indigenous versions of local self-government.

Various meanings were being attached to the term: Neo-Confucian self-cultivation; local elites attending to local affairs; a way to protect communities from intrusive state power; a means by which localities could be integrated with the state, either through new bureaucratic positions filled by local persons or by the electoral processes of a constitutional state; or a way to ensure local security. Local self-government, as a concept, was almost too accommodating.

The Chinese attempt to grapple with the meaning of terms like *self-government* was no less momentous or contested than other efforts throughout the long century of revolution, reform, and counterrevolution that began in the American colonies in 1775. The United States, France, England, Germany, Russia, and Japan contributed to the debate before China joined in. For Thomas Jefferson, one of the first theorists to use self-government in a political sense, the reference was limited initially to the rights of state governments vis-à-vis the federal government. By 1820, twenty-two years later, Jefferson had extended the meaning to refer to the "generation of 1776" and their attempt to "acquire self-government and happiness" in the struggle for independence.[21] Jefferson's later equation of independence, self-government, and sovereignty was used far less in the nineteenth century than his first, which described the relationship between different governmental jurisdictions in one country. The lexical lineage that was more concerned with power relationships within a state was the one, however, that attracted the attention of governments in Asia. They looked, for example, to Prussia's experience in the early nineteenth century.

King Friedrich Wilhelm III, shocked by the virtual collapse of the Prussian state during the Napoleonic wars, invited Karl vom Stein to pursue a wide-ranging reform agenda during a hectic fourteen-month period in 1807–1808. One of these reforms was defined by a 208-article regulation for reorganizing municipal government that was drafted during the summer and fall of 1808 and approved in November. Stein, who had planned similar regulations for rural areas and for the establishment of a parliament, was soon forced from office, but subsequent Prussian attempts at local administrative reform would reflect his influence.

English approaches to local administration, particularly what Stein took to be the relatively light hand of the state in local affairs, had intrigued him during his travels in England in 1786–1787. As a protégé, colleague, and friend of Stein, Ludwig von Vincke, wrote in 1815: "[I]t relegates a great mass of business to the inhabitants, and leaves them to the exercise of their own judgment and energy." Elsewhere Vincke argued: "The Home Secretary [in England] only corresponds with the (local) authorities in extraordinary emergencies, such as rioting. . . . [He] exercises absolutely no regular control over the Justices of the Peace."[22] German interest in the English model continued, especially in the researches and writings of the eminent Prussian scholar, jurist, and politician Rudolf Gneist. Like Stein's pupil Vincke, Gneist emphasized the role played by justices of the peace, but in a very different fashion. Gneist's interpretation of English local government and his role in Prussian and German reforms at midcentury became relevant to affairs in Asia when his student, Albert Mosse, travelled to Japan and advised officials in 1886–1887 as they drafted regulations for local administration.

On the Continent, and indirectly in Asia, it was Gneist who popularized the term *self-government,* which he often left in English in his writings. He granted that the term was not used by the English in the eighteenth century, but he idealized this period as an era of "magisterial self-government" that was embodied in the justice of the peace. Appointed by a royal commission of peace, justices were "the life and soul of the district administration" according to Gneist.[23] He may well have borrowed the term *self-government* from the English barrister and polemicist J. Toulmin Smith, whose decentralist campaign in the 1850s helped doom the General Board of Health. The board, a centralized authority created by an Act of Parliament in 1848, had been directed to address malodorous and dangerous conditions plaguing English cities. Such a board was needed, according to one proponent, because of the notorious and "utter failure of the system of local self-government for sanitary purposes."[24]

But this pejorative and parochial use was reversed by Toulmin Smith, whose book titles, while ponderous, capture the decentralist pith of his work. In less than a decade he published *Government by Commissions Illegal and Pernicious: The Nature and Effects of all Commissions of Inquiry and other Crown-appointed Commissions: The Constitutional Principles of Taxation; and the Rights, Duties, and Importance of Local Self-government* (1849), *Local Self-government and Centralization: The Characteristics of Each; and its Practical Tendencies, as affecting Social, Moral, and Political Welfare and Progress* (1851), and *Local Self-government Un-mystified: A Vindication of Common Sense, Human Nature, and Practical Improvement, against the Manifesto of Centralism Put Forth at the Social Science Association, 1857* (1857). The summation of Smith's scholarly work, which was sprinkled throughout these polemical essays, was *The Parish* (1854), a work cited by Gneist. But the Prussian scholar used Toulmin Smith's language more than his ideas, for Gneist was convinced a well-ordered state needed a central authority with a strong presence in local affairs.

Gneist was not the only political observer on the Continent at midcentury to try to bring some meaning to "self-government." Alexis de Tocqueville left untranslated the English phrase "self-government" in the following passage, translated from the French, in *The Old Regime and the French Revolution* (1856): "I am satisfied that only a government which relied wholly on its own strength, and invariably dealt with individuals singly, as that of the old régime did, could have maintained the ridiculous and insane inequality which existed at the time of the Revolution. The least touch of self-government would have soon altered or destroyed it." This was a rare use by Tocqueville of the still-novel term. More often, in a manner reminiscent of Jefferson's first use, Tocqueville wrote about liberties exercised by national, provincial, and local groups (*libertés provinciales, liberté nationale,* or *libertés locales*).[25]

So even before "self-government" was exported from Europe to

Asia it was used contrarily. Toulmin Smith, as befits a founder of the Anti-Centralisation Union, was a vehement foe of central power. At the same time a German exiled in London during Smith's heyday, Lothar Bucher, published a book in German in 1855 that included a chapter entitled "Selfgovernment, Zentralisation". While paying homage to Toulmin Smith's *Local Self-government and Centralisation*, Bucher argued the opposite position. Bucher, who would become the chief aide to Bismarck in 1864, was shedding liberal inclinations in the 1850s and becoming a foe of parliamentary government. But in one liberal-inclined passage he explained that self-government had to be more than a centrally-devised program that left insignificant administrative affairs in the hands of local people. Instead, he argued that a true understanding and implementation of self-government required a political revolution in thinking about the relationship between locality and state. Bucher went on to dispute Toulmin Smith, arguing that establishing self-government and centralizing administration were not precisely antithetical.[26]

Bucher's analysis of England influenced Gneist, who also decried the growth of representative governments in the nineteenth century. Gneist would not even use the word *self-government* in his description of local electoral and administrative reforms that were part of this process, since they only encouraged, he thought, parochialism and selfishness. Instead he called this false *Selbstverwaltung* (self-government or self-administration). Gneist contrasted "magisterial self-government" *(obrigkeitliche Selbstverwaltung)* with the economic or commercial (or representative) self-government *(wirtschaftliche Selbstverwaltung)* of the vote-crazed nineteenth century. For Gneist magisterial self-government was the beginning and end of what he meant by self-government[27] and sometimes in his German texts he even contrasted eighteenth-century "self-government" with the false nineteenth-century "Selbstverwaltung."[28]

These theoretical flourishes did not appear in the regulations Gneist's student Mosse helped draft in Tokyo in 1886–1887 that set the tone for Japanese local administration until 1947. Yamagata Aritomo, who had invited Mosse to participate in the drafting process, was convinced that earlier drafts would have failed to persuade

Western countries that Japan had Westernized enough to justify the renegotiation of the unequal treaties that had granted them extraterritoriality and tariff-setting rights.

The Prussian system, which still bore the influence of Stein's 1808 regulations, was adapted by the Japanese. Eventually described as institutions of "local self-government" *(chihō jichi)*, councils elected by Japanese at the prefectural and local level were designed to serve as depoliticized venues for local administration in the spirit of Gneist's "magisterial self-government." Yamagata Aritomo emphasized the importance of the state, insisted that local administrative reforms precede national constitutional reforms, argued that local government should be in the hands of impartial bureaucrats, and stressed a concept of citizenship that put duties ahead of rights. The Japanese regulations that so influenced Chinese policy makers were promulgated in 1888 and 1890.[29]

But however authoritarian the Japan model appeared, it advanced the international debate on local self-government, for it associated these local reforms with the larger program of establishing a constitutional government. This elaboration of "local self-government," which linked individual citizenship, local administrative reform, and the establishment of constitutional government, went far beyond the historical experience Continental theorists had pointed to. In the England of the Magna Carta of 1215, for example, barons forced King John to recognize only the "ancient liberties and free customs" of London and other cities. Neither individual persons nor rural populations mattered much. Even in the United States, where one of the first uses of *self-government* in political discourse can be found, the term remained a reference to intragovernmental relations throughout the nineteenth century. Although scholars eventually began to equate local self-government with individual liberty, as did Amasa Eaton in 1900 when he wrote that local self-government was "part of the unwritten constitution, one of the common law rights brought over from England by our ancestors and never surrendered,"[30] the point of contention in the United States during the latter half of the nineteenth century was the relationship between local municipalities and state governments.[31] There was little or none of the concern, becoming paramount in Asia, about the relationship between citizens and the state as mediated by local self-government institutions.[32]

By 1905 "self-government" was, East and West, overburdened with meaning. Action in China did not strip away any of its contradictory nuances, but the local self-government movement left traces numerous enough to allow reconstruction of its history up to the end of the dynasty. Thought led to action as more and more persons outside a small circle of government officials, expatriates, and returned students began to pay attention.

In the summer of 1905 Japanese and Russian troops had fought to a draw in their struggle for supremacy in Manchuria, the strategic corner of the Eurasian landmass. The imperial court in Beijing, seeing its homeland overrun by foreign troops, called for advice from senior government officials and made three important decisions: to dispatch two high-level government delegations on worldwide tours to study the governments and societies of Japan, the United States, and several European nations; to conduct a special palace examination in the Forbidden City of men who had studied a Western curriculum in Japan in their specialities; and to abolish the time-honored civil-service examination system.

The government might have preferred more dramatic and direct action, but few officials thought China could dislodge Russia and Japan from Manchuria. Instead, a cautious strategy that appeared to postpone triumph to a distant future was put on the table. But a second look reveals policies that were actually quite audacious. The same government that shrank from challenging formidable armies of Japanese and Russian soldiers on fields of battle in Manchuria was now trying to transform an educational system and a mindset that had brought wealth, power, and prestige to a lucky few and filled the heads of millions more men with dreams that seldom died. An assault on foreign armies armed to the teeth would have been less perilous.

The political landscape was remade. Not only were Qing officials finally able to express openly their interest in Western-style constitutionalism, but the entire government was now committed to awarding degrees to students who had studied in Japan in order to facilitate their entry into public service. The subsequent abolition of the examination system brought even more prominence to the so-called Western learning. Although degrees would still be granted in a transitional period, they went only to candidates who had mastered a Sino-Western curriculum taught in new-style schools. At the highest levels of education, however, there were few of these schools in China; Japan consequently attracted the ambitious. For those left behind the future was bleak; years of study of Confucian classics while in pursuit of degrees granted after competitive exams at the prefectural *(shengyuan)*, provincial *(juren)*, and metropolitan *(jinshi)* levels had prepared them for a world that was no more.[33]

The end of the examination system also had an impact on politics, since Confucian knowledge and administrative power often went hand in hand in late imperial Chinese society. The most successful candidates, those who won the *jinshi* degree in Beijing, were given the best posts among the approximately 20,000 slots in the Chinese bureaucracy, which stretched from Beijing to remote county seats. Even *juren* were qualified to fill some of these positions, but *shengyuan* status counted for little beyond one's home county, of which there were about 1,700.[34] Recipients of any one of several lower degrees could, however, be bright lights in the constellation of non-statutory administrative jobs available at home. These local notables were joined by *jiansheng*, men who usually had purchased this degree after first receiving a honorary *tongsheng* degree from their local magistrate in recognition of passing a non-competitive qualifying exam. These groups of *shengyuan* and *jiansheng*, the so-called *sheng-jian* stratum, were fixtures in the field of unofficial administration that local magistrates relied upon but were invisible, by design, to Beijing. Just below the *shengjian* was the largest group—about 1,000 to 1,500 per county by one estimate—who participated each time in the qualifying round of the examination system. These students, still commoners, were called *tongsheng*.[35]

When the examination system was abolished in 1905, *tongsheng* and *shengyuan* lacked even the glimmer of hope possessed by *jian-sheng, juren,* and *jinshi,* who at least had a small chance to gain office without mastering the new Sino-Western curriculum. A new opportunity for *shengyuan,* and an additional one for *jiansheng,* appeared on the horizon, however, shortly after the old path that led to Beijing was blocked. When the government-mandated local self-government councils began to be elected in 1909, one could find on lists of council members the names of many *shengyuan* and *jiansheng.* But others were not so lucky, especially *tongsheng* and other influential commoners residing in the countryside. This elite stratum of commoners, which could include, to use labels of a succeeding era, rich peasants and small landlords, was ignored in the Qing government's local self-government policy. But this had not always been the case, for earlier efforts, official and unofficial alike, had sought to include this group in their plans.

For example, Shanxi governor Zhao Erxun targeted them in one of his reforms of 1902–1903. Zhao, whose Shanxi reform was precursory, was one of two provincial officials (Yuan Shikai was the other) directed by the court in 1906 to establish prototypes designed to extend government administration into the countryside. The contrast between the way Zhao planned to court *shengyuan, jiansheng,* and influential commoners like *tongsheng* with the manner in which the central government cast the last group aside shows both the complexities of elite structures and the danger of ignoring any one section. For Zhao Erxun and others, this realm beyond the reach of officials was often seen as the world of self-government, which was contrasted to the world of bureaucrats (*guanzhi;* lit., official rule) and the administrative system (*guanzhi,* lit., official system) bounded by the walls of government compounds known as yamen.[36]

This dichotomy paralleled the old statecraft distinction between centralized bureaucratic monarchical rule (*junxian*) and feudalism (*fengjian*). Late-nineteenth-century statecraft theorists like Feng Guifen had hoped that their reform proposals would imbue the centralized monarchy with the positive aspects of feudalism. Power was not to be completely devolved, but these thinkers wanted the state to encourage local development with a light hand. This was precisely the spirit Huang Zunxian displayed in Hunan in 1898 and Zhao Erxun brought to Shanxi in 1902. They were not alone; but when the age of constitutionalism dawned in China in 1905, the terms of debate were changed. The old ways and thoughts had to be abandoned. China's new citizens, shaped from the passive and yielding clay of imperial subjects, would begin their metamorphosis with firsthand political experience at home. The process was maintained in provincial capitals, where assemblymen continued to hone their skills. Finally, the best representatives were sent to Beijing by an electorate thoroughly familiar with ideas like representation and practices like elections. Many activists in and out of government argued, then, that local self-government was the foundation of constitutional government. China's old subjects would become its new citizens.

The frantic search for patriotic citizens that typified the Qing dynasty in its final days, when numerous councils and assemblies were established, proved to be deeply flawed by an extremely restricted understanding of elite society. But earlier, in tense but slightly calmer times, a less ambitious but very illuminating attempt was made to reach out to rural China and bring a far broader range of its most respected subjects into a new relationship with the state. In the minds of some people back in the summer of 1905, the answer to China's crisis had been found as much in Zhao Erxun's Shanxi reform model of 1902–1903 as in foreign models. Paradoxically, Zhao's authoritarian program, which revealed greater concern for institutional reform than finding citizens, was far more attentive to the complexity of local society than most of the programs drafted in Beijing in later years. Zhao was convinced that China's only hope was to bring rural elites into new structures of power that reached to Beijing. He sought flesh-and-blood subjects that rarely entered into the calculations of the returned students who would begin to dominate policy-making in Beijing in 1907. These returned students and their patrons broke the promise of local self-government and provided common cause to a new army made up of abandoned men whose lifelong dreams of winning Beijing's imperial favor had vanished overnight. Beijing, by ignoring their existence, had created formidable enemies.

PART ONE

*Setting the Scene, 1902–1906*

# ONE

# Zhao Erxun's Search for Local Leaders in Shanxi

Zhao Erxun was the first Qing governor to describe his reform programs as means to foster local self-government. Yuan Shikai, who was yoked with Zhao in the court's 1906 order to conduct experiments in local administration in Zhili and Manchuria, publicized Zhao's attempt in 1902–1903 to change the relationship between local communities in Shanxi and the state.[1] Being first is not the reason, however, for bringing attention to Zhao's long-forgotten reform program in Shanxi. These reforms are noteworthy for their attempt to illuminate rural elites, the importance placed on trying to change the way officials dealt with local communities, and the effort to blend current practice, past precedent, and new ideas from Japan and the West. Unlike countless officials and activists who would chant "local self-government is the foundation of constitutional government" as if it were a mantra, Zhao's well-considered program and cautious use of self-government as a descriptive category in the pre-1906 period shows one way in which critical problems in local administration were approached before the age of constitutionalism.

The venue for Zhao's innovations was Shanxi, an inland province in north China far from the Western-influenced treaty ports scattered along China's coast and major navigable waterways. The province had just witnessed or played a part in several headline events. In 1900 her people saw the Empress Dowager, the Guangxu Emperor, and the rest of the imperial entourage who had fled the capital when the Allied invasion of China reached Beijing. Moreover, the people of Shanxi gained notoriety when news of the violent deaths in the province of nearly two hundred Western missionaries and family members and thousands of Chinese Christians in that terrible year became known. The Allies demanded, and received, retribution. Yuxian, the Shanxi governor who had been cashiered late in 1900, was castigated as the butcher of Shanxi; Western demands for revenge were finally satisfied when reports of his execution in Lanzhou, where he had been exiled, were received. A few persons in Shanxi had already paid with their lives, but most Shanxi inhabitants became subject to a decade-long burden of a 500,000-tael (ounces of silver) indemnity that was used to establish a Sino-Western university in the provincial capital of Taiyuan. This agreement was reached by Cen Chunxuan, who replaced the disgraced Yuxian, and Westerners led by the eminent missionary and advisor Timothy Richard.[2]

Zhao Erxun became the financial commissioner in Cen's provincial yamen on 16 May 1902. Second in command to Cen, Zhao was formally appointed acting governor on 5 August 1902, a month after his superior was transferred. With this assignment Zhao continued his methodical climb up the ladder of Chinese officialdom. He had first won notice in 1874 with the receipt of the highest civil service examination degree (*jinshi*) at the age of thirty and gained a coveted post in the prestigious Hanlin Academy in Beijing. Zhao Erxun became a member of the Censorate, the "eyes and ears" of the emperor, in 1882 and five years later he received his first provincial post. Tours in Guizhou, Anhui, and Shaanxi preceded his Shanxi service.[3] Zhao was in charge only five months, but this was more than enough time to manifest his vision and energy.

Zhao's Shanxi remained deeply troubled as the repercussions of the violence of 1900 continued. Besides the new tax burden placed on Shanxi's peasants, the countryside was scourged by demobilized soldiers and bandits according to monthly reports from county magistrates.[4] Zhao wrote: "Recently, incessant disorder has led to famine, and everything is lacking. Repeated taxations have caused the livelihood of the people to crumble."[5] The dozens of cases of local disorder included endemic armed conflicts over water rights along the Fen River, which bisected the province, and tax protests in two counties in southern Shanxi.[6] The people of Shanxi, reportedly once virtuous and timid *(liangnuo)*, were now ruthless and cruel *(diaohan)*.[7]

The new governor, the fourth in three years, was convinced that the debacle of 1900 was rooted in the government's blindness and indifference. Magistrates, provincial officials, and Beijing bureaucrats had been unaware of the tinderbox that was Shanxi, Zhao argued, because of a breakdown in communication between villages and county yamen.[8] The mutual security network *(baojia)* had failed and Zhao redirected attention to it with a provincial order in October 1902 that highlighted the rewards that would be given to competent reeves.[9] Seldom did these men possess much stature and influence and usually they were armed with little more than words and hope; Zhao knew more was needed. But who really ran things out in the Shanxi countryside? Zhao could find few clues in the local gazetteers because those elite-compiled local handbooks for magistrates did not say much about the organization of rural society in Shanxi. Zhao's predecessors in the governor's yamen did leave a few clues about formal community organizations that met ritual and local security needs. In an 1856 memorial Wang Qingyun described fortresses, between ten and a hundred per county, that dotted the Shanxi landscape. Each of these had temples to local deities that were managed by local elites in accordance with their own regulations.[10] And Zhang Zhidong wrote in an 1883 memorial that every village *(cun)* customarily had at least one *she* (literally, shrine). In some villages there were two or three *she*, each of which was associated with a temple *(gongmiao)*. The leader of the *she (shezhang)* was the effective leader of his community, according to Zhang.[11]

Not much had changed in the two decades since Zhang Zhidong left Shanxi. Zhao Erxun was able to confirm this with information provided by Wu Tingxie, the prefect in Taiyuan and a longtime resident of Shanxi. Wu's responsibilities for administering the prefecture's nine counties, an area that was especially violent in 1900, combined with administrative experience gained while an assistant Shanxi subprefect earlier in his career, added to the store of local knowledge that informed the advice he gave Zhao and the documents he drafted for the governor.[12] Informed in part by Wu Tingxie, Zhao emphasized variations in both the size of subcounty administrative jurisdictions and the names of their respective leaders. For example, leaders called *sheshou* could be responsible for anywhere from a few villages to several dozen. Sometimes these leaders were self-proclaimed; others served either by rotation or selection. And in parts of southern Shanxi, Zhao pointed out, one could still find rural constables (*xiangyue*) who were responsible for just one village.[13] Gentrymen (*shenshi*) often managed larger areas referred to as *xiang* and were called *gongzheng* or *gongzhi*.[14]

Zhao Erxun wanted to standardize these customary practices and try to incorporate the goals of the mutual security system into a different structure of authority in the Shanxi countryside. He planned to identify respected local leaders who would occupy a new, government-recognized position. For ideas Zhao could draw on two sources besides the extant organizations described to him by Wu Tingxie. These included statecraft ideas that had been developed in reform circles in the nineteenth century. And in 1902 he could also look to Western and Japanese models. Besides the prominence given to works like Huang Zunxian's study of Japan, the beginning of the flood of information about the world outside China could be tapped by Zhao.

The indigenous reform milieu had begun to be defined in 1826 with the compilation of *[Huangchao] Jingshi wenbian*, a compact anthology of statecraft essays and documents that were sometimes quoted by Zhao and Wu such as Gu Yanwu's seventeenth-century essays on subcounty administrative reform and the Yongzheng Emperor's rejection of Ortai's 1729 proposal to establish a post for rural leaders he called *xiangguan*.[15] The statecraft prescriptions in the writings of Feng Guifen were also prominent at the turn of the century because a posthumous collection of his essays had been circulated by imperial command among high government officials in 1898. Zhao might have found ideas in Feng's essay on subcounty administrative reform where he proposed that two levels of subcounty leaders, selected by groups of one hundred and one thousand families, should settle petty legal disputes and handle other local affairs.[16] In addition to the influences of Gu Yanwu, Feng Guifen, and the corpus of statecraft thought contained in subsequent versions of *[Huangchao] Jingshi wenbian*, Zhao could have read Sun Yirang's *Zhouli zhengyao* (The political essentials of the Rites of Zhou), which was published in 1902.[17] Sun called for local landholders, to be selected by groups of one hundred or more families, to replace yamen functionaries and to serve in the post of *xiangzheng*. Sun himself was influenced by Gu Yanwu's famous dictum about the need for a legion of minor officials and the description in the *Rites of Zhou*, compiled before the reign of China's first emperor, of responsible rural leaders called *xiangguan*.[18]

But Zhao was also looking beyond the Shanxi countryside and the Chinese past to the West. And it was here that Zhao Erxun entered into the debate about self-government carried on by men like Thomas Jefferson, Toulmin Smith, Lothar Bucher, Alexis de Tocqueville, Rudolf Gneist, and, in Asia, Albert Mosse. Zhao, like Gneist, was most intrigued with the position of the English justice of the peace. Zhao compared Chinese county magistrates to Gneist's royally appointed but locally active central authority.[19] Both justice and magistrate were officials *(guan)* in Zhao's mind. But in finding a model for the local leader he styled *shezhang*, Zhao emphasized the elections by the people *(minju)* used to fill other positions in English local administration.[20] What most intrigued Zhao was the way the royally appointed justices of the peace were found among local men of wealth, power, and prestige. This would have been illegal in China, however, for magistrates were not allowed to serve anywhere in their native province.

Zhao tried to capture the essence of the English model in a newly defined position that combined familiar practices, formal elections, and government legitimation. His *shezhang* were to be "elected" *(gongju)* just like parliamentarians in the West, although Zhao's preferred means looked more like familiar Chinese selection methods.[21] Local men of property should "elect" a slate of nominees from which magistrates selected community leaders. In this way Zhao tried to realize what Gneist had called magisterial self-government in which locally prominent and respected men served in important administrative positions. But this enlightened authoritarianism was, in England at least, already anachronistic. The complete redefinition of the role of English justices of the peace in the last two decades of the nineteenth century had extended the principles of representative democracy to local administration. Neither Zhao nor Rudolf Gneist would have found much merit in the reforms of 1888, when justices lost their administrative power or the changes six years later when popular election replaced royal appointment as the means for selecting justices who were now expected to respond to local interests.[22]

Zhao froze English administration in its pre-1888 state because he needed to obfuscate his use of the term "official." Zhao recognized that in England popular elections and royal appointment were both used to designate local officials. But in Shanxi Zhao had to maintain the fundamental distinction in Chinese political practice between centrally appointed officials like magistrates and popularly selected leaders like *shezhang* who would not, Zhao said again and again, be officials. Nonetheless, in practice Zhao's *shezhang*, legitimated as they were by centrally appointed magistrates on the recommendation of local communities, occupied a no-man's land between officials and the people.

With his curiosity about the English model Zhao signalled that foreign ideas and institutions were worth considering. Privileging neither East nor West, he tried to solve a perplexing matrix of problems. But Zhao was convinced that more than a formal Western-style electoral process was needed to successfully redefine the relationship between state authority and local communities. Zhao thought that institutions, processes, and ideas should be imported, but he knew that the Chinese social context made careful modifications mandatory. His blending of new ideas and old precedents situated Zhao between a total dependence on foreign models and an unthinking obedience to the past. The most important example of Zhao's future-oriented flexibility is his conception of local elites. Although Zhao used the familiar term *shenshi* in the sense of gentrymen whom he expected to continue to "rule the people," he was convinced that commoners might be selected and magistrates were warned that these respected men did not deserve displays of contempt or arrogance.[23] *Shengyuan* and *jiansheng*, along with *tongsheng* and other literate commoners, should be treated equally and politely.

Zhao's attempt to create a new type of leader in rural Shanxi was one of the last reforms he promulgated during his term of office. Earlier Zhao had tried to eliminate the pernicious influence of yamen functionaries *(mending)* who controlled access to government yamen, create police forces in urban areas, encourage local leaders to reallocate community resources for the purpose of establishing new-style schools, and publish a provincial government gazette.[24]

With his directive of 6 January 1903 Zhao Erxun tried to create a quasi-official post at the subcounty level. Given the long-standing and constantly reaffirmed imperial policy that prohibited officials from serving at home, this was a delicate proposition indeed. These reforms allowed local leaders to retain their posts, but change was imminent. First, Zhao wanted to standardize the size of the population under the control of local leaders *(shezhang)*. Local conditions might affect the number,[25] but the ideal was ten villages. One *shezhang* should manage the public affairs of a hundred or so families. In some cases, however, villages were as large as market towns and might require two *shezhang*. But the ideal size of the population under the rule of a *shezhang* was about five hundred persons.[26] It would be neither large enough, one could observe, to command sufficient resources to oppose the county government, nor so small that an excess of quasi-officials clogged the countryside. Second, local leaders were asked to submit themselves to a selection process with final authority vested in the local magistrate.[27]

With his so-called *xiangshe* reform Zhao sought to define, select, outline the responsibilities of, and specify the rewards and punishments of, local leaders. Zhao hoped community leaders would be found among the degree-holding ranks of *shengyuan, jiansheng,* or higher, but he embraced commoners like *tongsheng* as well as anyone who was literate.[28] Commoners received the nod when degree-holders were absent, failed to make the nominee list, or were unacceptable to the magistrate.[29]

Local leaders were selected *(gongju)* by the magistrate from lists of names nominated at special gatherings of those who owned at least ten *mu*[30] (a little less than two acres) of land. The top vote-getter still had to pass muster at the county yamen and some would fail, for Zhao's concern about a selection process corrupted by bribery, coercion, or cajolery prompted him to reserve final judgment for the magistrate.[31]

The responsibilities of these leaders included oversight of all aspects of local administration, education, and public works; reporting the names of insubordinate persons; mediating petty local disputes; and, if necessary, joining with other local leaders to resolve disagreements between communities.[32]

The regulations make it clear that community leaders were not officials. The rank associated with an office, not the office itself, was reward enough. Zhao Erxun's leaders, much like Feng Guifen's description of local militia heads, were men who "were not officials but were close to officialdom."[33] There were many reasons why Zhao refused to grant official status to local leaders. The nondegree-holding status of some local leaders at a time when a degree was still a prerequisite, in most cases, for government service, made this status problematic. Also, if the government did not control the status marker, powerful but disreputable men could easily become officials. Finally, officials had to be paid and the government fisc lacked room even for yamen clerks and runners.

Zhao cautioned that "the people rule the people, but power still resides in the official" but his system of rewards drew people toward the ranks of officialdom. Degree-holders were rewarded with yamen posts; commoners gained rank equal to that of an assistant magistrate or could even become eligible for formal government service.[34] The *shezhang's* quasi-official status was objectified by the seal presented to them by magistrates for authenticating documents.[35]

But there was a contradiction. Zhao wanted a rural post where leaders could be "close to the people," as the clichéd description of county magistrates went, at a time when none of these overburdened officials could realize that ideal. *Shezhang,* who would "rule the people" like the rural officials *(xiangguan)* of antiquity, were desperately needed. If power remained in the magistrate's hand, could local leaders, however well-respected and earnest, solve problems with authority alone? This was the dilemma Zhao faced. When governments lost touch with rural society, dangers lurked. In his discussion of the English model of local administration he emphasized the importance of popular participation in selecting local officials. His reforms were an attempt to blend that idea with past Chinese practices. But in the end Zhao's chief worry was about names: these men were not officials, he assured the court.

But Zhao's authoritarian program was tempered by a conviction that educated men in the countryside enticed by official status markers to accomplish the good deeds they tended toward anyway,[36] could aid in a transformation of China that had to begin in myriad rural communities. The insults and punishments meted out to well-respected and influential commoners by arrogant yamen functionaries was contributing to a crisis of leadership: "Those who rule are not good, and those who are good do not rule."[37] Zhao wanted to rely on these local leaders because he distrusted most magistrates and was certain that the few who were worthy of respect were overwhelmed by the demands of the job.[38] His denunciation of the officials at the lowest tier of government influenced by personnel decisions in Beijing was blistering:

> A majority of the officials in Shanxi lack initiative. In poor and remote counties they loaf with despicable characters and do virtually nothing. The experienced and severe say: "My acts are my law; who needs permission from higher officials?" The avaricious make plans for selfish gains. The worries of the peasants? Who has time to ask? So orders are virtually ignored; and when trouble comes, no one checks it out. The government slowly vanishes while the people's misery grows day by day.[39]

Given this tense relationship between provincial and county yamen it was difficult for Zhao to rely on magistrates, a fact that also softens the authoritarian tone of his reforms. Besides limiting the discretionary powers of magistrates to select local leaders, he insisted that money raised by rural communities to establish new-style schools could not be touched by county officials and functionaries.[40]

Zhao levered magistrates with the symbolism of imperial power. When his memorial about some of his Shanxi reforms was rescribed for comment to the Bureau of Government Affairs (Zhengwu chu) on 25 November 1902, Zhao immediately distributed copies of the memorial to all of his Shanxi magistrates.[41] It was as if Zhao were trying to show these officials the handwriting on the wall in Beijing.

The imperial state in practice was not the hierarchy-bound monolith it appeared to be in theory; there were many centers of power and authority. Although Zhao was able to institute numerous reforms, he still respected and needed symbolic power centered in Beijing. A late-Qing provincial governor was powerful, but not omnipotent.[42] Significantly, the enlightened authoritarian Zhao Erxun tried to check the petty despotisms of local magistrates by forcing magistrates to legitimate and empower local leaders who were nominated by local property holders.

Zhao's state, defined daily by communication and action by thousands of individual officials and non-officials, bore little resemblance to the metaphorical ship of state his fellow official Liu Tieyun evoked in *The Travels of Lao Can*, a novel that portrayed a foundering Qing state. Zhao was not trying to repair and expand a behemoth of state power to the fringes of rural society. But he did fear that government was slowly vanishing much as John Locke worried that English government in the seventeenth century was dissolving because of inaction.[43] In China Zhao surveyed a province where magistrates refused to follow orders, investigate local conditions, or apprise superior officials of their actions. His loss of faith in magistrates led to his *xiangshe* reform, which created new lines of communication and control that could, if necessary, bypass local magistrates entirely. The state for Zhao needed less in the way of symbols and pomp displayed by pretentious county yamen and more action by magistrates and reciprocal communication between rural society and imperial authority.

Zhao Erxun and Wu Tingxie believed in the strength and integrity of local communities and their program sought to identify and reward local society's leading lights. These leaders, neither officials nor private citizens, would receive government directives and authenticate their documents with government-supplied seals, and yet the position would be unsalaried and the person selected would be nominated by their peers. The boundary between state and society would be imperceptible.

Zhao's Shanxi reforms were publicized throughout the empire and the Bureau of Government Affairs, which was responsible for reform proposals, reviewed and approved the *xiangshe* reform, even though at least one censor had asked the throne to abolish it. But Zhao was already in Hunan, serving as governor, by this time.[44] The issues Zhao thought were central in Shanxi following the Boxer uprising did not, however, disappear in Shanxi or elsewhere. The need for responsive local leaders, a desire to lighten the workload of over-burdened magistrates, and a hope for clear lines of communication between villages and the Forbidden City were no less important two years later when the Shanxi program once again was a topic of interest among high level policy makers.

While Russian and Japanese armies were stalemated in Manchuria in the summer of 1905 and diplomats from both countries were struggling toward peace halfway around the world in Portsmouth, New Hampshire, Chinese officials, who had not even been invited to observe the negotiations, plotted to regain control of China's northeastern corner. Shen Jiaben, the preeminent legal scholar of the late Qing, reminded the court of Zhao's reforms in a plea for provincial and subprovincial administrative reform in Manchuria contained in a July 1905 memorial. Shen cited the precedent of Zhao Erxun's Shanxi reform and mentioned the Japan model of elected prefectural assemblies before proposing that imperial civil administration take the place of Manchu military command in the ancestral homeland of the imperial house. Shen also recommended that the government identify and recognize leaders of local communities *(xiangshe)*.[45] Shen was certain China could reestablish control in Manchuria if only the emperor and his people were reunited. If the realities of rural life became known to Qing officials while the people were told

about China's international plight, then the country would become
stronger.

Shen's memorial bore fruit. In August 1905 the throne approved
the recommendation by the Bureau of Government Affairs to establish a cadre of government-recognized leaders of local communities
in Zhili. The bureau recapitulated the argument: the people's feelings
needed to be heard within government circles and the wishes of the
government had to reach the people. Overburdened magistrates in-
evitably delegated their responsibilities to yamen clerks and runners
who treated rural residents as their "fish and meat." Subcounty official positions had been filled in the past by local elites *(shishen)*
who were publicly selected *(gongju)*. The bureau urged the court to
establish responsible administrative positions in the countryside and
it asked that some title other than *xiangguan* be used.[46]

Zhili governor[47] Yuan Shikai did little in 1905 with this mandate
but a year later he was chosen, along with Zhao Erxun, to develop
a provisional local administrative reform that would establish *xiangguan*. This imperial order came in response to a memorial by Shanxi
censor Gu Yuan that had taken aim at Zhao Erxun's *xiangshe* reforms. Gu Yuan had belittled Zhao Erxun's tortured attempt to
avert the use of the term *xiangguan*,[48] the staple of statecraft thinkers
like Gu Yanwu and Feng Guifen in their discussions of local administration in the Zhou and Han. Zhao Erxun had carefully distinguished his reforms from the proposal rejected by the Yongzheng
Emperor in 1729 that called for establishing *xiangguan* at the subcounty level, but Gu Yuan confidently proposed to establish this
very post. He suggested that each county be divided into four sections headed by a *xiangzhang*, a local person selected by the people.
Under the *xiangzhang* were several boards of advisors *(xiezhu yuan)*,
also selected by the people, that settled disputes such as those pertaining to land and marriage. These boards would also suggest locally funded projects.[49]

The influences Gu Yuan alluded to in his memorial, which included statecraft ideas, current practices, and foreign models, continued to inform discussions on local administrative reform. Reiterating
the Chinese precedents for this course of action, Gu Yuan echoed

Gu Yanwu's argument that a well-ordered realm required numerous officials.[50] But the emphasis had been shifting since Zhao's Shanxi days in favor of foreign models, especially Japanese models for administrative reform. Yuan Shikai, for one, had been championing Japanese reform models. In 1903 he had dispatched the Tianjin prefect to Japan to study penal administration,[51] and in 1905 Yuan sent sixty-eight men to Japan to study local administration.[52]

When the Bureau of Government Affairs commented on Gu's request, they mentioned Zhao Erxun's Shanxi efforts, their response to Shen Jiaben's 1905 proposal about *xiangshe,* and one of Zhao Erxun's recent memorials in which he discussed administrative reforms he was now pursuing in his new post in Fengtian. After cautioning about how easily these reforms could be exploited by local despots who would only oppress the people, the bureau called for Yuan Shikai and Zhao Erxun to establish prototypical positions of *xiangguan* that could provide models for all of China.

This proposal received an imperial rescript of approval[53] and this time Yuan acted. Still governor in Zhili, he established a self-government bureau in the north China treaty port of Tianjin on 29 August 1906.[54] Yuan linked this directive to Gu Yuan's proposal about *xiangguan,* claiming "the way of local self-government is [the same as establishing] *xiangguan.*" Yuan was dissembling, since the term *xiangguan* was a staple of statecraft essays and "local self-government" was now being discussed in terms of constitutionalism. Yuan strengthened this latter emphasis by appointing to the bureau men whose studies in Japan had exposed them to Japanese and Western ideas about politics and government. These men had much in common with Zhao Erxun and Wu Tingxie, but their program differed significantly. The Shanxi model, while referring to Western institutions, stressed the importance of current practice and statecraft theory; in Tianjin the use of Western models, as glimpsed in a Japanese setting, was favored.

# TWO

# Yuan Shikai's Foreign Model for China

The Tianjin County Council, which met for the first time on 18 August 1907, came to power on the basis of China's first Western-style election. The thirty-member council was elected by a process that had begun earlier in the summer involving thousands of participants in Tianjin county.[1] It was no accident that these events took place there, for the city from which the county was administered, Tianjin, was a treaty port with a longstanding reputation for reform. This was the base of Yuan Shikai's power and influence.

Yuan, who governed the province that surrounded the separate Beijing metropolitan region, had been groomed for this role by his mentor and patron Li Hongzhang. Li, the influential and reform-minded official whose tenure in the seat now occupied by Yuan brought him renown and respect among Westerners, had established Tianjin's reputation as one of China's more progressive cities. Paradoxically, Tianjin's proximity to the areas devastated by the xenophobic Boxer uprising of 1900 enhanced this reputation, for a series of changes begun under Allied occupation in 1900–1902 continued after the Allies returned the city to the Chinese on 15 August 1902.[2] Yuan Shikai and his subordinates took over the newly designated provincial capital, where the old walls had been torn down, a decade before Shanghai's would be destroyed, and replaced by streetcar lines. Symbols of the new continued to be added to the city's landscape.

The audience for the publicity Yuan generated about his economic, administrative, and social reforms was both domestic and international. An American consul in Tianjin commented: "By his wholesale introduction of modern conveniences and methods Viceroy Yuan has shown how much can be accomplished toward the betterment of the conditions of the people in a short space of time even in China. . . . [I]t is to Yuan Shih-k'ai, who had the courage and wisdom to successfully carry out plans made by a foreign military government, that the credit for securing to Tientsin the reputation of being the most progressive and enlightened city in China rightfully belongs."[3] Yuan shrewdly manipulated events that might add to his stature. Toward the end of the summer of 1905 he gave a reception in his Tianjin yamen for President Theodore Roosevelt's daughter Alice. She was greeted by Chinese officials as well as their wives and daughters. The presence of women astounded a Western correspondent: "It is a bold move on the part of our advanced Viceroy. We believe His Excellency is honestly desirous of bringing China into the line of real and true progress—into line with Western nations so far as her venerable social customs will permit."[4]

Like Canton, Tianjin was a treaty port, commercial center, and provincial capital, but the gateway to the populous and fertile north China plain was distinguished by its proximity to Beijing. The city was just a short trainride from the capital and provincial-based reform efforts could be transformed quickly into national policy; officials stationed in Tianjin could craft urban and provincial policies in the morning and still make it to the Forbidden City for an imperial audience before sunset. This reciprocation would be especially apparent in 1906–1907.

When Beijing ordered Yuan to establish new positions for rural leaders *(xiangguan)* in Zhili that could serve as models for the rest of China, he seized the moment. He failed to follow directions but this year, unlike 1905, he acted. In mid-August Yuan sent a telegram to the Bureau of Government Affairs, the Beijing agency that had recommended this action to the court a month earlier, in which he immediately sought to diminish the old statecraft nuances of the *xiangguan* reference by proposing instead that urban notables *(yishen)* and rural managers *(cundong)* meet and discuss local affairs, thus establishing the basis for lower-level assemblies *(xia yiyuan)*.[5] Yuan soon directed subordinates to organize elections for local deliberative councils *(yishihui)* and administrative boards *(dongshihui)* in Tianjin county. This would be a preview for China; two years later similar orders were issued by Beijing to the empire.

Yuan Shikai began remaking the political landscape in ways that Zhao Erxun had taken pains to avert. Yuan's prestige emboldened him to experiment with a Western-style council election in Tianjin county even though the court had simply directed him, along with Zhao, to create new positions for government-recognized rural leaders. Zhao, now governor in Fengtian, maintained his authoritarian stance while Yuan tried to foster democracy in one county in China. Yuan, envisioning the foundations for constitutional government and China's regeneration, styled his reforms "self-government" and attached that label to a new bureau he staffed with returned students. Yuan's goal was nothing less than to establish China as a great power in East Asia and he knew that this required a state that could protect its own *(zishou)* territory and rule *(zizhi)* its own people.[6]

But Yuan was ambivalent about the meaning of self-government and sometimes he seemed of one mind with the more explicitly authoritarian Zhao Erxun. Yuan meant *zizhi* to convey more than the vague sense of a country's being responsible for its people; he was certain that China needed to borrow Western models that granted "self-government" to the people in arenas that were beyond the reach of officials *(guanzhi)*. Although this formulation echoed the statecraft ideas used by provincial officials like Zeng Guofan, who levied local militias to augment government armies during the Taiping Rebellion,[7] Yuan wanted his new bureau in Tianjin to look to the future. He was not disappointed, for the returned students he appointed to the bureau ignored old heroes like Zeng Guofan in favor of men like Japan's Yamagata Aritomo.

Yuan's protégé Jin Bangping accepted Yuan's offer of the position of bureau codirector. In his first comments to the bureau Jin, who had specialized in legal studies while attending Waseda University in Tokyo, outlined his and Yuan's vision: "If constitutional government is to be established, we must first begin with local self-government. This goes without saying. . . . His Excellency, who is convinced that local self-government is the critical aspect of a constitutional government, has taken the first step by establishing the self-government bureau to do preparatory work."[8] Jin thought this reform would improve China's relative power in the family of nations, enable China to establish sovereignty over her own territory, and restructure government so as to reunite ruler and ruled. Like Yuan's, Jin's ambition would not have been contained by Tianjin's walls even if they had still been standing. The bureau's mandate addressed China's international role and its sovereignty as well as the more concrete challenge of enticing people to vote and play a role in local affairs.[9]

And even that last mandate had broader implications. Service in this bureau was an extraordinary opportunity, Jin insisted, for a model would be created for all of China to follow.[10] Yuan's gift and penchant for self-promotion ensured that Jin's actions were noted throughout China. Besides coverage in newspapers like Beijing's *Shuntian shibao* and *Jingbao,* the bureau received publicity in national journals published in Shanghai like *Dongfang zazhi* and *Zhengyi tongbao.* Of course Yuan's own provincial gazette, *Beiyang guanbao,* did not miss the story. And the still-mightiest channel of all, which carried imperial edicts and other communications from Beijing to all corners of the empire and gathered in return memorials from high-ranking officials, called attention to the Tianjin bureau within a fortnight of its founding.[11]

Unlike Zhao Erxun's Shanxi experiment, which took form out of publicity's eye and without reference to central policy making, the Tianjin program both influenced and was affected by Beijing. Two days after the bureau was set up the court proclaimed in its momentous 1 September 1906 edict that China should enjoy the fruits of constitutional government. This announcement ended a summer's-long debate in Beijing, in which Yuan Shikai took part, about the recommendations made by the high-level commissioners who had covered much of the globe in their firsthand investigation of Japan, the United States, and selected European countries earlier in the year.[12] Two of these commissioners, Duanfang and Dai Hongci, submitted a comprehensive memorial on 25 August 1906 that included a brief for the importance of local self-government as the basis for establishing a constitutional government.[13]

The crescendo of documents—the commissioners' memorial, Yuan's directive, and the court's edict—continued in the months to come. The Tianjin self-government model was repeatedly publicized in the official and unofficial channels that crisscrossed China. Yuan, who formed the Tianjin message, had been instrumental in creating the medium. By 1906 his provincial gazette, *Beiyang guanbao,* had attained a reputation throughout China as a source of information about the Qing court and Yuan's yamen in Tianjin; ideas and actions by other reform-minded officials; and news from Zhili, other provinces, and the world.[14]

Yuan's gazette and its many imitators[15] transformed the policy-making environment in China. Beijing, the cynosure in the constellation defined by the court-centered memorial system, was beginning to fade. Rather than merely repot Beijing policy, reform-minded officials used provincial gazettes to publicize their own efforts. Circulation of these gazettes defined an empirewide reform network that Beijing chose not to compete against until the fall of 1907. Until then provincial gazettes like *Beiyang guanbao,* first published on 30 December 1902, dominated the reform network. Furthermore, *Beiyang guanbao* served both as a mouthpiece for Yuan's reform-minded allies in Beijing and a source of information for friend and foe alike.[16]

Yuan used *Beiyang guanbao* to influence metropolitan policy-making in the months following the 1 September 1906 edict on constitutional government. He had access, for example, to Duanfang and Dai Hongci's August memorial, a document so sensitive that the court retained *(liuzhong)* it in the Forbidden City. Grand Council secretaries noted only the date and the memorialists' names in their record book *(Suishou dengji)* in which all incoming memorials and subsequent imperial action were registered and, usually, summarized. In the past this would have limited knowledge about the memorial to a narrow circle. But Yuan Shikai, who was a reform ally of Duanfang, used *Beiyang guanbao* to publicize it nonetheless, for on 3 October 1906 his gazette described its contents. Even metropolitan officials relied on this provincial gazette to learn about the retained memorial.[17]

*Beiyang guanbao*'s prominence and influence was established before 1906. Reforms carried out in Zhili, for example, were referred to by a Shanxi prefect in his request for permission to publish a vernacular gazette, *Shanxi baihua yanshuobao*. The prefect cited Yuan's approval, published on 6 January 1903, of a request from Wanquan county to establish a primary school. The Shanxi prefect used this Zhili example to buttress an argument that a vernacular gazette and a lecture circuit would address Shanxi's illiteracy problem.[18] Another indication of the weight of Yuan's gazette during the period when he virtually monopolized this network of communication comes from Sichuan where the former Shanxi governor Cen Chunxuan, who was governor in Sichuan from August 1902 to April 1903, ordered 530 subscriptions to be distributed to provincial and subprovincial officials.[19]

Few people would have known that Yuan was helping to publicize a message crafted in part by persons who had been banished from China in 1898. The Duanfang memorial given such prominence by Yuan Shikai, for example, contained the work of Liang Qichao. Duanfang had gained indirect access to Liang through a network of Chinese students studying in Tokyo during his short stay early in 1906.[20] Once again Liang's message had breached the walls of the Forbidden City. Although Liang's advice was cloaked in anonymity, thousands of other expatriates like Jin Bangping had been returning to their homeland as power in Beijing flowed back to the reform-minded faction. This helps explain why Yuan, so hesitant in 1905, acted so decisively in 1906. The Tianjin Prefecture Self-government Bureau became a showcase for returned students at a time when the court had repeatedly encouraged provincial officials, in confidential court letters, telegrams, and edicts emanating from the Forbidden City in 1906, to use such talent.[21]

Most members of the Tianjin bureau were selected on the basis of credentials collected in Japan, but all of them possessed still-important and more familiar degrees. Three *jinshi* and six *juren* topped the list. Besides Jin and the Tianjin prefect who headed the bureau, the remaining twelve members included four current officials and eight expectant officials. At least five of the men were natives of Zhili.[22]

The social and intellectual milieu of bureau members was familiar to people like Zhao Erxun and Wu Tingxie. What distinguished the bureau was its open use of Japanese models of local administration and a Western-style electoral process. Policy makers in Taiyuan and in Tianjin alike tried to strengthen the tie between the state and local communities, but Jin Bangping and his associates, with the support of Yuan Shikai, looked to foreign models and processes for answers to the same questions.

This new orientation owed much to the experience and contributions of China's returned students. Jin Bangping was one of the most eminent of this new breed. A native of Anhui, he had been sent to Japan by fellow provincial Li Hongzhang in 1899 on a Zhili province government scholarship. After graduating from Waseda, one of Japan's best private universities, Jin returned to China with high hopes. But Jin's Waseda degree counted for little since examination degrees, not law degrees, remained a prerequisite for office. Even Yuan Shikai failed to get Jin a post in 1904. A year later, however, Jin opened doors for himself with his splendid performance in a special palace examination conducted in Beijing in July 1905 for fourteen returned students with expertise in Western learning. After Jin received his new-style *jinshi* degree in law and administration, Yuan was able finally to add him to his staff.[23]

Yuan had been preparing the ground with care for the programs Jin and his colleagues put in place. One of the staunchest advocates of Chinese study abroad, Yuan had followed Li Hongzhang's lead in sending people to Japan. By mid-1905 more than a hundred men from circles of elites or officials in Zhili had been studying in Japan.[24] Yuan and his students were not alone.

In the opening up of China after the disaster of the Boxer uprising, which had discredited the conservative faction, more and more Chinese went overseas, especially to Japan, to study. The number of Chinese students in Japan, sent by family, community, or government in the decade before the 1911 Revolution, peaked at between 7,000 and 8,000 in 1905–1906.[25]

The pioneers in this group had attended regular classes in some of Japan's best universities, including Waseda, Chūō, Meiji, and Imperial. The Qing government recognized their achievements with special exams in Beijing held in 1903 and in 1905, when Jin triumphed.[26] A precedent had been established. In September 1905 the old civil service examination system was abolished and new-style examination degrees, like a *jinshi* for law or economics, could be won only by men like Jin Bangping who had studied overseas. By the end of the dynasty 161 new-style *jinshi* and 1,213 new-style *juren* degrees would be awarded.[27]

Not all of these students were in their late teens or early twenties. The Zhili contingent, for example, also included older men who were officials, expectant officials, and degree-holders. Men in this category, studying primarily at Japanese law schools,[28] returned to play significant roles in county yamen, provincial offices like the Tianjin Self-government Bureau, and metropolitan ministries in the final years of the dynasty. Many of these students graduated from a special program offered in Tokyo at Hosei University. This course at one of Japan's premier law schools, established after a series of discussions between the Chinese government and Japanese educational officials, was favored by Yuan Shikai.[29] Ninety-four students began an accelerated course in law and administration *(fazheng sucheng ke)* in May 1904; and by the time the fifth and final class of 385 students graduated in 1908, the number of graduates had increased to 1,145. Eminent Japanese professors, assisted by translators, lectured on law, administration, finance, and foreign affairs during each three-month term.[30] After returning to China, graduates shared their knowledge with colleagues in new government bureaus or taught students in provincial-level law schools. Their students, in turn, became instructors in local self-government schools at the county level.

Chinese law schools *(fazheng xuetang)*, although first conceived as a specialized arena in a newly developing educational system, were politically significant. In effect they served as new-style schools for expectant officials awaiting a job. Regular schools were closed to anyone over the age of thirty *sui*, but students as old as forty-five *sui* could matriculate at Chinese law schools.[31] Local self-government schools, in turn, were important adjuncts of law schools that often shared personnel and covered similar material. Law schools trained expectant officials; self-government schools were set up for local degree-holders and gentrymen. Both kinds of schools, especially at the provincial level, were important venues of action for this special category of China's returned students. They were pioneered in Tianjin, first at the law school established in 1905[32] and then, a year later, at China's first so-called local self-government school *(difang zizhi yanjiusuo)*, which was established by Jin Bangping's bureau.

Yuan's broad interpretation of his court-given mandate in 1906 allowed him to turn to the law faculty in Zhili as he placed men on the self-government bureau staff. These men were eager to turn thought into action. And for inspiration they looked, naturally, to Japan. Men like Jin Bangping and his colleagues, prodded by Yuan, were as intrigued with Japanese models as Zhao Erxun had been with extant rural organizations. When Yuan Shikai told Beijing in August 1906 that he would try to create assemblies where urban notables and rural managers could discuss public issues, he had ordained the orientation the Tianjin bureau would take in September. The bureau's regulations were on Yuan's desk waiting for approval five months later. Unlike the Shanxi reform documents, which reflect the local knowledge of Zhao's ally Wu Tingxie, the Tianjin regulations contain few hints about current structures of power in Tianjin prefecture. Instead, the bureau produced a modified version of the Japanese regulations for city, town, and village administration promulgated in 1888. The Japan model, which included provisions for a Western-style electoral process and the separation of legislative and executive powers, had been lectured on at Hosei University.[33] This model became part of the Tianjin regulations in 1907 and would be prominent in the imperial regulations promulgated in 1909–1910.

Indeed, the Japanese influence on the Tianjin program is apparent in three major efforts that can be documented: writing the regulations, training a cadre of representatives from each county in the prefecture to assist local magistrates, and publicizing the reforms.

If the Japanese angle should be noted, so too should the elitism of the Tianjin program, reminiscent of Hunan's ill-fated Nanxue hui that heard Huang Zunxian's call for local activism in 1898. Jin Bangping and his colleagues drew upon their Japan experience at the outset as they established an ad-hoc committee *(qicheng hui)* to draft regulations. The bureau reached out to elite circles in Tianjin as they contacted the education office *(quanxue suo)* and the Chamber of Commerce and asked for representatives. Notables without ties to either group were selected by the bureau.[34] On 16 December 1906, when the committee opened the first of nineteen deliberations on the regulations, sixty people had gathered,[35] including Zhang Boling, who would found Nankai University, Wang Xianbin, the salt merchant who headed the Chamber of Commerce, and his associate, Ning Shifu.[36] The expansiveness of the bureau's attempt to attract a broad array of local notables to the committee in this early self-government initiative is noteworthy, especially so since in later years members of educational and commercial groups could be ignored by dominant cabals of degree-holders whose elitism made Tianjin look like a participatory democracy.

The returned student and expectant magistrate Wu Xingrang[37] led bureau members in drafting regulations. These were printed for the self-government committee, which amended and then voted each article up or down at meetings held in the Tianjin prefecture yamen. Revised regulations were then submitted to Yuan Shikai. By mid-February 1907 the committee had completed its work and by the beginning of spring Yuan approved the *Shiban Tianjin xian difang zizhi zhangcheng* (Provisional Tianjin county local self-government regulations) for use in the upcoming county council elections.[38] Within a month, an earlier draft of these regulations was published in *Zhengyi tongbao*, the same journal that had published Zhao's Shanxi reform documents.[39]

But even before this eminent group had met, the bureau established the basis for communicating its program to selected elites who lived outside Tianjin city. County magistrates in Tianjin prefecture were directed to send students to the Local Self-government School in Tianjin city. The three counties farthest from Tianjin were asked to send six students each; the three closest had a quota of eight. In Tianjin county, eight students from areas outside Tianjin city were selected, since city-dwellers already had convenient access to information about reforms.

As with most initiatives under Yuan's umbrella, the school developed a national reputation. Within months of its founding *Dongfang zazhi* published an essay produced at the school in the special December 1906 number on constitutionalism. A year later the school would win accolades from a Canton journal as being one of the two most visible advocates for reform, the competitor being Shanghai's famous Society to Prepare for Constitutional Government (Yubei lixian gonghui).[40]

The Local Self-government School, co-located with the new-style normal school, opened on 13 October 1906, six weeks after the founding of the bureau, with a class of fifty students. Members of the first class ranged in age from twenty-three to fifty-nine, with almost half between the ages of twenty-four and thirty-four. A majority of the fifty students held the lowest of the degrees *(fusheng)* included in the *shengyuan* category. Others held different kinds of *shengyuan* degrees. There were also six *jiansheng*, at least six expectant officials, and two *juren*. One student was a warden in a county yamen. The students were to be selected from circles of local elites *(shenqi)* from each county, with gentry-managers *(shendong)* especially sought after because of their influence in molding opinion in the countryside. When space was available, auditors who had registered their names with the bureau were invited to attend.

Four months of classes, held from 8:30 A.M. until 12:30 P.M. each day, covered materials relating to self-government, elections, census, local finance, educational and police administration, economics, and law. These topics were taught by returned students, who were supposed to be graduates of Hosei University. Four bureau members were among the seven teachers of the first class.

Final exams awaited students at end of term. The results were even scrutinized by Yuan Shikai. Students with satisfactory grades returned home to serve as assistants to the county magistrate in self-government affairs. The first class of fifty, along with fifty-nine auditors, was tested on 22–25 January 1907. Eighty-six men passed; twenty-three continued their studies with the second class.[41]

The degree-holders attending classes at the school were but a slice of an already small section of the population. But the bureau did not forget the rest of the population in the county. Soon after the bureau was founded, four men were selected to go out and lecture to people about self-government, constitutional government, and administration. They used the lecture halls *(xuanjiang suo)* that had been established in Tianjin city earlier in the year as part of the educational reforms mandated by an imperial edict of 13 May 1906.[42] The goal was to give lectures throughout the county,[43] but the first lectures on local self-government were given to men in Tianjin city only.

The bureau relied on lecturers to use familiar idioms and metaphors to explain regulations and other documents. Lecturers wrote their own speeches, and copies were collected by the bureau and then published in order to help rural elites explain reforms to peasants. A few speeches appeared in the first issues of a gazette published by the bureau,[44] and in March 1908 a compilation of lectures was issued.

Lecture topics included the origins of the self-government bureau and the purpose of the lectures. One lecturer mentioned that local self-government was the basis for constitutional government. He highlighted the role of "returned students from Japan" in the bureau and told how they had sponsored classes in new-style schools, established a local self-government school, and were publishing a gazette. The speaker thought "these methods would make it possible for everyone—poor, rich, rough, or refined—to understand eventually."[45]

The public's tepid response to the first lectures in Tianjin city prompted some bureau members to think that special schools were needed. And others were sure all of these efforts would fall short. Emphasizing instead the powers of persuasion offered by popular culture, one petitioner in 1906 asked Yuan Shikai for permission to establish a society to write new operas to be performed in the countryside as a way to popularize various reform programs.[46]

In addition to classes and lectures, the bureau emphasized publishing in order to reach beyond the city. Besides the lecture compilations, the bureau also published *Fazheng guanhua bao* (Law and administration gazette), beginning in the early fall of 1906. This monthly carried transcripts of lectures, regulations, explanations of regulations, and essays.[47] Unlike the widely circulated *Beiyang guanbao* or *Beiyang fazheng xuebao* (Beiyang law journal), which was edited by bureau member Wu Xingrang,[48] the bureau's gazette was intended for a local audience alone. This gazette, which was composed in the vernacular *(baihua)*, was inspired by an idea pushed by the president of Hosei University,[49] who may have discussed it with Yuan Shikai during his 1906 visit to China,[50] and certainly broached it in classes held in Tokyo.[51] The gazette's compilers planned to explain topics like constitutional government and local self-government. Magistrates in Tianjin prefecture were slated to receive fifty copies of each issue for distribution to gentry-managers in the countryside *(xiangcun shendong)* and to teachers in new-style schools for study and lecture purposes.[52] Such outreach, according to bureau member Qi Shukai, depended upon the local elites who would implement local self-government to explain carefully the reforms. He worried that fearful or obstinate peasants would refuse to cooperate. Qi was convinced that peasants would help out as soon as local elites had persuaded them that the new programs represented a departure from the past.[53] Local elites who rose to the challenge could crib from model speeches such as the ones published in late 1906 on the public nature of self-government, its precedents, and its place in the administrative structure[54] or from vernacular self-government gazettes published by county governments.[55]

The self-government bureau also sent out compilations of documents associated with planning and preparation for self-government in order to provide material to each county yamen in Tianjin prefecture to guide preliminary studies of local conditions. The first compilation, which was approved in late 1906 by Yuan Shikai, included directives, petitions, regulations, and namelists of the self-government bureau and Local Self-government Committee.[56]

The bureau publicized its program throughout Tianjin prefecture and, if rural elites cooperated, down to the village level. Lectures, schools, and publications all combined to educate the people. Without education there could be no local self-government, and, ultimately, no constitutional government in China.[57] Although precedents existed for each of the programs just described—the *xiangyue* system of lectures on imperial maxims, the structure of education at the county and subcounty levels, and the official gazettes published in Beijing and the provinces—the bureau's activities were inspired by foreign models, especially the one from Japan; and from the ad-hoc drafting committee and the regulations they produced to the lecture circuit, schools, and vernacular gazettes, the justification for action was found outside China's borders. The returned students in the bureau repeatedly distinguished their efforts from anything that had ever taken place in China. The framework for constitutional government was being imported; Tianjin's elitest democrats were not interested in camouflaging their reforms with old rhetoric and programs as Zhao Erxun and Wu Tingxie had in Shanxi.[58]

But Zhao, who was now governor in Fengtian, continued to think in his familiar authoritarian ways even as he began to use the same language and programs being popularized by Yuan's bureau.[59] Although Zhao, who had also been directed by the court to develop new prototypes for rural administration, looked to Tianjin for ideas, the cautiousness he had displayed earlier in Shanxi was no less evident now. Local security and control, not constitutionalism, were high on Zhao's agenda. Zhao delayed action on his imperial mandate until the end of 1906, when he named the top officials to the Fengtian Local Self-government Bureau. By the time the Fengtian bureau finally met, in early March 1907, the Tianjin bureau had already completed drafting its council election regulations, graduated the first class from the self-government school, established a lecture circuit, and published several issues of its gazette. Zhao justified his caution in a speech given at the opening session of the bureau: "Conditions in Fengtian are not comparable to other provinces. If we hastily establish local self-government, magistrates will have difficulty selecting people to organize it. . . . The enterprise before the bureau at this moment can only be called 'preparation,' not 'implementation.' "[60] Because Zhao worried that the purpose of the reforms would be lost unless it were guarded by regulations and a trained cadre, he insisted on a measured approach. Zhao would not boast, as Yuan did later in 1907, of an elected county council meeting for the first time. Instead bureau members in Fengtian spent the next eighteen months training investigation teams and dispatching them throughout the province to assess local conditions. After eight months of courses in subjects such as law, economics, administration, local self-government, census methods, statistics, Fengtian's geography, and mathematics, 108 investigators dispersed to all parts of the province. Their studies of topics like weather, population, education, administration, agriculture, commerce, mining, transportation, and customs lasted until July 1908, when their data, organized into reports, maps, and tables, were presented to provincial authorities.[61]

The Fengtian and Tianjin self-government bureaus established in 1906, in accordance with an imperial order that simply asked that *xiangguan* be established, began the process of defining what local self-government meant in practice. Yuan Shikai's returned students had free rein in Tianjin prefecture, and in less than a year they had worked themselves out of a job as the newly elected Tianjin County Council began to attend to local affairs. But whereas the Tianjin bureau had been committed to reaching out beyond the city in hopes of enlisting both rural elites and peasants in the battle to create a new and powerful China, in Fengtian, Zhao Erxun's provincial self-government bureau sought information rather than citizens. In the event, although both bureaus were established by provincial officials at the request of the central government, it was the Tianjin model, not the Fengtian model, that Beijing wanted other governors to emulate. Thousands of returned students like Jin Bangping and Wu Xingrang were eager to participate in reform efforts in Beijing, provincial capitals, and county seats.

The Zhili and Fengtian programs were both under the watchful eyes of Yuan and Zhao. But the language of local self-government policy, especially the connection to constitutional government often heard in 1906, was sometimes seized by local elites as justification to found their own self-government societies. Personal impulses soon found a voice in numerous local organizations. Indeed, the Qing government, with its calls for associations for commerce, education, and agriculture, had provided a limited basis for politicizing functional roles in society. Local self-government reforms, especially in 1906–1908, were part of this environment, a social setting in which the remarkable penchant of the Chinese to form associations with common goals was often evident. Some local activists along with officials at the local, provincial, and metropolitan levels thought they knew what self-government meant. Everyone had different thoughts on who should be making policy and how fast change should come. The Shanxi, Tianjin, and Fengtian models had numerous competitors, none of which was fashioned under guidance from Beijing ministries. From 1906 until the end of 1908 the contest was wide open and took turns that would have astounded Tianjin's returned students.

PART TWO

*Localism, Centralism, and*

*Provincialism, 1906–1908*

# THREE

# Local Elites in Corporatism's Realm

Yuan Shikai, along with Zhao Erxun in Fengtian, may have been granted the official monopoly for model-making, but local elites and officials elsewhere in China did not necessarily wait for the results. Much hope was projected upon the edict of 1 September 1906, which blasted through walls that had often blocked local initiatives. Wealth and power of foreign countries, according to the edict, were due in part to the practice of soliciting public opinion on important matters.[1] Chinese elites responded quickly. They gathered to celebrate the news in cities like Shanghai, Canton, Shantou, and Beijing, as well as Tianjin. In the capital representatives from groups of officials, teachers, journalists, merchants, and degree-holders, confident of their stature, influence, and power, celebrated the edict and discussed a format for future meetings open to the public in which men would represent the consensus of their particular circle.[2] The liberating effect of the edict was also reflected in the spirited founding of new organizations by men eager to profit by the news from Beijing. Metropolitan authorities quickly tried to channel the energy. Within weeks they told provincial officials to prepare for constitutionalism by establishing self-government bureaus like Yuan Shikai's in Tianjin.[3] This order was repeated three months later to most provincial officials. In addition, Beijing called for councils of local elites (shenshi hui) to deal with public matters.[4] Instructions from Beijing and action in the provinces continued. By mid-1907 officials and gentrymen (shen) in Manchuria, Zhili, and Jiangsu were discussing mutual concerns in formally established discussion offices *(yishi ting)* and in Manchuria officials were told also to establish self-government societies *(zizhi hui)* for local elites *(shimin).*[5]

Beijing piled order upon order well into 1907. By the fall of that year the Tianjin County Council was already in session and Yuan Shikai and his protégé Jin Bangping, reassigned to Grand Council posts in Beijing, were now literally at the center of imperial power. Moreover, some of Jin's fellow returned students in the newly established Ministry of Interior had become much more aggressive in facing down men as powerful as Yuan, claiming the prerogative to direct reform programs throughout China. But their victory, which came at a heavy price, was preceded by numerous orders from elsewhere in Beijing. After a high-level planning commission had issued provincial reorganization regulations in July 1907 that called for county councils,[6] a circular again directed provincial officials to help prepare for constitutionalism by first establishing self-government bureaus like the one in Tianjin.[7] More of the same came in September, when the Grand Council instructed officials to set up self-government bureaus and councils in flourishing areas,[8] and in October, when the court told provincial officials to create councils *(hui)* in county and prefectural seats.[9]

Then Beijing fell silent. The Ministry of Interior, which the court recognized in late September 1907 as the sole source for self-government regulations, took almost a year to complete its draft. But the various calls for action in 1906–1907 were never rescinded. Having won its bureaucratic power struggle in Beijing, the ministry downplayed the reports it received on local initiatives.

In August 1908, however, just as they were making final changes to the draft, ministry officials extended their campaign for control to the people. They circularized China: "Recently degree-holders and gentrymen *(shishen)* in every province have been sending reports about initial efforts at self-government. Their privately drafted regulations are improper, for they mistake the meaning of 'self-government' and overstep its boundaries. If this reform is not done carefully at the beginning, then corruption and maladministration will be inevitable."[10] Local self-government initiatives were permissible only in Tianjin prefecture's counties; the rest of China had to wait for the imperial regulations. The editor of *Dongfang zazhi* commented: "It is very clear that the officials at the Ministry of Interior think it would be best to have just one self-government system *(zizhi zhi)* drawn up." [11]

The very people so electrified in September 1906 by an imperial edict were now being admonished by stern Beijing bureaucrats at the Ministry of Interior. Five months later, in January 1909, the imperial regulations would indeed finally be promulgated but the impatience already apparent in August 1908, which had been building ever since the issuance of the constitutionalism edict, was overpowering. Local elites, sometimes in concert with officials, steadily prodded the court to advance the date for council elections from 1912 to 1909. This force had been intensifying throughout 1907–1908. While the Ministry of Interior was trying to turn the Tianjin model into imperial policy, elites throughout China, who refused to temper the energy and excitement displayed during the fall of 1906, began making plans of their own.

Given the variety of actors among local elites, the view from Beijing of this action was remarkably, even dangerously, imprecise. Terms like *shenshi, shimin,* and *shenshang* evoked merely general images of degree-holders, local notables, merchants, and educated commoners. But the variety of action and the diversity of initiatives outside Beijing were as misleadingly homogenized in these Chinese compounds as they would be by such English terms as *local elite* or *gentry.* Not one elite, but many were vying for power and authority. The Beijing concourse in 1906, where men from diverse circles gathered, was part of a significant pattern of action and thought throughout China in 1906–1908. Complexes of motivation also were varied. Some elites responded to Beijing; others tried to lead it. In between was a scattered host where loyalties could be directed toward community, county, province, or nation.

The period between the September 1906 edict and the January 1909 promulgation of the self-government regulations was typified by a remarkable range of initiatives in China, the traces of which make it possible to describe what "local elites" could mean and better see the submerged confluences that can easily be misidentified as simply a "local initiative." A Chinese form of local corporatism—where local power was divided among functionally-specific groups—was on display but scarcely noticed, especially by returned students and their patrons in Beijing who influenced and would continue to influence, local administration and politics in China.

The outline of this portrait of activist local leadership can be glimpsed in one survey of late Qing newspapers and journals that reported the founding of 658 societies *(hui)*, 70 percent of which were in the fields of commerce, education, and politics. Most of these societies were founded in 1906–1908 as the constitutional age began.[12] What a society's formation owes to Beijing's lead and to local initiative is difficult to assess. Some of the 265 chambers of commerce, for example, may have been formed by restless merchants seeking autonomy and influence, but others were dutifully established in accord with imperial regulations promulgated in January 1904.[13] A similar case could be made for educational societies, which Beijing called for in July 1906.[14]

The form of chambers of commerce, educational societies, and even agricultural societies was stipulated by Beijing. But the state's role was less direct in the case of political organizations, which made up more than 10 percent of this particular list. No explicit directive came from Beijing to establish societies directed to constitutionalism or local self-government, but many activists thought the constitutionalism edict was signal enough. In Shanghai Zhang Jian and Zheng Xiaoxu quickly formed the Society to Prepare for Constitutional Government, which, along with the Tianjin initiative,[15] soon became a renowned and influential "constitutional" society. At least forty-five groups, about half of the "political" category in this survey, bore the words "self-government" or "local self-government."[16] The directives, telegrams, and instructions about constitutionalism and self-government from Beijing in 1906–1907 became an informal extension of earlier calls for chambers of commerce, educational societies, and agricultural societies. It was as if each functional group within local society were being asked to participate in local affairs in designated organizations.

Another survey took a second look at "self-government" societies and found further evidence that increased the total to fourteen bureaus and perhaps as many as sixty study societies. Although 80 percent of these organizations, established in 1906–1908, were located in noted centers of reform and innovation like Zhili, Jiangsu, Zhejiang, and Guangdong, there were similar efforts, ranging from Fengtian, Jilin, Heilongjiang, Shanxi, Shandong, and Henan in the north, to Hubei, Hunan, Anhui, and Jiangxi in central China, and Fujian and Guangxi in the south. And even this list is incomplete.[17]

The figures found in these two studies are based on surveys of sources like Shanghai's monthly journal *Dongfang zazhi* and Beijing's daily *Shuntian shibao* and could be expanded were additional sources like provincial gazettes, gazetteers, and archives to be consulted or reconsulted. For example, to the provinces discussed in the latter survey on self-government initiatives, Sichuan could be added. The provincial gazette *Chengdu ribao* tells of a self-government bureau and school in Chengdu, the provincial capital, and a number of other initiatives, some of which took place outside urban centers like Chengdu and Chongqing. Although the latter did establish a local self-government school on 11 August 1908,[18] there was also activity eighty-five miles to the southwest in Lu department where a returned student had organized a self-government study society *(zizhi yanjiu hui)*. Among its programs was a lecture series with presentations every two weeks.[19] Back in western Sichuan, a degree-holder in Mian department, about one hundred miles northwest of Chengdu, asked for and received permission from the Sichuan Provincial Self-government Bureau to establish a self-government lecture hall.[20] Finally, *Chengdu ribao* reported that someone in Jiangyou county, about fifty miles northwest of Chengdu, with the help of various circles, established a self-government school.[21] The Sichuan initiatives are but a sample of the voluminous data still buried in provincial gazettes (see Appendix A).[22]

Other facts can be gleaned from retrospective accounts in county gazetteers. Such sources for twelve counties in southern Jiangsu, for example, reflect self-government initiatives taken prior to 1909.[23]

In Jiading, just west of Shanghai, two groups tried to obtain pro-

vincial approval for their initiatives in the summer of 1907. The Jiading Local Self-government Bureau *(zizhi ju)* included a copy of its
regulations in a petition to Chen Kuilong in July. He approved the
bureau but limited its activities to investigation and study. Another
Jiading group was denied permission to establish a local self-government election bureau *(difang zizhi xuanju ju)*.[24]

A survey of gazetteers and provincial gazettes would uncover
dozens, maybe hundreds, of titles of new organizations that
sprouted in 1906–1908. Another category of sources, imperial archives, yields not only more new evidence but also, in some cases,
extremely detailed accounts. The archives also contain passing references to initiatives away from the provincial capitals of Sichuan, Hubei, and Fujian,[25] as well as ones sponsored by officials in the capitals of Yunnan, Heilongjiang, and Guangdong.[26] In addition, the
Ministry of Interior received numerous reports from local elites,
channeled through provincial yamen, about their initiatives; and
these sometimes provide more insight than do sketchy newspaper,
gazette, or journal reports. The best-documented cases took place in
Suzhou and Jilin city, while a handful of others comes from Beijing.
These were local elite initiatives, a third type of reform action in the
late Qing, that takes a place next to official-dominated initiatives like
Zhao Erxun's Shanxi and Fengtian programs and more explicit official-elite efforts like the Tianjin bureau. In Suzhou and Jilin city
high-level officials were significant, but discreet, influences. Most of
the Beijing initiatives, on the other hand, were much less ambitious
examples of municipal reform-planning that often included officials.
Although similar in some respects to the Tianjin model, the urban,
non-constitutional focus of these capital initiatives exemplifies a
fourth type.

Using a wider variety of sources, including newspapers and journals, provincial gazettes, gazetteers, and archives, yields an even
greater range of self-government initiatives prior to 1909 than the
first surveys suggested. Only Xinjiang, Gansu, and Shaanxi in the
northwest and Guizhou in the southwest lacked initiatives.

In late 1906 and early 1907, when most of the following initiatives
began, there were two certainties: that China was on the road to-

ward constitutionalism and that provincial officials should use the Tianjin model to begin preparing the population for this momentous change. Since the Tianjin bureau was well publicized in provincial gazettes like *Beiyang guanbao,* journals like *Dongfang zazhi,* and newspapers like *Jingbao,* there was plenty of information for officials and elites alike. *Jingbao* noted that Tianjin officials supervised a program that invited elite participation, worked hard to publicize its cause, and tried to diminish the influence of yamen clerks and runners. To reach these goals the Tianjin bureau drafted regulations, investigated local conditions, and published vernacular reports.[27]

In the southern Jiangsu city of Suzhou, prominent and well-connected persons in and out of government circles really did not need such guidance. Here the initiative was seized by nonofficials and former officials, *jinshi,* and returned students who received permission from provincial authorities, symbolized in the seal supplied by the governor to authenticate documents, to hold the first meeting of the Jiangsu Local Self-government Investigation and Study Society (Susheng difang zizhi diaocha yanjiu hui) on 31 March 1907.[28]

Fei Tinghuang, a degree-holder from Suzhou who had studied at Hosei University and was fluent in Japanese, had been teaching at Jiangsu Law School when he heard about the constitutionalism edict.[29] Fei convinced some of his colleagues and friends, including the *jinshi* Jiang Bingzhang,[30] that Suzhou needed a self-government society. This core group of founding members recruited more than one hundred persons to join the society.[31] In addition, four supervisors *(huidong)* were selected from those gentry-managers living outside Suzhou. Supervisors, who had to be publicly recommended by their communities *(you gongzhong tuiju),*[32] could be as distinguished as their urban colleagues. One was a *jinshi* who was a friend of society president Jiang Bingzhang and, like Jiang, had been a Hanlin compiler in Beijing.[33] These supervisors could be found in "scholar-gentry" villages, typical of the Jiangnan region, where generations of scholars and degree-holders, relying on rents from extensive landholdings or income gained from teaching, trading, practicing medicine, or carving seals, had flourished.[34] The society reached outward through its supervisors, who helped implement programs and also met with the standing committee each month, and looked upward to the provincial yamen representative, Zhu Jiabao, the overseer responsible for implementing the society's decisions. The overseer was also notified of the semi-annual general meetings in advance.[35]

The rhetoric used in Suzhou was typical for the time. Constitutionalism and local self-government were allies, an idea that Fei Tinghuang had first heard in classrooms at Hosei University. Instructors at Jiangsu Law School had been lecturing on Japanese reforms in local administration.[36] But the weight of the past half century, during which Jiangsu local elites tried to wrest administrative and fiscal control of rural areas from clerks, runners, and tax farmers,[37] was heavy and easily overwhelmed these untested and foreign ideas. Indeed, Suzhou had produced the eminent late-Qing statecraft advocate of local elite activism, Feng Guifen, and his calls to formalize the unofficial administrative roles of gentry-managers appeared to be on the verge of realization; the society's founders looked forward to the day when "investigation and study" would be dropped from their organization's title.[38]

It was this past, more than Japanese-derived theories, that framed the Suzhou society. No local elections were being planned here, as they were in Tianjin. Nor were plans being drawn up to encourage rural elites to participate as equals. Just four rural supervisors were invited to meet with the urban standing committee in return for helping to implement the committee's decisions. This desire by urban elites to dominate rural society also influenced the organizational structure and stated goals of the society. The largest society subdivision, with forty-three members, was the investigation department. It was supposed to conduct a census, investigate local finances and administration, survey local customs and habits, and assess education and commerce.[39] In years to come there were numerous attempts in many areas in southern Jiangsu to accomplish tasks like these and many countryfolk, in their violent opposition, brought notoriety to Jiangnan.[40]

The Suzhou society looks like an elite-dominated but urban-oriented version of Zhao Erxun's Shanxi model. In both cases an authoritarian model was proposed by officials or elites that checked the power of local magistrates and formalized the unofficial administrative roles of local elites in either urban or rural settings. In the background of both models was the ghost of Feng Guifen, an overpowering presence that obscured the foreign models that intrigued, but did not convince, both Zhao Erxun and the Suzhou activists.

Jilin city, the capital of Jilin province, hosted yet another distinctive local initiative that left behind a cache of documents. While Zhao Erxun was setting up a self-government bureau in Fengtian to begin a cautious program of investigation that would last until the summer of 1908, nearby in Jilin a group of local activists, with the permission of the provincial yamen and the assistance of a few yamen personnel, responded to the constitutionalism edict by convening a meeting of the new Jilin General Local Self-government Study Society (Jilin difang zizhi yanjiu zonghui).

The Manchu bannerman Songyu, who was elected president at a meeting held on 6 January 1907 at a gentry-managers' office *(shendong gongsuo)* in Jilin city,[41] had given up a military career in Heilongjiang when he headed home after hearing the news in September 1906.[42] There he quickly generated support for his society; over one hundred people had joined by the day of that first meeting in January. Within several months about six hundred persons added their names to the membership roll.[43] Most of the fifty men in the leadership core were lower-degree-holders, some of whom were expectant officials, and two had been students at a law school in Jilin; a dozen of them had experience in Japan, including two men who were still studying at Waseda and Hosei universities.[44]

The ambition of the Jilin activists exceeded their compatriots in Tianjin and Suzhou. They made plans to investigate local conditions and discuss findings, translate and publish documents describing foreign models, give lectures, and spur developments in public works, education, and commerce.[45] All of this would be duly reported to officials. For Songyu, at least, the provincial yamen was a crucial ally. In the spring of 1907 the society greeted Jilin's first civil governor, Zhu Jiabao. Zhu, who had overseen the Suzhou initiative, was taken with Songyu and advanced his cause.[46] By October 1907 lectures on self-government, constitutionalism, elections, and census-taking were being given at three locations in Jilin city,[47] and two months later elites arrived from outlying areas to begin a course of instruction at the local self-government school. In 1908, at the height of the golden age of official-elite cooperation, the society was sharing tax collection responsibilities with the local Chamber of Commerce.

And then it all came undone. Beijing transferred Zhu Jiabao to Anhui, over the protest of Songyu and others, who would commemorate Zhu's achievements by erecting a monument; the next governor would not receive similar honors. On 11 October 1908 he abolished what was now the Jilin Local Self-government Society ("Study" had been dropped from the title a year earlier),[48] which had been exercizing legislative and executive powers.

But Songyu quickly found new outlets for his energy and ambition, shifting his attention from local to regional and national issues like the railway rights recovery movement and a national movement to petition the government for the early convening of a parliament.[49]

Songyu's quick transition was made possible by the evident cosmopolitanism displayed by the Jilin society from the very beginning. Songyu took the constitutionalism edict to mean that local activism and national reform were of a piece. He returned home from Heilongjiang and was soon working with two other Jilin natives on the society project. Songyu and his associates, who took the world as their guide, reassured the Ministry of Interior that they were paying attention to both the Tianjin and Fengtian models. Songyu wanted to put this all together, create a Jilin model, and show the rest of China how things should be done.[50] When the new governor slammed shut the society's door, Songyu had several more to choose from.

The new Jilin governor would have been far more comfortable with the limited and government-oriented initiatives that had typified actions in Beijing in 1906–1907. These efforts are less well-documented than the Tianjin, Suzhou, and Jilin programs, but they are noteworthy because they were at the edge of the universe of constitutionalist rhetoric. Akin to pre-1909 merchant-dominated Shanghai reforms in urban administration, the Beijing examples show how initiatives could be culminations of trends rather than departure points. Unlike the previous case studies, the Beijing examples are fixed on urban China. Activists were uninterested in reaching out to the surrounding countryside and constitutionalism was seldom discussed.

The Ministry of Interior was responsible for municipal administration in Beijing. In May 1907 it requested summaries of local initiatives and in July received reports from police bureaus in the city. These indicated that most initiatives were led by merchants and were concerned with commerce or philanthropy.[51] In the report from the Outer City, which was south of the Forbidden City, organizations were divided into four categories: those established by officials, by elites,[52] by officials and elites, or by elites under the supervision of officials.[53]

The Municipal Government Discussion Society (Shizheng gongyi hui), organized in July 1906, was headed by a police superintendent and had thirty-nine members, mostly merchants; it provided a way once a month to bring together officials from the Central Police Bureau, merchants, and degree-holders *(shen)*.[54] A similar organization formed about the same time in the Inner City, which was near the Forbidden City, was the Municipal Public Welfare Society (Shizheng gongyi hui). Officials and elites gathered to discuss and plan projects in education and industry.[55]

There were only two organizations, established in 1907, that resembled some of the initiatives in the provinces. The first one, established in the Inner City, was the Local Self-government Study Society (Difang zizhi yanjiu hui), which had membership requirements similar to those mandated for the Suzhou society.[56] The society held its first meeting in August 1907 and selected forty-five leaders for various society posts. Some government officials were members, including Li Jiaju, who would soon be dispatched to Japan to head the mission investigating all aspects of Japanese society and government.[57] Within three months of that first meeting, the society published a primer on self-government *(Difang zizhi qianshuo)* and investigated the local population and local conditions.[58] Both the regulations and activities of this society were acceptable to the police bureau, which stated in its late November 1907 report that officials should lead the way.[59] The other society that resembled provincial counterparts was the Citizens' Self-government Study Society (Gongmin zizhi yanjiu hui), which met twice a month on Sundays in the Liulichang district of the Outer City according to its report to the police bureau.[60]

Although these examples from Suzhou, Jilin city, and Beijing[61] do give some meaning to "local elite initiatives," vagueness still remains. The activists involved, while interested in varying degrees with rural China, were primarily interested in urban change. Their rural elites are no less hazy than Beijing's *shenshi,* especially when that terrain is limited to degree-holders. But the activity sparked by the September 1906 edict and other government decrees, and the societies formed on the basis of local initiative alone, make it inadvisable to let the Suzhou and Jilin elites in particular stand for late Qing local elites in general.

When we move far beyond Beijing, stopping at provincial capitals and county seats, and study regulations, telegrams, petitions, and news accounts, a much more complicated picture emerges. Degree-holders, gentry-managers *(shendong)* of bureaus and offices, rural leaders of local security organizations *(baojia* and *tuanlian),* and students in new-style schools all have a place in these documents. "Local elites" could also include degree-holders with rank; members of chambers of commerce; members of education societies; members of local self-government bureaus, offices, and schools; leaders of old-style and new-style schools; and rural leaders. These persons, who could live and work in the county seat, market towns, and villages, were among the local elites who were displaying so much organizing energy in 1906–1908. These case studies from Suzhou and Jilin, dominated by degree-holders, were driven by one local elite among many. This list has been built up from a number of sources, most of which were produced in 1907–1910.[62]

Take, for example, the normative visions contained in regulations written in Sichuan, Anhui, and Jiangsu, and in self-descriptions by local elites as suggested by lists of individual names or "circles" *(jie)* appended to petitions submitted to the Sichuan provincial yamen about various local concerns. Regulations drafted in Chengdu for officially sponsored county self-government schools displayed a search for students who held official rank or degrees, had graduated from a new-style middle school or normal school, were involved in public enterprises, or had commercial and agricultural enterprises valued at one thousand yuan or more. Clues about the structure of county and subcounty administration can be found in lists of sponsors of students. The county's educational establishment, such as administrators and teachers at new-style schools along with the government officials charged with educational responsibilities, head the list. Degree-holders and merchants are followed by *tuanlian* and *baojia* leaders in the countryside. "Various bureau heads" of quasi-official offices in county seats with branches elsewhere also had the right to nominate students for the school.

The importance of functionally defined circles can also be seen in documents produced outside Chengdu. For example, the regulations drafted in 1909 governing the selection of an advisory assembly headed by the magistrate of Mian department lists possible sources of members: educational circles, local security officials, leaders of chambers of commerce and agricultural societies, and electors for the provincial assembly.[63]

Another case shows how circles remained distinct even after local councils were established. In Yunyang, a county located on the Yangtze eighty miles upriver from the Hubei border, signatories of a telegram dated 9 July 1910 included persons involved in education, local security (*jiaolian suo*), the agricultural society, industry, taxation, and local self-government (local council and local self-government school).[64]

A final example comes from Nanchuan, fifty miles southeast of Chongqing. A telegram to the provincial yamen dated 18 June 1909 concerning local defense problems was signed by the following persons or organizations: the educational inspector, the head of the education society, the head of police, the head of the chamber of commerce, and the leaders and some members of gentry bureaus for sericulture, industry and commerce, railroads, mining, and the *lijin* tax.[65]

Returning to normative views found in regulations, the plans for a consultative bureau designed to concentrate popularly selected persons from every county at the provincial capital of Anhui contain a detailed representation of elite society in Anhui counties. Ad-hoc county electoral colleges were supposed to include holders of official rank; degree-holders; degree candidates in the old examination system; local notables *(gongzheng shenqi);* graduates, teachers, and administrators of new-style middle schools and above; those associated with education societies, chambers of commerce, and other "self-government groups" *(zizhi tuanti);* and those whose capital exceeded one thousand taels.[66]

This description in a set of regulations anticipated the way elite society in Huichang county, Jiangxi, would be captured in a roll of 327 persons who were eligible to select men to be sent to the prefectural electoral college in 1909. Huichang electors were drawn from four districts and each person's age, residence, degree status, property holdings, or functional status (such as school teacher or local defense leader) was given. Degree-holders were numerous—198 of the 327 electors. Most of the remaining 129 qualified for the franchise on the basis of their property holdings; but sixteen, mostly school teachers and local defense leaders, were allowed to vote because of the roles they played in society. There was also some overlap: seven teachers were also identified as degree-holders *(fusheng).*[67]

Both the Anhui regulations and the Jiangxi electoral rolls suggest why the responses to Beijing's calls for political activity were framed in terms of functional circles: degree-holding, educational, merchant, agricultural, industrial, managerial, and governmental. This phenomenon typified elite self-conceptions and behavior beyond county seats and their hinterlands. The solidarities displayed by provincial elites in response to the constitutionalism edict remained important. In August 1907 Shanghai elites, for example, heeded a call by Duanfang, now governor-general in Jiangsu, to propose plans for establishing representative bodies at the national, provincial, and county level. Twelve different groups *(tuanti)* in Shanghai, with memberships ranging from several dozen to over a hundred, sent representatives to this general convocation. Education groups like the Jiangsu General Education Society (Jiangsu jiaoyu zonghui), merchant organizations like the Shanghai General Chamber of Commerce (Shanghai shangwu zonghui), and groups dedicated to the study of law and constitutionalism like the Constitutional Study Society (Xianzheng yanjiu hui) and the Society to Prepare for Constitutional Government took part. Working in a self-proclaimed spirit of official-elite cooperation, the general assembly submitted proposed regulations to provincial authorities that were forwarded to Beijing.[68]

The kind of constitutionalism imported into China by returned students had little room for the corporatist practices so evident in China in 1906–1908. Subjects needed to be turned into citizens, not into members of functionally-specific groups who gave up their political voice to their leaders. Many returned students would have been surprised to learn that respected Europeans in the late nineteenth century were almost convinced that civilization would end once all persons possessed the right to vote and play a part in public affairs. Fear of mass politics and socialist revolution led some to argue for a society in which "corporatist politics" were carried out by the leaders of "natural," functional groups.[69]

The intellectual foundations for this view had been established by German Romanticists earlier in the century who decried individualism and the political analogue in which sovereignty was invested in persons who collectively, through the franchise, determined the state's will.[70] Conservatives sought to revitalize the political role of vocational groups and strengthen regional autonomy in order to establish a check against both royal despotism and bureaucratic centralism.[71]

But the corporatist responses of 1906–1908 were ignored in Beijing, where returned students labored to draft both self-government regulations and ones for provincial assemblies. In both cases the emphasis was on the individual person, not the group. The corporatist pattern in local political life was, however, deeply engrained. In one of the era's great paradoxes, the centralizing actions of Western-style metropolitan ministries, when extended to a corporatist environment in county seats, split local elites into factions. Local elite began to compete against local elite, with each vying for metropolitan patrons; the centralization of policy making and administration served only to splinter. The local self-government program conceived and executed by the Ministry of Interior began this destabilizing process.

# FOUR

# The Center Readies Its Arsenal

The local self-government regulations issued by the Qing court in January 1909 symbolized the Ministry of Interior's ambition to centralize China's administration. It was a goal that owed much to Japan and the West. One of the foremost Chinese interpreters of these foreign models, Liang Qichao, complained that "on the surface the government seems to be a centralized one. However, the country is actually divided into innumerable small units and groups on the basis of either territory or biological relatedness or occupations."[1] Liang wanted to change China from what he thought was a vast territory of group-oriented parochialism to a state where the energies of public-minded "new citizens," imbued with a sense of solidarity and the capacity to form new kinds of civic associations, were on display. Liang's new group *(qun)* would be the nation-state.[2] Liang had sounded the challenge back in 1898 in Hunan:

> It is not merely to have rulers, officials, students, farmers, laborers, merchants, and soldiers, but to have ten thousand eyes with one sight, ten thousand hands and feet with only one mind, ten thousand ears with one hearing, ten thousand powers with only one purpose of life; then the state is established ten thousandfold strong. . . . When mind touches mind, when power is linked to power, cog to cog, strand around strand, and ten thousand roads meet in one center, this will be the state.[3]

China needed new citizens whose loyalties went beyond place, family, and occupation. But this was a perilous task, for persons usually were imbedded, as Liang had written, in familiar groups that often designated representatives to deal with the state. How could persons with strong group loyalties and a mentality long-influenced by Chinese local corporatism become new citizens whose primary loyalties were directed toward the state?

The diversity of local groups, which had only increased since the Qing call for chambers of commerce, educational and agricultural societies, and local assemblies, was the target of a unifying vision articulated by Liang and shared by many in China, especially the returned students who were in Beijing by 1907. Jin Bangping was one; others included Sun Pei and Lu Zongyu at the Ministry of Interior. Sun, like Jin, had studied law in Japan; Lu Zongyu, a native of Zhejiang and a Waseda graduate, had been awarded a new-style degree in the same special 1905 palace examination that had opened doors for Jin.[4]

Returned students had long prepared for this moment. Much of their time in Japan had been given over to translating, writing, and publishing articles on government, politics, and administration, a practice that continued as they returned to China. Lu Zongyu, clutching his newly won credential, shared his "Private Thoughts on Constitutional Government" with the readers of the Shanxi government gazette *Jinbao*. Lu soon gained a national audience after the essay, which argued that a constitutional nation required citizens *(guomin)* who had been introduced to the art of politics by practicing self-government, was published in *Dongfang zazhi* in November 1905.[5] By 1907 Lu was a highly placed official at the Ministry of Interior, where local self-government policy was being decided upon for all of China.

The Ministry of Interior, which had been created in November 1906, during the general metropolitan reorganization,[6] around the institutional nucleus of Beijing's year-old police bureau,[7] had slowly acquired jurisdiction of self-government policy for its portfolio. The ministry then tried to infuse the "local" part of the reform with a central authority that would have pleased Rudolf Gneist and his Japanese followers. Under the influence of returned students like Sun Pei, the ministry pushed for programs that would be managed from

Beijing. These metropolitan bureaucrats praised the Tianjin model, but tried to dissuade local elites and local officials from drafting their own rules. The men in Beijing were looking for unity in practice as well as theory. Local self-government was the foundation for constitutional government because it would unify China's diverse regions and localities. There could be initiatives in Tianjin, Suzhou, Jilin city, Shanghai, Canton, Beijing, and elsewhere; but the Ministry of Interior fought for and won the right to build the theoretical and administrative framework. The title given to a draft in the summer of 1907 captured the sentiment: "Uniform Simplified Regulations for Preparing for Local Self-government."[8]

What kind of unity was possible? Men like Wu Tingxie, the former Shanxi official now at the Ministry of Interior, knew rural China's diversity from personal experience. Wu, along with his colleague Lu Zongyu, urged his peers to collect as much local knowledge as possible before prescribing reforms. But could unity be achieved simply by collating diversity? Did unity require, instead, a penetrating vision from one source that prevailed over local differences? The arguments made by Toulmin Smith in England and Rudolf Gneist in Prussia were duplicated in China, where some praised and encouraged local autonomy while others hoped Beijing's policies would open local communities to the reach of the state.

Policy makers at the Ministry of Interior often referred to foreign models, but were less interested in the administrative histories behind them. Europe's transformations of the previous century, however, not the current structures of her governments, were more apposite to China's situation. In 1907 China was heir to familiar administrative practices that possessed a logic also found in cameralist theories taught at German universities in the eighteenth century. Baroque administrators-to-be had learned that harmony was immanent in a world of diverse appearances. Although this harmony could be deranged, state administrators need only eliminate the disturbant elements to restore harmony.[9] State activism was frowned upon and local communities, with their own slices of sovereignty, counterpoised the state.[10] Aspects of political theory in imperial China resonated with this cameralism. For example, the statecraft ideal of infusing the centralized bureaucratic monarchical state *(jun-xian)* with a feudal spirit displayed by local people taking care of local affairs *(fengjian)* is part of an argument combining apparent diversity with immanent unity. The intellectual foundation for these ideas can be found in Neo-Confucian thought, with a pedigree extending a millennia, in the concepts of *li* (principle) and *qi* (material force): "*li* is one but its manifestations are many."[11]

Just as Napoleon jolted the Germanic states from their cameralist complacency, so too did the crises China faced a century later. The Chinese, who were searching for a new kind of unity, were weary of cringing when Westerners mocked China's diversity by gibing that its provinces were really separate nations. Local self-government planned and managed from Beijing and inspired indirectly by Prussia's reforms in the nineteenth century, seemed to be the answer to some. From Baron vom Stein's fascination with the English model to Rudolf Gneist's voluminous writings on English "self-government," Prussian administrative reforms and some of their consequences were at least known in Asia by the late nineteenth century.[12] Stein's reforms of 1808 had been effective in Prussia, where relatively quiescent towns and cities already tied into regional and international economic systems, accepted a set of reforms that sought to connect them to the Prussian state. But centralizers in Beijing were unaware of a different scenario to the south in Middle Germany, where autonomous and economically self-sufficient "home towns" and their tightly controlled hinterlands had rejected state-initiated programs. After the Napoleonic crisis passed, in fact, local autonomy and its attendant diversities reappeared in Middle Germany.[13] But the unity-diversity problem remained. As cameralist baroque administration faded into a memory associated with the defunct Holy Roman Emperor of the German Nation, administrative specialists in Prussia and other German states sought a German unity that could survive future challenges from either France or England. Lacking the administrative and judicial system, the parliamentary cabinet system, or the political party system that were crucial to French, English, or American state unity, Germans kept looking for an appropriate and effective way to achieve unity while protecting diversity. But each approach was either rejected or failed.[14] A symbolic approach that began to be developed in the mid-nineteenth century, and one that continues to be significant, emphasized the idea of Heimat, an untranslatable term connoting "home" and "the familiar." The German nation, according to one scholar, was ultimately constructed by developing these intense local feelings in the context of translocal nationalism. Since the "nation" is too abstract truly to imagine, the palpable loyalty engendered by home territory or Heimat segued to a nation of many Heimat. In the end, again, unity in diversity.[15] This model for unity was absent from the centralizers' vision expressed by Liang Qichao at the turn of the century. His "innumerable small units" were the stumbling blocks, not the building blocks, of nationhood. Instead, Liang and most other observers in Asia and the West looked to institutional models of cabinets, judiciaries, and political parties derived from other Western experience for antidotes to China's crisis.

Beijing policy makers in 1907, who would have recognized the challenges faced by Germanic states in the nineteenth century, began to force uniform policies on diverse localities. Under the influence of returned students as well as unrealized ambitions of the imperial state, the Ministry of Interior also insisted on a surveillance and information-gathering function. Did China need this centralism? Could Beijing handle all the information? And did Beijing have the will and the ability to carry out its directives? China could not survive many more years of cameralist administration, but what could take its place? And, finally, who were the people and how should they participate in public affairs?

Answers to these questions were crafted under the influence of an ethos that can be identified with a significant section of China's returned students, some of whom were active in government ministries like Interior, while compeers tried to influence Beijing policy making from cities like Shanghai and Tianjin. Clues to their mindset can be found in internal Ministry of Interior documents and published essays alike. The most illuminating and portentous to take on these attitudes can be found in a petition to ministry officials written by staff member Sun Pei and a colleague. Sun, a *jiansheng* from Anhui, was just twenty-four but came to the ministry with a résumé that included two years of studying law in Tokyo.[16] He was joined by Xu Chengjin, four years his senior, who was a *gongsheng* from Guizhou. Sun and Xu explained how administration in other countries was shared by government officials who were appointed and by popularly elected leaders of self-government organizations. They said local administration in China could only be accomplished by a similar arrangement.[17] Writing early in 1907, Sun and Xu worried about the paucity of initiatives even though imperial instructions had been sent out. Beijing had to take the lead and show the way by doing the following:

> Principles for a provisional form of local self-government should be drawn up and sent to provincial officials for guidance.
>
> Provincial officials should establish self-government study societies *(zizhi yanjiu hui)* for the purpose of training gentry-managers *(shendong)* about the nature of local self-government.
>
> Local self-government should be implemented in stages, beginning with the provincial capitals and treaty ports, and then extending to every county.
>
> In Beijing, local notables *(gongzheng shenqi)* should establish a municipal assembly and begin public works. This is necessary because of Beijing's key role as a leading area for the rest of China.
>
> Provincial officials should be required to submit reports every three months to the Ministry of Interior concerning self-government activities.
>
> All subprovincial groups, such as self-government societies, should be required to send copies of regulations and other documents to the Ministry of Interior.
>
> All local assemblies for education and commerce should be required to send their regulations to the respective metropolitan ministry, as well as to the Ministry of Interior.

Sun and Xu called for detailed reports on local initiatives to be sent to Beijing so that maladministration and corruption could be prevented. They emphasized that the law must be followed in order to control corrupt local notables who might follow their own wishes and desires. In November 1907 this centralizing vision was evoked again in a memorandum of discussion produced by the ministry's Drafting Office. The influence of Sun Pei, who had since become head of the ministry's Local Self-government Section, is clear. This archival document is brief, and now quite fragile; insects have eaten away a few of the characters, but it is still possible to piece together policy discussions.[18]

The November memorandum of discussion mentioned two sets of articles: twenty-eight for planning and ninety for management. The working title for the first set, *Chouban difang zizhi jianzhang* (Simplified regulations for preparing for local self-government), corresponds to another extant document drafted by the Ministry of Interior. This earlier version of the Simplified Regulations describes temporary organizations, like the Tianjin Self-government Bureau, that were necessary to manage local council elections. This draft echoes Sun and Xu's concerns that had been expressed in their petition: the need for indoctrinating local elites about the meaning and significance of local self-government, emphasis on careful reporting of local initiatives to the central government, and control by local magistrates of all initiatives. To establish self-government it was necessary to elect local councils and executive boards. Bureaus, which would supervise the elections, would be appointed by magistrates in county seats throughout China. Seven people were required for each of the two sections of the bureau, one of which was responsible for investigations such as boundary-marking, census, and compilations of electoral lists, the other for managing the elections. A third group ran the local self-government school.

Plans for schools, which could be founded by both officials and nonofficials, were also described. Every county needed one official school with separate classes for gentry *(shen)* and other notables *(shi)*. The magistrate was asked to report the founding along with data like names of students and personnel, class sizes, fees and financial information, curriculum, and book information to provincial authorities. They would in turn compile provincial reports for the Ministry of Interior.

Local people could organize schools as long as they limited their activities to teaching about self-government. At least ten persons were needed to found a school, which required a magistrate's permission. The founders had to supply all the information requested in the above-mentioned reports, as well as their addresses and the address of the school. Again, Beijing asked provincial officials to provide summaries of all this information. The local magistrate was to monitor the organizations, and when local activists became too active, a magistrate could, with permission from provincial authorities, shut down the schools.[19]

The confidence in the ease with which central orders could be realized was shared by other returned students in Beijing. For example, those at the Constitutional Commission (Xiangzheng bianchaguan) were certain in 1908 that when local council elections were finally held, the new councillors would be graduates of new-style schools.[20] The perspicacity of these capital policy makers was lacking, in this instance, since few new-style schools in 1908 even accepted students over the age of thirty *sui*.

The tidy vision shared by these men was animated by a strong conviction that constitutionalism and elections could solve China's crisis of local leadership. Other returned students outside the ministry and Beijing had similar ideas and faith. For example, in October 1907 the ministry received a booklet sent by the Shanghai society responsible for its publication, the Society to Prepare for Constitutional Government. In it Meng Zhaochang criticized the way managers *(dongshi)* collaborated with evil clerks and runners from government yamen. In his preface to *Difang zizhi zhi gangyao* (An outline of systems of local self-government), Meng insisted that formal elections *(xuanju)* would identify a different set of leaders from those chosen by the old way of reaching an informal consensus *(gongju)*. He thought that by replacing the "old-boy" network with a system legitimated by the vote of the people *(zhong)*, the influence of gentry-managers would be undermined.[21]

An even more detailed description of the anticipated benefits of reform comes from Tianjin, where returned student and bureau member Wu Xingrang wrote that in the new age of constitutionalism safeguards against corruption were part of the institutions of local self-government. Wu, who helped write Tianjin's regulations for Western-style council elections, argued that the procedures used by local councils, especially the privileging of the majority's will, would eliminate selfish and prejudiced leaders. Elections would bring to power the very public-minded, educated, and progressive leaders China needed for social progress. If this was too optimistic, Wu assured his listeners that the separation of legislative and executive powers between councils *(yishihui)* and boards *(dongshihui)* would minimize the potential for abuse. He knew local leaders tended to exercise political power as an extension of the person or family; consequently Wu emphasized that the community, for which he used the Japanese loanphrase "self-government group" (J: *jichi dantai;* C: *zizhi tuanti)*, included everyone in an administrative jurisdiction. Council members represented everyone; the relationship between a council member and the persons in a self-government group was not like the one between a landlord and his tenants.[22]

The regulations Wu helped draft in Tianjin, influenced as they were by the Japan model, were similar to ones finally produced in Beijing. Tianjin documents were forwarded by Yuan Shikai and the court to the Ministry of Interior, where influential men like Sun Pei appeared sympathetic to many of the ideas and programs discussed by Wu Xingrang. Meng Zhaochang's ideas were also available, and well-received, at the ministry.[23] But Beijing's perspective did modify ideas. Those in the Ministry of Interior, at least, were intent on establishing centralized control of local administration; their classmates in the provinces, however, were partial to a state with a lighter hand. And for much of 1907 returned students in the provinces were not burdened by many specific instructions from Beijing. That would soon change.

The Ministry of Interior's eventual mandate took form in a volatile policy-making environment. Besides skirmishes with Yuan Shikai, the provincial reformer turned metropolitan official, it was not clear until the end of September 1907 that the ministry alone would be responsible for reform policy. But such certainty was not characteristic of the year. It was early in 1907 when ministry officials directed its Local Self-government Section (Difang zizhi ke), which was subordinate to the Administration Department (Minzhi si), to manage the establishment of councils and executive boards throughout China. Self-government bureaus, self-government societies, and self-government finances also fell under section purview.[24] But little was done to draft local self-government principles or regulations that could be relied upon by provincial officials nor were officials told to await Beijing's lead. A partial mandate was received in July 1907, when the ministry was identified as the source of guidelines for county councils. A call for these councils had been included at the end of a set of principles agreed upon by a metropolitan commission on 7 July 1907 to be used to guide reorganization of provincial administration.[25] This mandate was mentioned later in July by a discussion group in the ministry that had been convened to write the council regulations. In a memorandum dated 25 July 1907 the group mentioned the Tianjin model and commented, "[I]t is urgently necessary for this ministry to decide upon and send out regulations."[26]

The ministry group also suggested that a local self-government lecture society *(difang zizhi jiangxi hui)* be established in Beijing. Officials and elites sent by provincial officials would gather at the society to listen to introductory lectures and be briefed on the ministry's regulations for councils and boards. Afterwards they would return to their provinces to establish local self-government bureaus, which would be responsible for drawing up appropriate implementation schedules.[27]

The day after this memorandum was completed an item in *Shuntian shibao* stated that Shanqi, the president of the ministry, had requested Yuan Shikai to forward documents concerning the Tianjin council election regulations to the ministry.[28] The Drafting Office called for a self-government bureau managed by ministry personnel and modelled after the Tianjin Self-government Bureau to make preparations for establishing a local council *(difang yihui)* in Beijing. On 3 August 1907 *Shuntian shibao* reported that the Ministry of Interior had decided to form the Beijing Local Self-government Bureau.[29] A week later the ministry chose to use a slightly amended version of the Tianjin Self-government Bureau regulations.[30] The ministry was specially interested in the Tianjin model in the summer of 1907 after elections there had already taken place. It was not, however, the only Beijing audience for the Tianjin model, for the imperial court itself identified Yuan Shikai and Tianjin as the most important source of ideas and plans. And Yuan continued to influence this policy from Beijing as evidenced by the court's rescription of a broad-ranging memorial by Yuan on 28 July 1907 to the Bureau of Government Affairs. Commenting on Yuan's discussion of self-government policy, the bureau advised the court to direct provincial officials to use the Tianjin model in implementing local self-government in places where people were enlightened *(minzhi kaitong)* like provincial capitals and treaty ports.[31] Another memorial by Yuan Shikai that summer, which described Tianjin's recent council elections, included a copy of the Tianjin regulations and a request for the court to forward this material to the Ministry of Interior.[32]

Shanqi, the president of the ministry since 18 June 1907, was determined to control self-government policy making. Shanqi, also known as Prince Su, was honored among foreigners because of the role he played in protecting diplomats, businessmen, missionaries, and their families during the troubles in 1900 in Beijing.[33] He took seriously the claim that local self-government was the foundation of constitutional government. In the fourth month of his tenure he won his bureaucratic battle with Yuan Shikai and the Grand Council.

Shanqi had a reputation as an advocate of municipal reform;[34] and when he took over the ministry, he was well-situated to get formal reports of recent initiatives in Beijing. He could also see how Yuan's presence on the Grand Council and his association with the successful Tianjin model, combined with indifferent policy making at the Ministry of Interior, was dooming the ministry to insignificance. Unhappy with this state of affairs, Shanqi reshuffled the leadership of the Local Self-government Section in the Ministry of Interior in early September, placing the returned student Sun Pei in charge.[35] Shanqi continued his quest even as the Grand Council, under Yuan's influence, told the ministry to telegraph provincial officials about the Grand Council's decision to implement local self-government first in provincial capitals and treaty ports.[36]

With a handpicked man in the key ministry post, Shanqi coun-
tered with a memorial in which he and the ministry asked the court
to issue an edict that granted sole responsibility to the ministry. This
plea was prompted in part by the receipt on 26 September 1907 of
the namelists and regulations of the Jiangsu Local Self-government
Investigation and Study Society in Suzhou. A ministry official re-
marked that the Suzhou "regulations were not entirely in compliance
with existing regulations, but they were already being implemented
provisionally on the basis of the approval of the governor-general
and governor." But this official wanted the ministry itself to draft
the regulations.[37] This viewpoint was repeated in a comment *(tangpi)*
made by Shanqi when he authorized the submission of the memorial
requesting that the throne announce that the Ministry of Interior
was already working on regulations for local self-government;
Shanqi also called on the Suzhou society to revise their regulations
once the ministry had promulgated the official version.[38] Shanqi won
his battle in Beijing. On 30 September 1907 an edict stated that the
Ministry of Interior was responsible for drafting local self-government regulations;[39] previous instructions had directed the ministry
simply to draft general principles for establishing county councils.[40]

But the struggle for control had only begun between two officials
who had just assumed important positions in the Beijing bureaucracy. Shanqi led a newly established metropolitan ministry that was
responsible for a broad range of domestic affairs. Yuan Shikai's position was already redoubtable. Besides heading the Ministry of Foreign Affairs and sitting on the Grand Council, Yuan had won approval for the establishment of a new commission charged with
overall management of constitutional reform. The Constitutional
Commission (Xianzheng bianchaguan), a high-level body nominally
headed by two members of the Grand Council and responsible for
supervising all matters concerning the introduction of constitutional
government to China,[41] was established on 13 August 1907. It included Yuan on its board of directors and was staffed by many returned students and reform-minded officials, some of whom had ties
to him.[42] Yuan could also place his protégés on the staff of the still-
influential Grand Council. For example, Jin Bangping, reportedly

one of the brightest of his aides, was transferred to a staff position on the Grand Council at Yuan's request.[43] Yuan's advantage seemed greater given the Grand Council's proximity to the court. But Shanqi, whose ministry was located just east of the walls of the Forbidden City, also had access to the throne.[44] Was the Manchu Shanqi trying to check the Chinese Yuan Shikai? Perhaps, but it seems more probable that this was a turf battle between two reform-minded men. Yuan was better known for reform efforts; but Shanqi's early call for reforms in 1902 and the way he assisted Liang Qichao in 1907 when Liang tried to establish a study society in China, when juxtaposed with his reputation among foreigners and his efforts at the Ministry of Interior, had given Shanqi a reputation as a reformer too.[45] At issue in the struggle between Yuan and Shanqi was the level in the Chinese bureaucracy at which reform initiatives would be planned. Yuan, who had established his reputation on the basis of his provincial reforms, was still inclined, even though he was now in Beijing, to provincial discretion; it had served him well in Tianjin. But the bureaucratic in-fighting in mid-1907 that saw Yuan lose to Shanqi tended to diminish the role of both provincial officials and local elites in reform planning as Interior claimed a larger and larger role. Yuan, however, did not quit. Through his position on the Constitutional Commission he influenced the creation of the provincial assemblies that would be elected in 1909.[46] These bodies, not Shanqi's local councils, became the symbol for many of the court's commitment to constitutionalism.

Confirmed in its role, the ministry took almost a year to complete its version of self-government regulations for administrative seats, towns, and rural townships. In August 1908 this draft was sent for approval to the Constitutional Commission, where Shanqi's antagonist, Yuan Shikai, remained. Five months later, after a delay caused by the turmoil in Beijing following the deaths of the Guangxu Emperor and the Empress Dowager in November 1908, the regulations were approved by the Prince Regent on behalf of the infant Xuantong Emperor.[47]

The summer of 1908, when the Ministry of Interior finally completed its draft, drew particular criticism from Meribeth Cameron, a

pioneering scholar of the late Qing reforms: "No phase of the reform efforts of the later years of the Empire is more open to criticism than the hasty and uncritical copying of Western, and especially
Japanese, institutions, which in many cases took the place of hard
study of Chinese requirements and needs."[48] Cameron's critique
was especially apt for the self-government regulations, which were
heavily influenced by the Japanese regulations of 1888. But there
had been voices in the Ministry of Interior, at least, that had coun-
selled patience and study in 1907–1908. Returned student Lu
Zongyu had a role in writing a memorial from the Ministry of Interior that was rescripted back in March 1907. In its language and
ideas this memorial is reminiscent of the world described in the documents associated with the Shanxi *xiangshe* reforms. This was not
coincidental; Zhao Erxun's Shanxi associate, Wu Tingxie, was now
a high-ranking member of the Ministry of Interior, where he had
become second in command in the office responsible for drafting
legislation.[49] Moreover, Wu Tingxie may have discussed the Shanxi
reforms with Lu several years earlier, for both men were in Beijing
when Lu wrote his 1905 essay on constitutionalism in which he argued that China should study foreign models like Germany and
Meiji Japan and domestic models like Shanxi's *xiangshe* reforms and
the establishment of gentry bureaus *(shendong ju)* in Shandong.[50]

The Ministry of Interior had argued in its early 1907 memorial
that because the population was not ready for self-government, local
conditions had to be investigated first. Provincial officials were asked
to describe how local leadership varied. Armed with provincial reports on *xiangshe*, the Ministry of Interior could then draft appropriate regulations.[51] Attention to diversity was to precede unifying
legislation.

The ministry, which reached a national audience in the 12 May
1907 issue of *Zhengyi tongbao* and the 5 June 1907 issue of *Dongfang zazhi*, stressed the fundamental importance of China's rural areas in ensuring the unity of the people and officials. This unity, now
being redefined with a constitutional rhetoric, was undermined because local leaders were unaware of the government's reform agenda:
"The promulgation of previous legislation associated with the New

Policies has been mostly hidden from the leaders of *xiangshe*." Also, the state had to rely on local leaders, many of whom were inimical to the well-being of the people: "Those who serve are not good, and those who are good do not serve."[52]

The detailed local knowledge sought by the memorialists would be added to their present understanding about the diversity of local leadership in China. Beginning with three posts, given in a compendium of administrative law, connected with various local institutions for security *(baojia)*, taxation *(lijia)*, and imperial propaganda *(xiang-yue)*, the memorialists noted that these posts had been supplemented by a bewildering array of local leaders—thirteen different titles were mentioned—required to manage a wide range of local affairs, a change they dated to the mid-nineteenth century. There were leaders of local militia, managers *(dong)* in market towns and villages, and others who supervised *(jingli)* territories of various sizes: a village, a group of villages, or dozens of villages.[53] In fact, in counties far from provincial capitals, a rural constable *(xiangbao)* might manage *(guan)* an area approaching a section of a county.[54] This lack of uniformity extended to the way these leaders were selected, to whether their authority was designated by the magistrate, and to their social status.

Whether or not provincial officials responded to this request, policy makers at the Ministry of Interior appeared partial to documents and ideas imported from abroad under the auspices of a commission established on 25 November 1905 that was headed by five officials who scoured the world in 1906 for reform ideas.[55] This commission, which was the antecedent of Yuan's Constitutional Commission, was responsible for reform planning. On 6 February 1906 the commission directed Song Yuren, a reform-minded *jinshi* from Sichuan[56] who was an expectant Hubei official, to establish an office in Shanghai for translating books and materials that the commission would be sending back to China. Because the commissioners were not staying in Japan very long, nine staff members were directed on 10 February 1906 to remain behind and select and organize documents to be sent to Shanghai for translation. A memorial filed in November 1906 by the commissioners of the overseas mission stated that 67 of 434 titles of materials in Japanese and Western languages had been translated into Chinese. Descriptions of Japanese local self-government, including specific discussions of the codes of 1888 and 1890, appeared in the national government gazette *Zhengzhi guanbao* in October 1907.[57] But Beijing was the last to know. For example, Wu Xingrang's essays on and translations of Japanese laws pertaining to local administration had already been published, beginning in late 1906, in the Tianjin gazette *Beiyang fazheng xuebao*. Similar material had been covered in classrooms at Jiangsu Law School.

It was this body of information, not responses from provincial officials or independent investigators, that dominated policy makers at the Ministry of Interior in 1908. *Cheng zhen xiang difang zizhi zhangcheng* (Regulations for local self-government in administrative seats, towns, and townships), which was given imperial approval on 18 January 1909, called for two characteristic features in the Japan and Tianjin models: Western-style elections and a clean division of responsibility between deliberative councils *(yishihui)* and executive boards *(dongshihui)*. In Beijing as in Tianjin, the Japanese influence was clear. Besides the division of legislative and executive responsibilities, the Chinese borrowed from the Japanese, as the Japanese had from Germany, a Western-style system of elections. Ballot-casting electors, and those eligible to be elected, could include any literate male over the age of twenty-five *sui* who was a tax-paying resident of three-years duration in jurisdictions defined as administrative seats *(cheng)*, market towns *(zhen)*, and townships *(xiang)*.[58]

The influence of Japanese regulations promulgated in 1888 can also be seen in the requirement that electors must either be taxpayers or make voluntary contributions. Furthermore, the list of council functions (e.g., deciding matters pertaining to affairs of the area, promulgating local laws, raising funds, and making annual financial statements) are almost identical in content and order in the two codes.[59]

The regulations were divorced from the world of *xiangshe* first discussed by Zhao Erxun and Wu Tingxie in Shanxi in 1902, mentioned by Lu Zongyu and Shen Jiaben in 1905, and emphasized once again by the ministry early in 1907. As Wu Tingxie had acknowledged in the ministry's memorial of March 1907, the titles and functions of the leaders of these subcounty jurisdictions varied across China. Whether such information was ever collected is unknown, although Zhao Erxun, while governor in Sichuan, did refer to the memorial,[60] but the local self-government regulations reveal little about metropolitan conceptions of local society.

What ambition was evident in the desire of this metropolitan ministry to write relevant and uniform regulations for all of China's diverse regions! The ministry tried and its penchant for uniformity augured the future; cameralist administrative practices were becoming a part of the past. The world of *xiangshe* mentioned in the ministry's March 1907 call for local investigations was not to be found in these Japanese-influenced regulations. But in provincial yamen diverse realities were all that mattered, especially in 1907 and 1908 when conflicting signals from Beijing about the propriety of local initiatives created confusion. Well before the promulgation of these regulations, provincial officials were under pressure to sanction a variety of local initiatives. Returned students in the provinces pushed for change as eagerly as did their peers in Beijing while provincial officials tried both to heed Beijing's centralizing demands and to focus the energies of impatient activists. China was spacious, but was there room enough for the localism of a Suzhou, the centralism of Beijing, *and* provincialism?

# FIVE

# Provincial Officials Channel Elite Activism

Without responsive provincial and local yamen the centralism sought by the Ministry of Interior could only be an idea in search of a country. Provincial governors were needed to collect and summarize information provided by local magistrates for Beijing's convenience and relay metropolitan instructions to county yamen. But to act merely as concentrator and conduit would neither fit the self-image of provincial officials nor meet the daily challenges of their office. These officials were among the chief sponsors of local initiatives, a fact conveniently ignored by the Ministry of Interior in August 1908 when it ordered provincial authorities to clamp down on self-government initiatives.[1] At times high officials only watched from a distance, as in Suzhou and Jilin city; but as Zhao Erxun had shown in Shanxi and Yuan Shikai in Tianjin, they could be movers.

This was more than state activism. Much like the cooperation between officials and elites characteristic of Tianjin election preparations in 1906–1907, official-led initiatives often relied upon the energies of expectant officials in ad-hoc provincial bureaus and local men in so-called gentry bureaus. The pattern of these now-familiar relationships had been established in previous decades when provincial and county yamen delegated authority to managers of tasks in local administration. Local self-government planning was added to the long list of duties already being accomplished by officials and elites working in concert.[2]

But the court's call in the fall of 1907 for all plans to emanate from Beijing gave Shanqi's centralism precedence over Yuan Shikai's plan to allow provincial and local officials to develop specific initiatives as conditions permitted. Beijing, while now denying officials outside the capital customary powers and prerogatives, was still riven with conflicts over the relative merits of centralism and provincialism. This debate, personified in the struggle between Shanqi and Yuan, diminished the ability of the newly founded Ministry of Interior to claim its victory. And official-led initiatives in the provinces, which remained numerous, proved to be tenacious. Moreover, the new reform-planning bureaus and the medium of new-style gazettes pioneered by Yuan Shikai when he was governor of Zhili made it possible for Qing officials outside Beijing to stay in the fray. These official-led reform initiatives, along with private initiatives, would threaten to impinge upon the center-led reforms that began in 1909. Back at the beginning of the constitutional age provincial and local officials had no need to depend on bureaus and gazettes to buttress their power, for Beijing seemed willing to rely on persuasion alone to coax officials into the role of centralism's agent. Early discussions on provincial reorganization, for example, were characterized by a spirit of partnership and cooperation. The Compilation Commission (Bianzhi guan) meeting in Beijing in the fall of 1906 for the purpose of preparing schemes for both provincial and metropolitan administration was careful to canvass provincial governors about various proposals, including one for establishing elected councils. On 12 January 1907 a new commission of metropolitan officials and delegates sent by select provincial officials assembled in Beijing to consider ways to improve administration in counties and provinces.[3]

But talks quickly broke down, and an audience with the Empress Dowager shortly after deliberations began sapped purpose even more. The commission was trying to draft proposals for provincial reforms; but the court, along with some metropolitan officials, was more interested in completing the metropolitan reorganizations that had begun back in November.[4] Moreover, some provincial officials opposed the commission itself; in consequence, discussions finally ceased in early April, and delegates returned to the provinces.[5] Stasis turned to crisis, however; and in the summer of 1907, as the court began to transfer prominent provincial officials like Yuan Shikai and Zhang Zhidong to new posts in Beijing,[6] obstacles were skirted and the commission reconvened.

Provincial reorganization regulations, which took their place alongside the plans promulgated in the fall of 1906 for new Western-style central government ministries, were finally announced on 7 July 1907.[7] Responsibilities for self-government planning for council elections were divided between provincial yamen and the Ministry of Interior. But three months later, the court, having ignored Yuan Shikai's advice, placed the prerogative for policy planning in the hands of Shanqi and the ministry alone. Signals from Beijing were too mixed and local elites too impatient, however, for any provincial governor to step aside simply because Beijing wished it.

The emperor's men in the provinces sometimes discreetly misread Beijing's demands, which were often unenforceable anyway, and teased general goals into sanctions for particular programs. They were not playing for power; they simply knew what Beijing found difficult to admit: delay and repression would serve only to heighten and deepen disenchantment. Duanfang, the official whose memorials steeled the court for reform in 1906, admonished the dilatory throne in August 1907: "In recent days reckless people have begun to oppose constitutional government. In order to stop the minority that incites disruptive 'parties' of anti-Manchu sentiment, we must yield to the majority's hope for reform. . . . The parties of disorder will then be unable to deceive and incite the ignorant populace. Since their power will fade, there will be no need for us to suppress them."[8] Duanfang spoke from wide experience and possessed a reputation for administrative and educational reforms that he had won during tenures in Shaanxi, Hubei, Hunan, and Jiangsu, and would polish in Anhui and Jiangxi.[9]

Zhao Erxun was another provincial official who responded in 1907–1908 both to Beijing and the people he ruled. For example, when the Ministry of Interior issued its August 1908 proscription of local initiatives in self-government planning, Zhao's yamen in Sichuan tried to satisfy both Beijing's centralizers and Sichuan activists:

> In accordance with a Ministry of Interior directive that has been received, all activities such as establishing self-government bureaus should be delayed until the ministry's memorial is approved. Regulations may not be drafted independently. However, the Provincial Self-government School regulations and regulations for other schools that have been approved by the Sichuan Provincial Self-government Bureau and the governor remain in effect.[10]

Zhao Erxun, the cautious authoritarian, had no intention of waiting for Beijing's school regulations, which would finally be promulgated in May 1909, for he faced intense pressure in the post he had assumed in June 1908.

Zhao had seen several changes in the relationship among counties, provinces, and the capital since his Shanxi tour, but the capital's new reform policies served to push him into uncharted and dangerous territory. Zhao's initiative of 1902–1903 was conceived in Shanxi and received praise and publicity from Beijing; in 1906 while in Fengtian he had been directed by the court to create a reform model to be used there and elsewhere in China. By 1908, however, Beijing was telling Zhao and the rest of his colleagues in China to stand still and wait for further instructions. Zhao knew, as did Duanfang, that the times called for action. Their challenge: to support provincial reform programs while demonstrating loyalty to a Beijing that was beclouded with strange rhetoric and idealistic plans translated from foreign idioms.[11]

And there was plenty of talent competing for influence from the provinces; neither returned students nor reform ideas were being monopolized by Beijing. Men like Yuan Shikai and Zhang Zhidong left behind many of the foreign-trained administrative specialists they had patronized in recent years, while governors like Zhao, Duanfang, and Cen Chunxuan continued to attract reform-minded men to provincial capitals; governors could also place chosen people in local yamen. Even without such particular magnets, the role claimed in general by provincial yamen in the constitutional age made these government offices as attractive, in the minds of some returned students, as any Beijing ministry. The self-government bureaus ordered up by Beijing in the fall of 1906 were obvious venues; but there were others, including law schools, self-government schools,[12] and various ad-hoc reform bureaus and offices that were called for in 1906–1908.

Returned students jostled with expectant officials for these posts; and, in some cases, an expectant official was also a returned student. For example, the Sichuan native Shao Congen was both a graduate of Hosei University and an expectant official who had been assigned to Shandong. But he decided instead to return to Sichuan, where he held posts like supervisor *(jiandu)* at the Sichuan Law School and taught at the provincial self-government school.[13] Joining Shao at the school was another Sichuan native and Hosei graduate, Xiong Zhaowei.[14]

Shao Congen, like his compeers in Tianjin Wu Xingrang and Qi Shukai, was an unusual expectant official. Most of these men had never left China and their stature in the constitutional era was shrinking. At a time when regular officials were being caricatured venomously in popular "novels of exposure" *(qianze xiaoshuo)*,[15] expectant officials were vulnerable indeed. Even the central government took aim. The metropolitan censor Zhao Binglin encouraged the throne to weed out incompetent or superfluous expectant officials, and his ideas were incorporated into regulations promulgated in early January 1908 that established a testing program for them.[16] Officials-in-waiting for regular county or prefectural jobs, as well as those placed in probationary *(shiyong)* posts, were liable to be tested in provincial capitals. Depending on the results, they could return to their posts, become students at provincial law schools, or be cashiered and sent home. Testing commenced later in the year. In Zhili, for example, at least forty expectant officials were reviewed and examined by provincial officials. Special personnel forms were sent to Beijing that recorded each expectant official's test result, degree status, rank, native place, date of arrival in the province for duty, and job description. Seven men were released after they failed the exam. Archival evidence demonstrates that similar tests were given in Shandong, Shanxi, and Hunan.[17]

This self-analysis by the Qing bureaucracy may well have been as unsettling as the vituperative attacks in novels of exposure. But its pertinence in a study of local self-government reforms rests on the connection in 1907–1908 between law schools, where expectant officials received further training, and local self-government schools. These schools, it should be added, were usually staffed with returned students like Shao Congen and Xiong Zhaowei.

Expectant officials, however, were too expectant to be satisfied with more training. Along with degree-holders, they, not returned students, came to dominate the lower reaches of the personnel lists of the various offices in provincial yamen responsible for reform planning.[18] For example, the Guangdong Constitutional Government Preparation Office (Guangdong xianzheng choubeichu) included, along with high-ranking provincial officials (financial commissioner, educational commissioner, censor, salt commissioner, industry intendant, and police commissioner) and the heads of the self-government and judicial reform bureaus, eleven members of the provincial yamen staff (mostly expectant magistrates or prefects).[19] Another list, from the Henan Provincial Assembly Preparation Office (Henan quansheng ziyiju choubanchu), gives the names of fifty-eight members, of whom forty-three were either officials or expectant officials. The fifteen other members were degree-holders: twelve *juren*, one *fusheng*, one *gongsheng*, and one *jiansheng*. Most of these degree-holders were election managers *(sixuan yuan)* who went to prefectural seats to explain the provincial assembly regulations to local elites.[20]

Although ad-hoc bureaus in the provinces, like the various commissions in Beijing, created new bureaucratic space for expectant officials, degree-holders, and returned students, many men in the last group wanted nothing more than to make bureaus obsolete. This intent, part of the general goal of centralizing administration, was shared by some metropolitan officials. Many familiar administrative relationships were questioned in yamen in county seats, provincial capitals, and Beijing. The centralizers looked especially at the quasi-official ad-hoc administrative bureaus that were so important in the latter half of the nineteenth century and which influenced the form of reform bureaus in 1907–1908. This widespread phenomenon was brought to Beijing's attention in a telegram sent by Zhang Zhidong early in 1907. Zhang, who would soon end a quarter-century of service in provincial yamen, said there were gentry bureaus in most counties. He provided examples from Sichuan, Guangdong, Shanxi, and Henan.[21] Zhang's claim is corroborated by the Sichuan telegrams cited in Chapter Three, which were signed by county leaders of gentry bureaus *(jushen)* for sericulture, industry and commerce, railroads, mining, and taxation. This was not a new trend. It was China's mid-nineteenth-century crisis that prompted a devolution of power in the areas of taxation and local security to local elites. This phenomenon of state-sanctioned local activism can be traced further to the mid-eighteenth century in the area of irrigation and water control.[22] Bureaus were driven by the energy of local notables in counties and expectant officials in provincial yamen but always remained subservient to officials. Or so went the succinct argument put forth by Zhang Zhidong. But the system had become unworkable according to Censor Shi Fujin, who argued in his memorial of 25 January 1907 that bureaus and offices should be abolished and their responsibilities centralized. Shi complained that "forests of bureaus and offices, bearing all kinds of different names, had been established in every province."[23] To discuss these bureaus was to address the troubled relationship among county magistrates, clerks and runners, and local elites. Bureaus established with the approval of magistrates often checked the feared and unofficial power of county yamen functionaries. These institutional innovations were a reflection of and contributed to the local corporatism of Chinese society.

Bureaus in provincial and county yamen shared the same administrative history and both were targets in the constitutional era. But they were also, in the minds of some reformers, the building blocks for a new order. Moreover, the fates of new Western-style self-government councils and old gentry bureaus were inextricable. In the fall of 1906 the Compilation Commission, which was influenced by returned student members like Jin Bangping,[24] had proposed to provincial officials that elected deliberative councils *(yishihui)* discuss county affairs and that executive boards *(dongshihui)* be established to assist the county magistrate in carrying out the decisions of the councils. Councils and boards would then be established in market towns and townships.[25] This was an element of Western-style constitutionalism. But Zhang Zhidong, who had yet to be summoned to Beijing, suggested in his response that the word *hui* (society) in the name of these bodies be changed to *ju* (bureau). Familiar gentry bureaus were the precedent, Zhang thought, for the proposed councils and boards. To use *hui* invited unwanted comparisons with illicit secret societies like the Jianghu *hui, lianzhuang hui,* the Sanhe *hui,* and the Gelao *hui,* all of which were "societies that made chaos."[26]

Zhang Zhidong was comfortable with careful delegation of power to bureaus; but a returned student in Tianjin, a member himself of the soon-to-be-abolished self-government bureau, told listeners on 18 August 1907, the day marking the opening of the Tianjin County Council's deliberations, that the wide scope of council responsibilities, its permanent existence, and its formal connection with constitutional government distinguished it from the ad-hoc and nominally transient bureaus such as those for grain, police, sanitation, minting, and taxation.[27] Nevertheless the tendency of officials like Zhang Zhidong to equate the purposes of old appointed bureaus with new elected councils was a common one; it would prove difficult to repeat the success enjoyed by the Tianjin Self-government Bureau in contrasting bureaus with the county council in 1907. Bureaus, caught between state and society, proved hard to leave behind.

But the advantages of ambiguity and careful misinterpretation seized by Zhang Zhidong to turn a completely new institution into a familiar friend were also apparent to returned students in Beijing, who transformed an imperial order to establish new ad-hoc consultative bureaus in provincial capitals into a sanction for Western-style elections for provincial assemblies. An edict of 19 October 1907, which reminded officials of the goal of electing county councils, called for "consultative bureaus" *(ziyiju)* in provincial capitals. These new bureaus would help unite officialdom and the people through discussion of local affairs. One more bureau in the forest of bureaus and offices some might have thought. Officials and nonofficials alike in Sichuan, Anhui, and Jiangsu, who drafted regulations describing the selection process for these bureaus, planned to invite men from every county to serve in this new bureau in the provincial capital that would assist the governor; bureau members would aid "government by officials *(guanzhi)*." Other provincial officials, including those in Guangdong, Guangxi, Hubei, Jiangsu, Shanxi, Zhili, and Fengtian, made plans for consultative bureaus; these bureaus became active in all but Hubei.[28] Meanwhile in Beijing, the Constitutional Commission, a center of returned student influence, had different ideas about the *ziyiju* mentioned in the October 1907 edict. On 22 July 1908 regulations drafted by the commission were promulgated in Beijing that would guide the Western-style elections of twenty-one provincial assemblies in 1909. Those provincial officials who were busy establishing consultative bureaus *(ziyiju)* in 1907–1908 would have to scramble after they learned that Western-style provincial assemblies (the same *ziyiju*), not another ad-hoc bureau, were to be established in 1909.[29] The bureau plans were dropped and new preparations for provincial assembly elections, which turned about one hundred returned students into assemblymen,[30] began instead.

Although some policy initiatives were being taken from the hands of provincial officials, these proud men were neither content nor confined to serve Beijing only as concentrators and conduits. In some cases officials were convinced that they must at least appear to encourage reform-minded loyalists, a group they had been nurturing. Partly in response to Beijing's previous instructions,[31] some provincial officials had been creating a reform-minded clientele through the efforts of yet another new bureau, the late Qing publishing bureau. Yuan Shikai's *Beiyang guanbao*, which had been circulating in Zhili and throughout China since late 1902, came from such a bureau. His gazette had become a model for other provincial officials, men who shared his vision for *Beiyang guanbao*: "to discuss principles of government, break old habits, enlighten people with knowledge, unite the wills of those above and below, and advance toward wealth and power."[32] Between 1902 and mid-1907 provincial gazettes were also established in Hunan, Shanxi, Jiangxi, Jiangsu, Sichuan, Anhui, Hubei, Guangdong, Shandong, Guangxi, and Henan.[33] The court again encouraged this trend (and two Beijing ministries published their own gazettes[34]); by 1911 provincial gazettes would be published in all provinces but Xinjiang. Adding these titles to lists of more specialized government gazettes, like Tianjin's *Fazheng guanhua bao* and related serial compilations,[35] yields a total number of just over one hundred (see Appendix A).

Although marked by a strong government flavor, gazettes, like gentry bureaus, sometimes reflected the energies and interests of nonofficials. The intertwining of official and private interests was apparent, for example, in Hunan. After Duanfang assumed the governorship in December 1904, he learned that the trimonthly gazette *Hunan guanbao*, which had been founded in April 1902 by private interests in Changsha with the permission of the governor,[36] was in financial trouble. Although the gazette had readers in county yamen throughout Hunan, subscriptions were proving difficult to collect. But even with its troubles, the gazette was noticed as far away as Japan. The Hunan expatriate Chen Tianhua wrote, in May 1903, a two-part critique published in the radical Shanghai journal *Subao* and entitled "On the Corrupt and Rotten *Hunan guanbao*." Chen criticized the gazette's contents, which included edicts, memorials, official announcements, petitions, and items from the Shanghai newspaper *Shenbao*, for being too limited. Chen prodded the gazette to add essays and more news and to slip free of the restraining hand of provincial authorities.[37] Chen may not have been satisfied, but publication continued. Finally, however, provincial authorities had to step in and save the gazette. Duanfang bought out the shareholders and changed the name to *Changsha ribao*. First published on 19 April 1905, the restyled gazette was distributed throughout the province, with estimates of copies per issue ranging from 1,000 to 3,400.[38]

New-style government gazettes like *Beiyang guanbao* and its imitators at the metropolitan, provincial, and subprovincial levels differed significantly, Chen Tianhua's critique notwithstanding, from old-style gazettes, which were vehicles for edicts, memorials, and regulations only.[39] New gazettes also included articles reprinted from other government gazettes and the popular press, petitions by local elites, directives from provincial officials, announcements, and even advertising. In many respects they were a realization of Liang Qichao's 1896 call for publications with world news, new government policy, and information on Sino-foreign problems.[40] New-style gazettes combined the chief function of their predecessors, announcing policies, with the purposes of the press advanced by reformers in the 1890s: describing and discussing government measures and shaping public opinion.

Government publication of periodicals was part of the general expansion of publishing activities at the end of the Qing. These gazettes were competing with numerous private periodicals and newspapers. Yuan's *Beiyang guanbao* blamed the private press *(sijia zhi bao)* for misleading the people and claimed that government gazettes were needed to inform them of new developments in government and education.[41] The new medium made it possible for officials to create provincial constituencies for reform,[42] much as Yuan had been nourishing a national audience, even in the years when so little was being decided upon by Beijing.

In 1906–1908 the focus of reform activities was in the provinces: Beijing talked, provinces acted. Self-government bureaus, consultative bureaus, law schools, self-government schools all took form in, and were publicized from, provincial capitals under the watchful eyes of yamen personnel. Some of these officially sponsored programs were called for by Beijing; others were being improvised. This pre-1909 provincialism takes a place alongside the localism of initiatives like those in Suzhou and Jilin city and the centralism on display by policy makers in Beijing.

Among the actions publicized in provincial gazettes was the creation of law schools, established for expectant officials, in provincial capitals. These law schools, which began to be opened in 1905, developed connections with the official-led self-government planning initiatives beginning in 1907. The model, which was established by Yuan Shikai in Zhili, was recommended by Beijing to all China on 5 September 1905. A more detailed order was sent out on 26 June

1906 by the Ministry of Education.[43] Law schools began to be established, such as the ones in Suzhou[44] and Jilin, and by 1910 there would be forty-seven law schools, both official and private, throughout China with a reported total of 12,282 students.[45] In the midst of this explosive growth, law schools developed an early association with the self-government reforms, for in 1907 law school classes established for nonofficials sometimes became the nucleus for new self-government schools. A number of schools were established well in advance of the Ministry of Interior's May 1909 regulations, and by the end of 1911 provincial governors would claim that about seven thousand students had graduated from schools in every provincial capital and about forty-seven thousand from over a thousand local schools in all provinces but Gansu and Xinjiang (see Table 1).

As with new-style gazettes, law schools, and self-government bureaus, the prototype for self-government schools had been established by Yuan Shikai in Tianjin. Others emulated this model, which took form in October 1906. The schools proved useful to officials who wanted to meet demands for action by local activists while still trying to persuade Beijing that it really did retain the initiative. One of the best-documented provinces in this respect is Sichuan, where the governor established such a school in preparation for opening the provincial consultative bureau called for in the October 1907 edict. He directed county officials to send men to Chengdu where the school opened in May 1908, and by September 321 students had journeyed to the provincial capital from most parts of Sichuan, although eight of the independent jurisdictions *(ting* and *zhou)* directly subordinate to the provincial yamen did not send anyone.[46] In addition to calling for students from each of Sichuan's 143 counties, an important provision was made for other people to attend classes.

While magistrates could select *(xuansong)* students, other potential students living in Chengdu could also be recommended *(baosong)* for the school by local notables *(gongzheng shenshi)*. Provincial authorities, who wanted self-government school students who were wealthy or possessed impressive scholarly abilities but wanted to keep opium addicts away, allowed men already living in Chengdu to become students at the school. This school was attached to the

Sichuan Law School, which had been in operation for over a year, and had two classes of students: one of sixty expectant officials; one of 240 degree-holders, ranging from *juren* to *jiansheng*.[47] This second class of men, from areas outside Chengdu, may well have been a source of some of the students who matriculated at the new self-government school.

The difference between the two classes at the law school was outlined in a petition, submitted in August 1908, by an expectant official who was a student at the law school. He noted that the purpose of the class for expectant officials was to develop their capacities for "official rule" *(guanzhi)*; degree-holders at the law school, who studied the same materials, were preparing for roles in supervising self-government *(zizhi)*.[48] This second purpose was shared by the new school for self-government, whose eight instructors were supposed to be graduates of Japanese law schools.[49] At least two teachers, Shao Congen and Xiong Zhaowei, both of whom had graduated from Hosei University, matched this requirement.[50] The returned students who taught at the Sichuan Provincial Self-government School (Tongsheng zizhi yanjiusuo) were to explain self-government methods, nurture administrative talent, and prepare a foundation for constitutional government. But there was a more specific purpose. The people dispatched by county authorities or selected from among the absentee local elites residing in Chengdu were also being trained to help establish a provincial consultative bureau *(ziyiju)*. Even though consultative bureaus were finally redefined as provincial assemblies in the June 1908 regulations that were promulgated in the midst of the first eight-month term of the self-government school, many students were sent back to their native counties to prepare for provincial assembly elections. Of the 144 persons dispatched to explain these electoral procedures throughout Sichuan in early 1909, sixty were graduates of the school. The other eighty-four were graduates of the class of degree-holders at the Sichuan Law School.[51] In addition to providing this assistance, graduates of the school could become teachers in self-government schools in county seats.[52]

Other provinces were also experimenting with new bureaus and schools. In Hubei, for example, Zhang Zhidong sent officials up north to study the Tianjin model in late spring 1907; at the same time the Hubei Law School was established. There were also places in Wuhan, which attracted over a thousand students, called *gongmin yangcheng suo* (schools for nurturing citizens).[53] In January 1908 the Hubei Provincial Self-government Bureau, based on the Tianjin model, was established.[54] Chen Kuilong, who became governor in March 1908, decided to add a self-government class *(zizhi yanjiu ban)* to the provincial law school because there was a shortage of personnel qualified to carry out the census mandated in August 1908. After the first class was graduated at the end of 1908, the name was changed to the Self-government School and the enrollment quota was set at three hundred. Students, whom the governor expected to be intelligent degree-holders and gentrymen *(shishen)* came from counties throughout Hubei. Large counties had a quota of five students; medium and small-sized counties were to send four students. There is evidence from at least one Hubei county that supports these claims. According to the 1935 gazetteer for Macheng county, located about seventy-five miles northeast of Wuhan, two Macheng students graduated with the first class and three with the second.[55]

Most of the well-documented initiatives in 1906–1908, like the officially sponsored Sichuan and Hubei programs and the elite-led initiatives in Jiangsu and Jilin described in Chapter Three, took place in provincial capitals. But the evidence from Sichuan, Jiangsu, and Hubei also included in Chapter Three demonstrates that official-led initiatives took place elsewhere. At the local level, however, documentation is often too inadequate to allow distinctions to be made between official-led and elite-led initiatives. There is one well-documented case for Jilin, however, that allows this exploration of official-led initiatives to continue at the prefectural level.

In November 1908 the returned student Li Shuen arrived in Binzhou prefecture, at the northern boundary of Jilin, to take up a post as temporary prefect.[56] Li had held a series of Jilin assignments since 1902, when he had purchased the rank of expectant official after returning from Japan,[57] where he had studied administration and education at Waseda University. Before his assignment to Binzhou, Li, a Jiangsu native of thirty *sui*, held positions in Jilin city and served as magistrate of a county to the west of the capital during 1907.[58] Li, who would have been aware of the Jilin initiative described in Chapter Three, had been an ambitious reformer while county magistrate and continued this role in Binzhou, where his reform initiatives included an attempt to prepare Binzhou for local self-government.

Li was dismayed by the appropriation of the term "self-government" by the local militia in Binzhou. Militia leaders had renamed their organization the Self-government Rural Militia Bureau (Zizhi xiangtuan ju). Li immediately abolished the bureau, which had been established in early 1908, and charged that the "gentry-managers *(shendong)* of this bureau were all ignorant about the method of self-government." In Li's mind self-government and the affairs of the local militia were "two completely different matters that should not be confused."[59] With some of the tax monies once controlled by the old bureau, Li established a self-government school with room for fifty students in the first class in the prefectural seat and appointed a returned student from Japan to head the school.[60] The reaction of the members of the abolished Self-government Rural Militia Bureau to Li Shuen's actions is not recorded in the new-style gazetteer compiled under Li's authority, but their distaste for Li's policies and programs can easily be imagined. Li Shuen also tried to replace decades-old patterns of subcounty administration with a Japanese model.[61]

But even the old patterns had been in flux. In the early Guangxu period (1875–1908) a network of local leaders had been selected *(gongtui)* by groups of ten families. In 1908, prior to Li's arrival, additional selections were made. Ten of these men gathered to select a leader for a group of one hundred families. The higher-order leaders then selected someone who assumed responsibility for a thousand families.

These decimal groupings would have been familiar to any reader of Feng Guifen's essays or students of old *baojia* regulations, but Li Shuen knew he wanted no part of these accepted patterns of local administration. He said this had nothing to do with self-government, and besides, some of these men were "ignorant country rustics." Li's plan was to send graduates from the self-government school to the countryside where they would give lectures and try to persuade the old administrative elite to help implement the new initiatives.[62] Whether deliberately or not, Li was bringing the pattern of the Tianjin model to Binzhou.

Swirling around the reform milieu, which was crowded with elite activists, metropolitan bureaucrats, provincial and local officials, expectant officials, returned students, and gentry-managers, were three powerful forces: localism, centralism, and provincialism. As in mid-nineteenth-century Europe "local self-government" was being used by centralizers and local autonomy advocates alike and by an array of activists in-between. On the eve of the January 1909 promulgation of the imperial regulations, the territory was very, very contested.

Provincial and prefectural officials tried to balance demands from Beijing above and pressure from local elites below. The influence of foreign models, especially Yuan Shikai's interpretation of the Japan model, is apparent. Foreign ideas continued to be publicized by returned students, some of whom were now officials or government advisors. Constitutionalism was the key for many returned students in Beijing and the provinces. To that end, Li Shuen established a school to proclaim the meaning of local self-government. Li's approach echoed the one being crafted in Beijing: local self-government would provide the training and perspectives required of new citizens, defined by age, sex, wealth, and residence, whose energies would build a stronger and richer China by establishing a constitutional government that brought together locality and center as well as ruler and ruled. Elected bodies at the local, provincial, and national level, closely supervised by officials, would create a new China where centralized administration would finally allow China to take its place in Asia and the world.[63]

But there were other ideas and other initiatives, the least visible of which were taken in county seats and market towns. Without a glance toward constitutionalism, the Binzhou rural militia that so disgusted Li Shuen had appropriated the "self-government" label for their own purposes, presumably local security. When Li Shuen abolished their bureau he was reversing decades, even centuries, of change in the relationship between local elites and the imperial state. Li, like Shi Fujin in Beijing, had no use for this tree in the "forest of bureaus and offices." But their colleague Zhang Zhidong saw opportunity where they saw obstacles, for Zhang sought to blend local initiatives with government supervision.[64]

The provincialism and localism that held China together in 1906–1908 while Beijing was trying to chart a path into the future became an anachronism on 18 January 1909, when the court finally promulgated its self-government regulations. The bureaus and offices of quasi-official administration were to give way to centrally mandated local councils that should attend to education, public welfare, public works, and agricultural, industrial, and commercial development. Public management carried out in the past by gentry-managers (*shendong*) would now be accomplished by councils.[65] Just as Beijing had dictated in 1908, contrary to the plans of some provincial officials, what the nature of provincial-level representative bodies would be, so too did metropolitan bureaucrats specify the terms of China's local self-government program. Unlike the fall of 1906, when a Beijing commission asked provincial officials what they thought of the new ideas for local reform, early in 1909 the center prescribed, in minute detail, what provincial and local officials should do.

# PART THREE

# State and Society Unravelling,

# 1909–1911

# SIX

# Local Councils in China

That symbol of Beijing's centralizing ethos, the first set of regulations for local self-government, appeared on 18 January 1909. Much of the variety of reform programs evident in 1906–1908 would soon be overlaid with a veneer of uniformity as provincial and local officials along with local elites bestowed Beijing-approved labels upon extant organizations. Although new metropolitan ministries were receiving directly communications from local elites, this centralizing tenor was balanced by the initiative of provincial yamen, which remained the site of a critical nexus between Beijing and the rest of the country. Those provincial offices established along the lines of the Tianjin model, usually called self-government bureaus, were rechristened self-government preparation offices (*zizhi choubanchu*) and told to oversee preparations for local council elections. They shared space on the reform horizon with offices that were coordinating provincial assembly elections, due to be held in the summer of 1909, according to the court's Nine-Year Plan for establishing constitutional government, a detailed list of events scheduled to occur between August 1908 and 1916. The first local councils, for example, were to be elected in 1912 and 1913 followed by county councils, with their countywide electorates, in 1913 and 1914.

The assemblies were elected as planned; local councils, however, began to appear as early as 1909. By the fall of 1911, according to more than one hundred periodic reports by provincial yamen and the summaries of data Beijing had extracted from them, there were about five thousand local and county councils.

This number can be known because provincial and local yamen along with ad-hoc provincial offices and local gentry bureaus collected and collated the kind of detailed local knowledge that had been yearned for by the Ministry of Interior since 1907 and was requested specifically by the Constitutional Commission in 1909. A responsive institutional structure, stretching from Beijing to county yamen, wrote reports for superior officials and also published gazettes and serial compilations for nearby audiences of officials and elites (see Appendix A and Appendix B). All aspects of the late Qing reforms were reported upon and summarized in numerous ways; but of these initiatives the most publicized and studied, especially outside government circles, was the provincial assembly program.

The assemblies, which were overseen, ultimately, by the Constitutional Commission, had metamorphosed from familiar ad-hoc bureaus into Western-style representative bodies. In the designs of many, these assemblies replaced local councils as the foundation for China's new constitutional government. When first proposed back in 1907, however, consultative bureaus had been placed between local councils and a national parliament on the pyramid of representative bodies. The assembly regulations promulgated in June 1908 reconstrued the foundation of the constitutional pyramid: the assemblies became the base and councils became, simply, local councils.[1] But local self-government remained the rhetorical foundation of constitutional government, and the bureaucrats in the responsible section at the Ministry of Interior might have still believed it, but institutionally, in January 1909,[2] councils mattered little in China's constitutional scheme. For some men, like Jilin's Songyu, it was easy to redirect energies from locality to province and nation. Indeed, activists in provincial capitals often applied the label "local self-government" to provincial assemblies. But those who lived outside provincial capitals or lacked connections in networks of provincial elites found that they had been rudely shoved aside. Provincial officials could sympathize, for they had been nudged from the center of action by Beijing bureaucrats. But in 1909–1910 provincial officials and local elites got even; they challenged both provincial activists and Beijing centralizers and once again insisted that local self-government and constitutionalism needed councils. Local electoral activities regained some of their old symbolism, especially by the end of 1910, and provincial officials reclaimed the prerogatives that Beijing had seized in 1907–1908.

A new round in this battle of wills began soon after the regulations were issued. Beijing reluctantly made a series of decisions, prodded by beleaguered provincial officials, to advance *(tiqian)* the time schedule for local elections; the original schedule for 1912–1914 never had a chance. Early in 1909 the Ministry of Interior ordered provincial yamen to classify all administrative seats, towns, and townships into five categories. Administrative seats of counties *(xian)*, departments *(zhou)*, and subprefectures *(ting)* had been called *cheng* (city) in the January 1909 regulations. Little distinguished market towns *(zhen)* from rural townships *(xiang)* apart from population size; *zhen* had a population of 50,000 or more and *xiang* had fewer than 50,000 inhabitants. The designations that followed could easily mislead; many a flourishing market town *(zhen)* presented a more urban character than distant county seats *(cheng)* with populations measured in the thousands, not tens of thousands. But the ministry's five new categories introduced some distinctions across China's landscape. Administrative seats and market towns were to be identified either as "commercially developed and flourishing" *(fansheng)*, "middling" *(zhongdeng)*, or "other"; and townships were to be divided into two categories: those near administrative seats and those in out-of-the-way *(pianpi)* places. Implementation was staggered, with the first councils now to be established in 1909 and the last in 1912.[3]

Provincial authorities began to classify their jurisdictions and entreated Beijing to advance the schedule again. Zhao Erxun, in a late spring 1909 memorial from Sichuan, insisted that Beijing must allow all local councils to be established long before the original completion date of 1914.[4] Self-government schools had already been established in Sichuan, and dozens of other places were requesting permission, while Beijing was just drafting regulations for schools.[5]

Authorities responsible for southern Jiangsu scheduled all administrative seat, town, and township elections for completion by 1911.[6] The Ministry of Interior telegraphed back in June 1909 under the returned student Sun Pei's signature, and insisted that Beijing's schedule, which would have delayed some township elections to 1913, be followed.[7] But the pleas and declarations continued. In the latter half of 1909 there was one occasion when provincial authorities informed Beijing that elites in six counties had requested permission to establish councils;[8] and in a provincial summary of events in this period, officials mentioned that several dozen townships in southern Jiangsu asked permission to hold elections. Approval was promised once voting rolls and maps of electoral districts were received.[9] Beijing failed to halt the onrush; all administrative seats in southern Jiangsu reportedly completed their elections by June 1910.[10] In 1909 and 1910 the difficulties in establishing local councils like Jiangsu's caused some provincial officials to focus instead on county councils,[11] especially after the February 1910 promulgation of the set of regulations for these bodies.[12] Shandong governor Sun Baoqi, for example, recommended in June 1910 that county councils be elected prior to making preparations for local councils. He suggested that self-government offices in county and prefectural seats with populations in excess of 50,000 be restyled self-government councils; township council elections should be delayed until educational and economic conditions had improved.[13]

A month later the Ministry of Interior sent out a packet of fourteen documents, two of which would have had the opposite effect. The ministry's packet, which formalized the changes made to the original 1908 schedule, included both an advanced schedule and one that abandoned the sequential plan that began in commercially developed administrative seats and market towns.[14]

But questions about priorities continued to be raised. In October 1910 the governor in Yunnan, Li Jingxi, argued that it was a mistake to try to implement both sets of regulations simultaneously. When everyone acts, chaos reigns, he warned. Elect county councils, then township councils. Li wrote, "It may be difficult to establish councils in one or two distant townships, but that should not threaten the whole program." It was easier to supervise county councils. Local councils, on the other hand, might be "pure local self-government," but the lack of qualified persons and the scheming of others was causing problems. In county seats, however, the embodiment of local self-government, county councils, could be supervised by the personification of "official rule" *(guanzhi)*, the magistrate. Li was confident people could then see what "local self-government" meant and that more funding would be available.[15] By the time the court rescripted Li Jingxi's memorial early in December, the governor in Hubei had also expressed concern about overloading the system and suggested that county councils first be established by the end of 1911, after which attention could be directed toward local councils.[16]

For some in Beijing the tone of these memorials should have been familiar. Earlier in the constitutional age, before Beijing's desire for cooperation gave way to dictation, provincial officials had been asked what they thought about the idea of elected councils. The responses that reached Beijing in early 1907 stressed how diverse China was. The idea was acceptable to most governors, but they insisted that there was no need for uniform policy or mandatory implementation schedules. They asked Beijing to trust their discretion, so that factors like the educational levels of the people and the quality of local leaders could be used to determine when the time for reform had arrived.[17] This moment of cooperation quickly passed. Late in 1907 Beijing directed them to share their prerogative with the Ministry of Interior, and in September 1907 even that had been taken from governors. By mid-1908 they were told to restrain local initiatives and in January 1909 Beijing presented its vision for local self-government; provincial yamen had been cast as agents of a centralizing ethos. But officials outside Beijing, who had little input into the regulations finally promulgated in 1909–1910, repeated their observations in those years and this time Beijing listened and quickly retreated from the ambit of its centralizing pretension.

At the end of 1910 the schedule for implementation was moved forward again and county councils, originally scheduled to be established in 1913–1914, began to appear. On 4 November 1910 a new reason for urgency had been added: after almost a year of a petition movement involving thousands of persons in and out of government, the court ordered a parliament to be established in 1913, three years ahead of schedule.[18] The court told the Constitutional Commission to revise the implementation schedule again for what was now, essentially, a six-year plan.[19] Ten days later the ministry revised its self-government implementation schedule one more time. It surrendered; control of the tempo of implementation was relinquished to provincial officials who, the ministry explained, understood local conditions better.[20]

The Ministry of Interior may have had to cede some of its authority to provincial officials, but it also saw an opportunity to renew its struggle with the Constitutional Commission. The ministry reminded the court, in a memorial of 27 January 1911, of the significance of these recent changes with respect to constitutionalism and self-government. Within the ministry itself there was a discussion about the connection between parliamentary elections and prior electoral activity at the local level.[21] For the first time since 1907, when the local self-government program suffered a de facto divorce from constitutionalism attendant to the struggle between Shanqi's Ministry of Interior and Yuan Shikai's Constitutional Commission, local self-government and constitutionalism were reunited. Although the 1908 regulations for provincial assemblies had not given a role to councils in provincial assembly elections, this return to old principles late in 1910 reinvigorated arguments that linked the two programs. County councils, in particular, came to the forefront once again.

China's new provincial assemblies, which were directed to cooperate with county councils, contributed to this development. They too called for county councils to be established quickly in light of the advanced schedule for parliamentary elections. For example, Anhui assemblymen petitioned Governor Zhu Jiabao, whom we last saw in Jilin, where Songyu and others had erected a monument in honor of his reform program. Noting that self-government at the county level was the "foundation of foundations" for constitutional government, the assembly called for county councils to be in session by October 1911.

The Anhui assemblymen had other concerns. They thought the financial burden on the provincial government would be lighter once county councils were established and they were convinced that the organizational base provided by the councils was required for the local reforms mandated in the old Nine-Year Plan to be accomplished.[22] Governor Zhu Jiabao was persuaded and urged Anhui's county councils to be in session by December 1911. This memorial received a perfunctory rescript on 16 April 1911.[23]

In Shandong provincial authorities took the initiative. In January 1911 they advanced the deadline for elections of county councils to October in some areas; by August 1911 there were reports that seventy-one county councils had been formed.[24] Nearby in Zhili, thirteen county councils had already been established by the end of 1910 and by mid-1911 the total had reportedly increased to 140.[25] By the fall of 1911, according to these reports from Shandong and Zhili as well as eleven other provinces, more than three hundred county councils had been established.

The provincial reports from which most of these numbers were derived were issued by governors every six months beginning in early 1909. Data were collated from various sources, including reform bureaus that were subordinate to the governors. Among these bureaus were those charged with organizing the provincial assembly elections held in mid-1909. At first, subprovincial local self-government programs were managed, at Beijing's request, by these offices, some of which were abolished after the assembly elections. In those cases provincial officials had created local self-government offices. After several months of confusion, in late 1909 Beijing itself finally called for self-government preparation offices to be established in provincial yamen.[26]

The data in semi-annual provincial reports incorporated information forwarded by an array of ad-hoc offices and gentry bureaus in provincial capitals and county seats. Self-government statistics, for example, were filed by the new provincial self-government planning offices. A good example of the beginning of the reporting channels between local yamen and Beijing can be found in south China. The Guangdong Local Self-government Preparation Office, headed by

the circuit intendant Wang Bing'en, provided data to the governor
for use in his reports. The data flow for events in the latter half of
1909 began with Wang's collation of numerous county reports. He
told the governor about class sizes and instruction terms at the self-
government school in Canton, named twelve counties with self-government schools, and listed thirty-three administrative seats and
towns that had been given the "flourishing" classification.[27] When
the governor summarized this five-hundred-character report, he cut
out 40 percent of the material, especially the placenames that Wang
Bing'en had provided. In Beijing the Constitutional Commission
summarized even more drastically in their report issued in the spring
of 1910. No Guangdong data appeared at all; instead, the commission simply implied that Guangdong's preparations were con-
tinuing.[28]

Hidden behind the few characters in provincial or national summaries was a much greater mass of material and number of actions.
For example, in the four Guangdong reports on actions taken between August 1908 and mid-1910 three provincial documents are
mentioned: a timetable for implementation in administrative seats,
towns, and townships; principles to be used in compiling voter rolls
for local elections; and a timetable for establishing county councils.[29]
But Wang Bing'en's self-government preparation office in Canton
produced far more than these three documents. The Guangdong
governor had been told about thirteen other documents, including
simplified versions of regulations for self-government schools and
examples of the forms to be used for census taking, reporting the
boundaries of election districts, and listing electors, that had been
produced during the eighteen-month period ending in mid-1910.[30]
This detailed information, which was found in serial publications
published by an ad-hoc reform office in Guangdong, did not make
it into the Guangdong provincial reports. Other provinces also recorded the progress of various reforms in numerous publications.
Some provinces, like Fengtian, Guizhou, Henan, Hunan, Jiangsu,
Jiangxi, Jilin, Shandong, Shanxi, Yunnan, Zhejiang, and Zhili, even
published specialized gazettes on self-government implementation
(see Appendix A).

At the very least this preliminary survey of statistics and reporting practices calls into question the dismissal of local self-government reforms by *The Times* (London) correspondent J. O. P. Bland or, in more recent years, the scholar John Fincher. Bland wrote:

> [N]either the Provincial Assemblies nor the Central Government have displayed the slightest interest in these still-born regulations or seriously endeavored to make them effective. . . . The *Rules for Local Self-government,* laboriously compiled with scissors and paste by well-meaning pundits under the Commission of Constitutional Reform, could have no possible meaning for the masses of China, and therefore no hope of fulfilment.[31]

John Fincher argues:

> [L]ocal-level assemblies were for the most part successful only on paper. Relatively few such bodies managed to assemble in the counties or municipalities except as societies devoted to the study rather than the implementation of official prescriptions for organisation or non-official exhortations to action, if even that. Moreover, those local assemblies which did become more than study societies must be sought in counties and municipalities close to the political and economic frontiers of China rather than deep within the internal strongholds of any traditional, landowning local gentry.[32]

The proclivities of Bland and Fincher were enough to keep them from seriously considering the implementation of the self-government regulations, but their conclusions were ordained by the limits of their sources. Neither of them exploited provincial reporting on subprovincial reforms, but the only road to an expansive appreciation of these reforms is marked with dozens and dozens of semiannual provincial reports that were published openly in a government gazette within weeks of their receipt in Beijing. These reports exist because early in 1909 the capital imposed formal requirements on provincial officials, who were told to submit reports every six months to a bureau at the Constitutional Commission that had been established to collate information about provincial and metropolitan reforms.[33]

Of the 138 provincial reports that should have arrived in Beijing by the end of 1911, 127 can be found in the imperial government gazette *Zhengzhi guanbao*, documentary publications, and in archives in Asia (see Appendix B). There are thirteen provinces with complete sets of reports; Shanxi has the fewest with four. Although some of the data in Shanxi's missing report for the first period is available in the national summaries filed by the Constitutional Commission and the Ministry of Interior, the data from the other ten missing reports, all of which should have been filed in the fall of 1911, are unavailable since neither the commission's nor the ministry's summaries, if in fact they ever existed, have been located.

What is the quality of this information? The local self-government reforms could tax the financial and personnel resources of even prosperous counties and sometimes there was pressure to produce results, and if that was too difficult, numbers alone. In Fujian, for example, when two county councils had not been established by a June 1910 deadline, the governor dispatched a team to investigate the counties and reprimand the magistrates.[34] Such impatience might have pressured some officials to fabricate results, but not all provincial yamen were so insistent.[35] And only twice in all of the categories of data on self-government provided by provincial authorities were results given that suggest mere cursory attention to detail. Although these Jiangsu and Anhui officials may have made too-sweeping claims about the number of councils established in administrative seats, provincial yamen usually produced discrete and specific data that can be aggregated and deserve credence.

Some of the authority of provincial reports can be demonstrated through corroboration by reform coverage in other sources for late-Qing history. The entire scope of local self-government reforms, which by definition took place in distant county seats as well as major cities, was usually ignored by journalists and diplomats, two important historical sources for the late Qing. But these witnesses recorded some of the most notorious cases of violence[36] directed against persons associated with the reforms, including managers, census-takers, and tax-collectors. Provincial officials, too, reported the bad news to Beijing. There are two especially well-studied cases where self-government personnel were targets of fury: the tax riots in Shandong's Laiyang and Haiyang counties in 1910[37] and the Chuansha department disturbance of early 1911 in Jiangsu.[38] The violence was reported by provincial yamen to Beijing. Shandong officials told the Constitutional Commission and the court that disturbances in Laiyang and Haiyang had caused delays.[39] The Jiangsu governor, in his reports, mentioned the Chuansha troubles as well as other hot spots like Huating, Rugao, Taizhou, and Zhenze. Later research on Jiangsu by Wang Shuhuai, based on contemporary newspaper and U. S. State Department reports as well as retrospective gazetteer accounts, verifies the governor's assessment of the most troubled sites.[40]

Most of the activity associated with the reforms, however, was neither violent nor, apparently, noteworthy. But sometimes even prosaic events like the graduation of self-government school classes were covered by nonofficial observers, whose reports support the data included in provincial reports. Zhejiang officials, for example, reported the graduation of two classes from the self-government school in Jiaxing county, situated north of Hangzhou on the Grand Canal.[41] These students were also mentioned in a dispatch of 30 November 1909 by the *North China Herald* correspondent in Jiaxing: "Our city has become quite active recently in the way of improvements and organization; not so much for local benefit as for the government at large. One is the establishment of what may be translated as a self-government school. It is not easy to find out just what is taught, but there are daily lectures on constitutional government and kindred subjects, such as will help to prepare young men to exercise intelligently the franchise."[42]

A similar kind of corroboration comes from Gansu, on China's periphery, whose fifth report told of a council that was established in Qin city in the latter half of 1910.[43] A *North China Herald* correspondent filed a report on 15 June 1911 about related developments in this administrative seat of Qin. "[The self-government] office is now very popular and has come into conflict with the local officials on more than one occasion," a correspondent wrote after telling of a case "when one of the police caused the death of a man on the street. The local officials tried to hush the affair up, but the self-government office would not hear of it."[44]

Further evidence of the reliability of these reports comes from Beijing, where officials acted on their skepticism and sent out investigative missions. The verdict after the return of four teams of investigators, one of which was headed by Lu Zongyu, in the spring of 1910: "In general the records in our files, the accomplishments reported by each province, and the facts enumerated by the deputies are in agreement." Two more missions were planned, one in the fall of 1910 and one in 1911. The last one would be cancelled, but in the fall of 1910 Beijing investigators again checked various aspects of constitutional reforms in provincial capitals, treaty ports, and other important economic centers. These emissaries scrutinized written records and interviewed responsible officials, the key elements in semi-annual production of provincial reports.[45]

A later analysis by the Ministry of Interior, dated 29 April 1911, demonstrated again the general accuracy of provincial reports in greater detail. The ministry compared provincial reports with the findings of the investigative missions of 1910. Of the ten provinces covered, the most serious discrepancies between the two sources occurred in Guangdong, Guangxi, and Jiangsu. In Guangdong, ministry analysts disputed the existence of eight of the sixty self-government schools that were reported open. For Guangxi they questioned the claims of thirty-seven of the counties that had reported establishing self-government schools.[46] The critique of Jiangsu continued the ministry's special concern about this crucial region. There was a glaring discrepancy between the ministry's findings and the Jiangsu governor's claim that councils and boards had been established by June 1910 in all thirty-seven counties subordinate to provincial authorities in Suzhou. The governor eventually supported this claim by submitting almost nine hundred names of council and board members. These namelists, which included the age and number of votes garnered by each councillor, did indeed arrive in Beijing, and have ever since remained part of the archives of the old Qing Ministry of Interior.[47] All of these hundreds of names notwithstanding, the ministry insisted that only Shanghai county had elected a council and the preparations for elections had been completed in just five counties and were ongoing in only two more.[48] But Jiangsu press accounts, in newspapers like Shanghai's *Shibao* and journals like *Dongfang zazhi,* echoed the claim of provincial authorities.[49]

A survey of Jiangsu gazetteers does little to clarify these contradictions, although sketchy evidence suggests that the ministry was too severe in its judgment. Gazetteer accounts for southern Jiangsu mention, for example, preparations for numerous township councils in Jiading[50] and a council in Yixing.[51] Gazetteers, unfortunately, have proven to be a disappointing source for a comprehensive study of the local self-government reforms. These events are covered in gazetteers;[52] but when one's focus is provincial in scope, these sources can illuminate only part of the picture. Zhang Yufa's study of Shandong, for example, shows the gaps, which exist because most counties had yet to publish a post-1911 gazetteer. Zhang Yufa used only twelve gazetteers for a province that had 106 counties. Zhang supplemented this gazetteer data derived from just 10 percent of Shandong's counties with specific information the Shandong governor included in a telegram he sent to the Ministry of Interior in which he mentioned that in June 1910 three administrative seat councils and two town councils were established. Zhang's attempt to build a database fell short, and he finally decided simply to cite a yearbook entry for events in 1911 that claimed for Shandong one hundred administrative seat councils and three town councils.[53] Zhang Yufa and Wang Shuhuai[54] used provincial reports for Shandong and Jiangsu in their studies because gazetteer coverage and diplomatic and newspaper reporting was just too sparse.

In the end we are left with the provincial reports, the most comprehensive source of information on reform implementation in the late Qing. The data on local self-government implementation presented in Table 1 are derived primarily from the provincial reports received in Beijing between March 1909 and November 1911 (see Appendix B). Although many of the local self-government initiatives

TABLE I  *Number of Students, Schools, and Councils as Reflected in Provincial Reports on Local Self-government Activities*

| | Provincial students | Subprovincial schools | Subprovincial students | Cheng councils | Zhen councils | Xiang councils | County councils | Period 6 report[a] |
|---|---|---|---|---|---|---|---|---|
| Anhui | 162 | 30 | — | 60[b] | — | — | — | no |
| Fengtian | 173 | 46 | 3,785 | 41 | 62 | 302 | 38 | yes |
| Fujian | 516 | 77 | 3,642 | 59 | 31 | 69 | 2 | yes |
| Gansu | 82 | — | — | 15 | — | — | 1 | no |
| Guangdong | 360 | 94 | — | 49 | 26 | — | 2 | no |
| Guangxi | 357 | 67 | 4,250 | 43 | 11 | 132 | 4 | yes |
| Guizhou | 2 classes | 60 | — | 64 | — | — | — | no |
| Heilongjiang | 144 | — | — | 15 | 3 | 22 | 1 | yes |
| Henan | 406 | 62 | 3,000 | 83 | 35 | 103 | 15 | yes |
| Hubei | 600 | — | 3,700 | 69 | 28 | 24 | — | no |
| Hunan | 406 | — | 2,819 | 33 | — | — | — | yes |
| Jiangsu-Ning | 1 class | 19 | — | 3 | — | — | — | no |
| Jiangsu-Su | 1 class | — | — | 37 | 20 | 300 | 20 | yes |
| Jiangxi | 546 | 52 | — | 71 | 54 | 774 | — | yes |
| Jilin | 142 | 13 | 390 | 13 | 1 | — | — | yes |
| Shaanxi | 255 | 89 | 400 | 73 | — | — | 4 | yes |
| Shandong | 216 | 1 | 5,499 | 105 | 5 | 1 | 71 | yes |
| Shanxi | 196 | 81 | 2,500 | 35 | — | — | 1 | no |
| Sichuan | 640 | 145 | 10,000 | 110 | 177 | 112 | 6 | no |
| Xinjiang | 72 | — | — | 12 | — | — | — | no |
| Yunnan | 417 | 170 | 3,284 | 32 | — | — | — | no |
| Zhejiang | 312 | 75 | — | 67 | 67 | 887 | — | yes |
| Zhili | 1,051 | 141 | 3,663 | 41 | 8 | 252 | 149 | yes |
| Estimated total[c] | 7,050 | 1,200 | 47,000 | 1,150 | 550 | 3,000 | 300 | yes |

*Sources:* Provincial reports and national summaries on various New Policies implementation, most of which were published in *Zhengzhi guanbao* (see Appendix B). Information for this table was also located in the following files from the Ministry of Interior and the Constitutional Commission.

Fengtian: See MZB, 172, for a namelist of approximately nine hundred board leaders at the *zhen* and *xiang* levels. Document dated XT3/12/22.

Fujian: See XZBCG, 14, for a manuscript table of schools, with founding dates and student totals. Sixty-one of these subprovincial schools were established by officials (*guan*) and sixteen schools, identified as public (*gong*), were established in five county seats, four *zhen*, and seven *xiang*. Fourteen of these sixteen schools were in Fuzhou prefecture. This manuscript arrived in Beijing on XT3/3/14.

Guangxi: See XZBCG, 13, for two extensive reports from Guangxi for Periods 4 and 6 that supplement Guangxi No. 4 and Guangxi No. 6.

Heilongjiang: See MZB, 177, for the names of 125 members of eighteen different boards sent to Beijing in 1911.

Henan: See MZB, 179, for a table listing schools, student quotas, school addresses, and founding dates for one hundred schools of which ninety-two schools had student quotas totalling 4,843. The figures in Table 1, however, are from Henan No. 4. See also MZB, 179, for a namelist of 205 graduates of the first provincial class, which was graduated in XT1/11.

Hunan: See MZB, 199, for a namelist of 226 students in the first provincial class, which was graduated in XT2/11.

Jiangsu-Su: See MZB, 189.2, for various lists of more than one thousand council members.

Jilin: Information on counties with schools and namelists from five of these counties as well as the provincial school can be found in *Jilin quansheng difang zizhi choubanchu diyici baogaoshu* (held by Beijing National Library).

Shaanxi: See MZB, 185, for a namelist of seventy-nine students from the first provincial class.

Shandong: See MZB, 181, for student namelists for the provincial school (216 names) and the school for Ji'nan prefecture (153 names). The figures for *cheng* and *zhen* councils are taken from a published report issued by the Shandong Provincial Local Self-government Preparation Office for Period 5. See MZB, 181.

Shanxi: See MZB, 182, for a XT1/9/25 report from the Shanxi governor in which the number of provincial students is given.

Sichuan: See MZB, 205, for nineteen printed forms on which information on student quotas, names of lecturers, founding dates, funding, and school addresses were entered. This booklet of forms from nineteen counties, which was sent to the Ministry of Interior on XT2/12/19, supplemented a compilation for the rest of Sichuan that had been sent to Beijing earlier.

Xinjiang: See XZBCG, 13, for a XT1/8/2 report listing thirty-six students in the first provincial class.

Yunnan: See MZB, 207 for a manuscript table giving the total number of provincial students in five classes as well as data on eighteen prefectural-level schools that were designated to accommodate students. These schools were called *zhuanxi suo*.

Zhejiang: See XZBCG, 14, for a manuscript table sent from Zhejiang on XT1/12/26 that gives a figure of 312 graduates from the provincial school. Zhejiang No. 2 and Zhejiang No. 3 describe the selection process for this class. County education offices (*quanxue suo*) and societies (*jiaoyu hui*) recommended over seven hundred students, of which 440 were invited to attend classes. See MZB, 191 for the Zhejiang Provincial Local Self-government Office report for Period 5 to the governor in which a reference to all counties having established self-government schools can be found. A copy was filed at the Ministry of Interior on XT3/3/16.

*Notes:* [a]The availability of Period 6 reports (covering XT3/1–XT3/int.6) is indicated in order to provide the reporting context for the *cheng* (administrative seat), *zhen* (town), and *xiang* (township) council figures. Whereas most of the schooling was done in 1909 and 1910, elections tended to take place only late in 1910 and in 1911. Thus, council totals for provinces without available Period 6 reports were probably higher. Even provinces with these reports may have had more councils, since many elections were scheduled to take place in September and October 1911, during the seventh reporting period. For example, the Jiading County Council, whose members are listed in Appendix C, was established after Period 6 and hence is not one of the twenty county councils indicated for southern Jiangsu. By the time Period 7 reports were due (March 1912) the abdication of the Xuantong Emperor and the end of the Qing dynasty had already been announced.

[b]Figures that are only implicit in a report are italicized in this table. For example, the fifth Constitutional Commission summary states that all councils in administrative seats were established in Anhui. Since Anhui had sixty subprefectures, departments, and counties, I have entered 60 in the appropriate column.

[c]These totals are conservative estimates, which round off the totals of each column to the nearest 50. Actual totals were probably higher. For example, it is likely that Hunan had about 50 subprovincial local self-government schools, given the number of graduates at that level; but I have not included them in the table or the total estimate.

reported upon had a history dating before 1909, provincial yamen were specifically reporting on the implementation of three main sets of regulations promulgated in 1909–1910, which regulated the establishment of schools (5 May 1909), councils in administrative seats, towns, and rural townships (18 January 1909), and the establishment of districtwide local self-government councils in subprefectures, departments, and counties (6 February 1910).

The reports suggest that the local self-government reforms were much more than "still-born regulations." There was action, especially in the steps leading to the formation of councils: classes held at various kinds of self-government schools, establishment of self-government offices in counties, and finally council elections. Although the creation of electoral districts and the compilation of voter rolls are rarely discussed, other sources can be used to supplement the provincial reports. There are two broad categories of information in the reports. One deals with provincial-level activity: the promulgation of documents and dispatch of reports to Beijing by self-government offices are mentioned. There are also data on provincial self-government schools and their students. The second category covers subprovincial activities: establishing offices, opening schools and instructing students, and electing councils. In addition, governors sometimes shared their thoughts about the reasons for successes and failures encountered.

About eleven hundred fifty councils in the 1,706 administrative seats of counties, departments, and subprefectures[55] were reported to be established. Market towns reported about five hundred fifty councils and townships about three thousand. These three figures, when combined with about three hundred county councils mentioned earlier yield a rough total of five thousand councils. Even allowing for exaggeration, this total would at least maintain the five thousand level if council foundings taking place throughout China in late summer and fall of 1911 could be determined along with the activity between February and August in the ten provinces for which these reports were missing.

These numbers, then, are testament to the institutional base established by the widespread initiatives of 1906–1908, Beijing's mania for data, the ability and willingness of provincial officials to collect and collate statistics supplied by local yamen, and the conviction that China's future depended, in part, on local action.[56]

These data, which suggest that the late-Qing self-government reforms were more than the well-documented slices of violence that plagued Shandong and Jiangsu, still require more of a context. Information buried in archives, gazetteers, and specialized late-Qing publications underlies these flat statistics; a portion has been recovered. Especially useful in this project is *Minzheng bu difang zizhi zhangcheng jieshi huichao* (Ministry of Interior's collected explications of local self-government regulations), a compilation of telegraphic traffic from 1909–1910 between Beijing and the provinces. The material in this publication, which will be referred to as *Collected Explications*, goes well beyond the realm of numbers.[57]

The process of turning China's subjects into citizens required answers to questions about place and belonging. The initiatives of self-government, in their need for voters from formal electoral districts, brought these issues to the foreground. In the problem-solving telegrams published in *Collected Explications* this most difficult process, which was glossed over in provincial reports, can be glimpsed. The regulations promulgated in 1909 stipulated only that councils be established in administrative seats, that the population in areas under the jurisdiction of town councils include at least 50,000 persons and that all districts with fewer than 50,000 persons be called townships. The Ministry of Interior sent out a request for electoral maps in May 1910. By late June, however, relevant and acceptable maps, tables, and reports had been received from only Shandong, Henan, Hubei, and Sichuan; Guangxi's map covered just two counties; and Xinjiang authorities had merely given placenames.[58] The call went out again, and throughout July of 1910 replies were received from all parts of the country.[59]

Officials complained that China's territory was not easily divided into self-government districts *(zizhi qu)*, especially those for townships; in southern Jiangsu familiar educational districts *(xue qu)* were sometimes used.[60] Although counties had often been subdivided into four *xiang* for administrative purposes in the past, the intention of planners in Beijing to limit their *xiang* to fewer than 50,000 persons often meant the familiar *xiang* were much too populous. And elsewhere extant *xiang* jurisdictions could be too small. Counties might have dozens, even hundreds of townships, especially when villages were defined as *xiang*. For example, in Fujian, market towns like Nantai and Baihu were at the center of more than a hundred *xiang* each, but other market towns had only a dozen. The question was: Should villages, suburbs, and towns coalesce? If so, how?[61]

This was one of the most troublesome sections of the regulations. *Cheng* jurisdictions, being limited to administrative seats, were problematic only with regard to determining the boundaries between them and their adjacent suburbs. And *zhen*, towns with 50,000 or more persons, were also discernible. But the *xiang* jurisdiction was ambiguous; Beijing planners, however, expected few problems. If they arose, the local magistrate should simply investigate and report his findings and recommendations to provincial officials (Article 3).[62] Although disputes over defining districts near county seats and market towns can at least be glimpsed, the challenges faced in drawing *xiang* districts are much more extensive and interesting, but are also much harder to document.

The imperial regulations specified that a *xiang* must include at least 2,500 people and sixty qualified electors who would elect, at the minimum, a six-person council (Articles 12 and 24). It was not easy, however, to go out into the countryside and, in accord with precedent, identify *xiang* with populations ranging from 2,500 to 50,000. Whereas Zhao Erxun, when viewing this reach of society in Shanxi in 1902 tried to rely on organizations that already existed, Beijing created an artificial category with no institutional base. And at the very least, any village with fewer than 2,500 persons was put on notice that a political identity could be created only after it coalesced with nearby villages. But such political will could cause problems, as people near Shuanglin town in Zhejiang found out. Their desire to be considered a township was challenged by Shuanglin notables who wanted to incorporate the suburban population so that Shuanglin could be considered a *zhen*.[63]

In time there would have been a representative body to deal with these problems, for county councils were designated as arbitrators (Article 3). But these councils were originally scheduled to be established *after* lower-level local self-government (administrative seat, town, and township) councils were in session. Temporarily, then, except in areas where county councils were established ahead of schedule, persons living beyond the county seat appeared to be left to work things out on their own. In the very last article of the election regulations, however, was the fateful stipulation that gentry *(shen)* appointed by magistrates would be empowered to supervise the first elections at *all* levels.[64] Self-government preparation offices in county seats, then, could dominate the districting done in the first stages of implementation. Elite activists in county seats, including gentry-managers, could influence township-level implementation. In fact, provincial authorities sometimes invited them to do so, especially in remote county seats. The Shandong governor, who worried about the low number of qualified electors in both towns and townships, asked for and received permission from the ministry to include all villages within five *li* of remote county seats in *cheng* electoral districts.[65]

Keith Schoppa points out that these boundary decisions "gave an area's elite the opportunity to make conscious choices about identifying its political and economic interests within a definite physical [and] political space."[66] Schoppa, who looked at cases in relatively urban areas centered on county seats in Zhejiang, assessed how elites within and without city walls lobbied for their interests. In Hangzhou, the suburban West Lake area remained outside the control of the city council; but in the Shuanglin case just mentioned, town elites prevailed in their attempt to incorporate nearby rural areas.[67]

Another example of a districting decision comes from Jiading county in Jiangsu. In the summer of 1909 local leaders were called together by the county magistrate to implement reforms, and discussion turned to the problem of Jiading city's western suburb (Ximen). Debate went back and forth, but they finally decided to limit the *cheng* jurisdiction to the city walls and grant township status to each of Jiading city's four suburbs. The first self-government preparation office outside Jiading city was established in Ximen and by the end of 1910 thirty-two more township offices were created.[68]

Another districting problem, especially in heavily-populated southern Jiangsu, concerned *cheng* councils in urban areas in which there were administrative seats for two or three contiguous counties. Wujin county and Yanghu county, both administered from Chang-zhou, faced this problem.[69] Although the regulations said there was no need for two councils, what was to be done when a council matter had to be referred to a magistrate (Article 10)? Would joint magisterial supervision be possible? Liang Qichao, for one, thought not.[70]

Even more fundamental than inscribing space with meaning was the question of a person's political identity: Who was a citizen? Who was being granted a political voice and a right to participate in local affairs by the regulations? Clearly the most problematic article in the local self-government regulations was the one describing who was eligible to vote in local elections (Article 16). There were more than twenty-two specific references to this article in the *Collected Explications*. Electors were to be men at least twenty-five *sui* who had lived in an area for three years or more and who paid at least two yuan of taxes annually. The residency and tax-paying requirements could be waived by local councils for eminent and respected persons. Furthermore, the person who paid the most taxes in an area automatically qualified as an elector, even if residence and age requirements were not met.

Queries from the provinces on this article concerned a range of issues, especially the tax-payment requirements. For example, past payments of the *lijin* tax, that transport tax borne by merchants, were hard to prove. Unlike the land tax and its various surcharges, fixed by parcel of land on a yearly basis, the *lijin* tax was paid only when goods moved and it was relatively anonymous. Provincial officials from Hunan, Jiangxi, and Jiangsu in particular were concerned.

Provincial officials also wondered about the loophole in Article 16 that appeared to allow women to be electors even though the franchise was limited to men. If the person paying the most taxes automatically was an elector, did that mean women could vote? The Guizhou Provincial Local Self-government Preparation Office issued a document that did indeed give the franchise to women—and children!—in such cases. The Ministry of Interior displayed little patience in its telegram of 29 August 1909: "This muddleheaded idea will lead to trouble in no time." The ministry referred Guizhou authorities to Article 18.2, where the use of proxies was described. Similar exchanges with Shanxi and Guangxi about the use of proxies were made in April and May of 1910.[71]

The focus on persons, not groups, in the regulations prompted some officials to ask the ministry how the franchise was related to individual members of a household. Were all men within a household eligible to vote or did each have to meet the tax requirement?[72] Similar questions were raised about businesses that were owned jointly.[73] Provincial officials from Henan asked about the stipulation for adding respected and eminent persons who did not meet all the electoral requirements. The regulations stated that these requirements could be waived by councils. But how could this be done, officials queried, if councils had yet to exist? The Ministry of Interior decided to give the responsibility temporarily to the preparation offices.[74]

The question of citizenship and minorities also appears in this telegraphic correspondence. Provincial officials in Fengtian asked how to handle Mongol populations whose leaders bore the responsibility for tax collection and whose tax monies were not accounted for in the ways outlined in the regulations.[75] And at the other end of China, Sichuan authorities were worried about the Manchus in the Chengdu garrison. Should they come under the jurisdiction of the Chengdu City Council? Yes, replied the Ministry of Interior on 9 August 1910, pointing out that Article 15 of the regulations stipulated that bannermen in Beijing, persons in garrisons, and merchant sojourners were all residents *(jumin),* and hence eligible to be electors.[76] Similar queries about Manchu garrisons came from Hubei, Guangdong, and Zhejiang.[77] In Zhejiang the problem was complicated by the existence of a Manchu Self-government Society that had been established in the fall of 1908.[78]

Other problems documented in *Collected Explications* and imperial archives will be addressed in the next chapter. But now, with an overall statistical picture of reform in place and some of the most vexing questions described, it is time to return to the narrative, necessarily episodic, describing local self-government's role in this epochal moment in Chinese history. It is unclear how much of this story is recoverable, but it is possible, in some cases, to associate events and people with statistics on self-government. The touchstones at the end are two councils, a city council in Sichuan and a county council in Jiangsu, among the thousands that were reported to exist by the end of the Qing.

Details about councils-in-action are difficult to find, but Sichuan again is rich in relevant sources. In this case there is evidence of the proud, and at times defensive, attitude of the Chengdu City Council and a demonstration of how difficult it was for old styles of political and administrative practice to give way to a new age. In December 1910 the problem was one of status as reflected in forms of address to be used by the council, provincial assembly, magistrates, and the governor. This debate reached Beijing in late February 1911 after being routed through the provincial assembly and then the governor's yamen.[79]

Forms of address had always been strictly ordered and hotly contested. Indeed, one of the first demands Westerners successfully placed in the treaties signed in the mid-nineteenth century was the right for Western diplomatic correspondence to be phrased in a way denoting equality with the Chinese bureau receiving the communication. The local self-government regulations heeded such long-standing concerns, insisting that councils symbolize their subordination to magistrates by using a petition *(cheng)*; magistrates issued directives *(yu)*. In their correspondence with a provincial assembly, councils were required to use deferential petitions but assemblies used *zhihui* (Article 107), a form which denoted equality. The relationship between assembly and councils was both equal and unequal.

The Chengdu City Council, however, demanded equality with both the magistrate and the provincial assembly. It asked for permission to use a *die* (note) when communicating with the magistrate.

The precedents for this, the council argued, were the forms of address used between the magistrate and various subcounty officials such as education authorities and assistant magistrates that were outlined in the official administrative compendium of the Qing dynasty. In turn, the council requested messages from magistrates in the form of an *yi* (communication), which was used for messages between magistrates and these same subcounty officials. As for the provincial assembly, the council wanted *zhihui* (notification), the communication form for addressing an equal, to be used in both directions.

The council members were nothing if not confident. But China's new citizens in Chengdu were still burdened by the old hierarchical customs they had borne as subjects. Although they refused to be treated like the emperor's old subjects, neither were they able to imagine a world of new citizens with equal rights. Instead, the Chengdu City Council occupied a no-man's land between government and citizen, and councillors represented themselves in documentary forms associated with subordinate officials.

Councillors certainly thought of themselves as social equals of magistrates: they portrayed themselves as the most respected and influential members of society, men who knew how to behave around officials. But the most telling and portentous passage in this petition concerns the relationship between Chengdu city and the countryside. In trying to define the proper relationship between the council and the magistrate, the Chengdu City Council explicitly contrasted its status and functions with those of heads of local security apparatuses (*baojia* and *tuanlian*), village compact *(xiangyue)* leaders, and yamen functionaries. The council encouraged the magistrate to continue treating *these* people as inferiors. One wonders what Zhao Erxun, who was administering Sichuan from his yamen in Chengdu, might have thought of this presumption. In his Shanxi *xiangshe* reforms, aimed at the kind of rural leadership being deprecated by the Chengdu City Council, he called on magistrates to treat *xiangshe* leaders, even if they were commoners, with respect and courtesy.

Much had changed in China by 1910, but some attitudes were unshakable. This was more than a matter of politeness and language; surely it was directed toward a day when bodies like the Chengdu

City Council would exercise political power over the hinterland. In the past this world had been managed by the welter of quasi-official bureaus and offices staffed at the pleasure of officials by those gentrymen who were *shendong* (gentry-managers). The Chengdu City Council, it appears, wanted this familiar authority to be exercised from council seats filled by Western-style elections. This was the dangerous mix of old and new brewed up by regulation-drafters.

It would not be long before the elites making up the Chengdu City Council and their peers in Sichuan and the rest of China witnessed, participated in, or learned about events that would be called the "fall of the Qing."[80] Sichuan was at the center of the storm, for the violent opposition by Sichuanese elites to Qing attempts to nationalize their railway companies had prompted authorities in Beijing to dispatch troops from Wuchang, just down the Yangtze from Sichuan, to quell the disturbance. Wuchang was undergarrisoned, then, when a revolutionary plot was exposed in the city on 9 October 1911. These desperate men, who were soldiers in New Army units, had nothing to lose and mutinied on 10 October; a beleaguered Governor Ruizheng, with few troops to command, fled the next morning; and an eminent local gentryman was coerced by the Hubei revolutionaries to lend some legitimacy to their new regime, which was declared on 11 October.[81]

Protests elsewhere quickly turned rebellious. The Hubei troops in Sichuan mutinied and confronted their commander. The doomed Duanfang, who had travelled around the world in 1905–1906 as part of the Qing constitutional study mission, who had argued constantly and effectively for constitutional programs, who had slipped the ideas of vilified expatriates like Liang Qichao into the Forbidden City, was murdered. Other dramatic and tragic events followed, but there was only scattered violence in most parts of China.[82] Reform implementation continued. Indeed, in Shandong, October 1911 was the month by which county councils were to have been elected, and many were. Throughout China more than three hundred county councils took their place in the fall of 1911 alongside approximately forty-seven hundred local councils.

Actions of local notables in these tumultuous days were sometimes framed by self-government councils and offices. In Jiangsu's Jiading County recent initiatives segued into revolutionary action. Activists like the _juren_ Huang Shizuo, with their attempts to establish local self-government institutions in 1906–1908, had prepared the ground. In 1909–1911 success had arrived. As we have seen, electors were identified and planning offices opened. In the summer of 1911 the county council election was held.[83] The first scheduled meeting of this body took place on 22 October.[84] Here China's turmoil was palpable. On 28 October the council authorized the organization of a local defense association _(mintuan)_. With the surrender of nearby Shanghai to revolutionary forces on 3 November, activities quickened in Jiading. The next day, civil and military officials were called together for a meeting at which they decided to organize a provisional militia _(linshi tuanlian)_ made up of water and land forces, police, local defense associations, and merchant-organized militias.

Throughout the drama of the last months of 1911 the persons and institutions of local self-government in Jiading played a role. One member of the county executive board was instrumental in organizing the militia.[85] On 9 November he was named vice-president in charge of financial affairs in the reconstituted county administration. Self-government organizations throughout Jiading were also useful; the calls to merchants in several market towns in Jiading county were delivered through local self-government offices. And on 6 November it was the county self-government office that declared the independence of Jiading from the Qing, an action marked by posting white flags on public buildings and the city gates.[86]

The importance of self-government institutions continued into the first two weeks of December. The county magistrate _(minzheng zhang)_ called at least two meetings of city and county self-government officials to discuss the question of establishing a new county council. Rather than call for new elections on what must have been an inauspicious moment, they decided to use the personnel of the old county council (see Appendix C). A meeting of this old council (with some changes in membership) took place the following week with twenty-two members present. Two weeks later, for unknown reasons, its proceedings were suspended;[87] this augured the future.

The balancing of localism, centralism, and provincialism needed purposeful men of good will and vision. And a bit of luck. Only sometimes, as in Chengdu and Jiading, were all ingredients available. The promise of the Qing local self-government reforms, while manifest in aggregate in 1909, 1910, and 1911, was also betrayed in particular instances. These betrayals sparked resistance, both measured and infuriated, that might be construed too easily as anti-dynastic rebellion, perhaps even becoming vignettes in the history of the 1911 Revolution. But the local arena, which had become the stage for contending forces, admitted no easy simplicities. Incontrovertible, however, was the quiet transfer of power in February 1912 from China's last emperor, who then withdrew to private courts and pavilions in the Forbidden City, to representatives of China's new Republic.

Reformers like Yuan Shikai and Lu Zongyu soon fell victim to their pasts. Yuan, the respected imperial governor, squandered his carefully nurtured national reputation as he played the role of republican president. Shortly after quelling an insurrection in 1913, he responded to complaints from his provincial governors about the presumptions of the councils and abrogated, in February 1914, the Japanese-influenced self-government program he had helped create back in August 1906 when he opened the doors of his yamen in Tianjin to men who had studied law and administration in Japan. In 1915 Yuan was ill-served by the Japanese who, taking advantage of the West's inability to maintain a strong presence in Asia while waging war in Europe, began reprising the aggressiveness they had displayed in 1894–1895. Yuan could only modify Japan's Twenty-one Demands and in May 1915 the Chinese government was forced to cede a bit more of its dwindling sovereignty. The golden age of Sino-Japanese amity was ending. In a delayed reaction so too were the careers of Lu Zongyu and other returned students wrecked. By the spring of 1919, when Japan was being rewarded at China's expense at the peace talks in Versailles, young Chinese in urban areas, spurred on by the next generation of returned students, who had come home this time from the United States and Europe, protested China's increasing subservience to Japan. Struck down, literally, in some cases, by this sweep of History were old returned students like Lu, the Qing Ministry of Interior official, along with his colleagues Zhang Zongxiang, Wang Rongbao, and Cao Rulin, all of whom had contributed ideas and energy to the late Qing reforms.[88]

The rush of events that swept over them reduced their late-Qing accomplishments to mere footnotes in the history of China's passage into the twentieth century, but their activities in 1905–1911 invite retrospect and have repaid study. Lu Zongyu and Sun Pei at the Ministry of Interior; Cao Rulin, Zhang Zongxiang, and Wang Rong-bao in the Constitutional Commission; Jin Bangping, who shuttled between Beijing and Tianjin; and scores more in the provinces like Wu Xingrang, Fei Tinghuang, Li Shuen, Shao Congen, and Meng Zhaochang may have sometimes misbegot regulations and programs based on the Japan model, and were often too impatient, but in their flawed reforms were the irritants that caused numerous recorded actions. The mutable society of late imperial China thus revealed demands a reconsideration of descriptive categories like rural and elite, for the logical steps that excluded rural China from the constitutional era become clear when portrayed on a wide canvas. Moreover, the failure of the self-government reforms was grand enough to both encourage and illuminate the first halting steps of China's new citizens. The fate of rural China, the future of the men abandoned by the abolition of the old examination system who were shut out of the self-government reforms, and the viability of new conceptions of citizenship were being determined.

# SEVEN

# Qing Policy, Rural China, and Elite Factions in the Age of Constitutionalism

In a drama with many plots, one main outline is just discernible, that of late-Qing self-government reforms fracturing local society along existing fault lines. At the intersection of Beijing's centralism and local corporatism are unstable combinations, especially at the local level, where contending sections of the elite quickly seek new allies in the capital. Another fissure opens after attacks by urban elites, which includes degree-holders, merchants, returned students, and the educated, on the gentry-managers who have monopolized control of the countryside and are now managing council elections in county seats and major market towns. This gap reminds rural leaders, among whom are other degree-holders and commoners, of their shared interests vis-à-vis towns and cities. Gentry-managers are the mobile pivot. Some are degree-holders; some are not. Some live in county seats and market towns; others live in villages.[1] But one thing is certain in the minds of self-government activists in urban centers: the responsibilities of gentry-managers should be assumed by elected councils. Who then will be the councillors? The power and influence of gentry-managers privileges them, but others clamor for a chance.

This contest, framed by a program designed to unify China, served only to divide. What details do we have? Little evidence of who the councillors were has survived and that which has points to the predominance of degree-holders. Most of these men, it is reasonable to infer, already possessed influence in county seats and market towns; for the regulation's definition of the smallest self-government district, the *xiang*, mandated populations ranging from 2,500 to 50,000. This was the most important and extensive district; for the market-town designation, *zhen*, was seldom used, in part because organizers thus averted the difficult task of drawing boundaries between *xiang* and *zhen*. Centered, most probably, on market towns, the *xiang* jurisdiction brought to the forefront men who would have been well known to thousands, sometimes tens of thousands, of persons. This could not have been a case of face-to-face communities electing village councillors.

In later decades of the twentieth century the county seats and market towns that sheltered the men who predominated in local councils would, in comparison with China's treaty ports, be lumped together with the villages beyond their walls. Philip Kuhn saw these two spheres and their increasing incompatibility in the twentieth century as follows: "[T]he modernizing process began to produce a new urban elite that found it increasingly hard to identify itself with the problems of rural China. The gap between modernizing and premodern cultures thus tended to become coterminous with the gap between city and countryside."[2] Begging questions about the meaning of modernizing and pre-modern cultures, the term "countryside" needs to be refined, for it is evident that the local self-government and constitutional reforms, as finally implemented, created sharp divisions within a part of Chinese society that in later years and from more distant vantages, became blurred into a homogenous "rural."

It is virtually impossible with the facts at hand to make any well-substantiated generalization about distinctions among councillors in administrative seats, market towns, and townships; but it is possible to suggest how Beijing policy makers, perhaps unwittingly, created two very different electorates, one whose interests were directed toward provincial capitals and Beijing, and one to localities. This implicit division of politics into higher-order and lower-order spheres implies the insignificance, perhaps even incomprehensibility, of one part of rural China in the minds of some Beijing policy makers. Furthermore, inappropriate qualifications for the franchise, given social and economic conditions in the Chinese countryside, barred from voting and participation many of the very kind of men once sought by Zhao Erxun and Wu Tingxie, who were convinced China's resurgence could only begin in its rural reaches. But local self-government electoral activities seldom appear to have extended that far.

Few of the citizens who could vote for councillors had been eligible to participate in the assembly elections; the regulations drafted by the Ministry of Interior identified a much broader electorate than the provincial assembly regulations written by the Constitutional Commission. Council elections were open to all literate men twenty-five *sui* or older who paid at least two yuan of taxes annually; the provincial assembly franchise, however, was limited to literate men twenty-five *sui* or older who met at least one of the following requirements: employment in an occupation, like teaching, that contributed to the public good; receipt of either a new-style education degree, *shengyuan*, *juren*, or *jinshi* degree, or official rank; or possession of capital or property valued at five thousand yuan or more.[3] Few qualified; but nevertheless in the six months of registration prior to the 1909 elections for provincial assemblies, 1.7 million names, or about 0.4 percent of the population, appeared on electoral lists.[4] The size of this electorate is about the same as that of the degree-holding gentry in the late Qing as estimated by Chang Chung-li.[5] But the nature of the electorate, if one of the few surviving electoral rolls is indicative, cannot be ascribed so narrowly.[6] In Huichang, a county in southern Jiangxi that was well removed from a treaty port or a major river system, there were 327 men eligible to participate in the first round of provincial assembly elections. The list included 129 commoners, most of whom qualified on the basis of their property holdings.[7] Members of this group, part of, if not equivalent to, the county elite, lived in Huichang city and elsewhere in the county.

The aggregate number of men who were registered to vote in China's council elections will never be known. And without an electoral roll comparable to Huichang's, it is impossible to describe the different participants in even one election. But clues have survived. The total number of men eligible to vote was much larger than the assembly electorate, as self-government activists were quick to point out. The Fengtian Provincial Local Self-government Preparation Office stressed this fact in one of the vernacular collections of documents it published and distributed in 1909–1910. Readers were told that the franchise for the assembly election required proof of assets totalling five thousand yuan, but council elections were open to anyone who paid at least two yuan per year in taxes.[8] The prediction in Fengtian that far greater numbers of persons could vote in council elections proved accurate. For example, in Jiading county, the county council electorate was three times larger than the one for the provincial assembly. Local organizers had compiled, in November 1908, a list containing 2,157 names of men qualified to participate in the first stage of the provincial assembly elections; in the summer of 1911 the number of county council electors was 7,644. (The Jiading gazetteer from which these data are taken give a total county population of about 200,000.)[9]

The difference between the electorates, defined by two Beijing agencies, shows one way in which "local self-government" could be divorced from "constitutional government." In 1906–1907 many had argued that participating in local elections and local government would provide valuable training for China's new citizens, leading them up a pyramid of representative bodies from locality to province to nation; in 1908 a wall began coming into view that divided localities from provincial capitals and Beijing. Most people eligible to vote in local elections had not voted for assemblymen, and even the minority who could vote in both elections did not necessarily send a local representative to the provincial assembly. No one from Huichang, for example, was elected to the Jiangxi Provincial Assembly, although the prefectural electoral college that included Huichang's electors did send assemblymen from nearby Anyuan, Xunwu, Xinfeng, Gan, and Yudu.[10] This two-step electoral process inclined provincial assemblies *(ziyiju)* toward provincial and national, not local, issues.[11] Paradoxically, the previous incarnation of *ziyiju,* the consultative bureaus planned and instituted on the basis of longstanding precedents by provincial yamen in 1907–1908, were more representative geographically in that members were to come from every county.

Councils, both local and county, and provincial assemblies belonged to different worlds. Local self-government councils were for localities; the assemblies were for provinces. Therefore, there were "local" citizens, a minority of whom were also "provincial" citizens. And even local citizenship was beyond the grasp of many, including merchants as well as the very group at the center of Zhao Erxun's Shanxi reforms, rural elites.

J. O. P. Bland had dismissed the reforms because of their neglect of the "masses," most of whom were in the countryside. The reformers, influenced as they were by Japanese and Western models, had no intention of creating a program for illiterate peasants [12] or those without property. They did, however, want local self-government to have at least some significance in rural areas. Indeed, the first Tianjin elections were planned originally to take place in areas outside county seats. [13] But problems popped up immediately, fulfilling warnings sounded by some of the men who had introduced the Japanese model to China.

The Tianjin bureau member Wu Xingrang, who had studied in Japan, foresaw that property or tax-paying requirements, which could be found in Japanese regulations, would bar those whose contributions were most needed. In an essay published in 1907 Wu pointed out that because taxes in China were based on landholding or commercial enterprises, persons who had the practical experience that needed to be brought to local self-government, such as those involved in local administration or education, might not have any tax liabilities in the counties they lived in and served. Similarly, literate locals could be too impoverished to have tax liabilities but were desirable councillors because of their status and talents. Wu also stressed how unsettling any attempt by the government to investigate a person's financial status would be. [14]

But Wu's warnings were unheeded in Beijing in 1907–1908; provincial officials began describing the consequences in 1909. Although the countywide electorate in the prosperous and densely-populated Jiangnan county of Jiading might exceed seven thousand in 1911, officials had previously told Beijing that electors were hard to find in some areas. In an exchange recorded in the Ministry of Interior's *Collected Explications,* the Hubei governor told the ministry that only a few persons in rural areas were being enfranchised. Based on a report by the magistrate in Zhangle county, just south of the Yangtze in Yichang prefecture, the governor emphasized how difficult it was in rural districts to find men who met the tax requirement. He illustrated this assertion with figures for the total land tax in Zhangle's thirty-four rural *bao:* about 190 *liang* (taels). Even in the thirteen *bao* near the county seat few qualified, let alone those in more remote districts. The governor did not say how these tax liabilities were divided; but even if they were apportioned evenly, fewer than one hundred persons outside Zhangle city would pay the minimum tax. The governor informed the ministry that including other categories of taxes, standard and special surcharges, would not solve the problem. As an example he mentioned the special taxes for education that often amounted to only several hundred *wen,* a fraction of two yuan. Shandong faced similar problems; the governor told the ministry about rural districts near county seats in which several hundred households might produce only forty to fifty electors.[15]

Inexplicably, numbers of electors could vary significantly even within a county. In Heilongjiang three *xiang* east of the prefectural seat of Suihua had 116, 1,036, and 1,038 electors each. The number of electors in Chengde county's twenty-two *xiang* ranged from 122 to 989. The average per *xiang* in this Fengtian county was 515. In Sichuan's Taiping county there were 1,050 electors combined in the county seat and nine *xiang.* Finally, figures from thirty-three *xiang* in Jiading county, Jiangsu, went from 61 to 985 electors, with a median of 195.[16]

The rural elites of concern to Hubei and Shandong officials were but one section of elite society in late imperial China and their existence is often overlooked in studies of elite activism in the late Qing, which have focussed on provincial and national elites that took part in the petition movement to convene a national parliament, provincial assemblies, and railway rights recovery movements.[17] But these activities were usually distinct from local activism. Elites in Suzhou, Jilin city, and Beijing could easily cross the line, but there were numerous other cases of local activism outside major cities, prompted by elites and officials, in Jilin, Sichuan, Hubei, and Gansu, that have been described in these pages.

Even "local" requires some elaboration. The "local" elites courted by Zhao Erxun, for example, may have had only a passing acquaintance with the men who finally stood for election in Shanxi's counties. Zhao's ideal face-to-face communities of 500 persons were essentially being overlooked in Beijing's regulations, which did not even offer the possibility of a political identity to villages with fewer than 2,500 persons. By juxtaposing Zhao's leaders with councillors, the need to add one tier to Philip Kuhn's model, which distinguishes national, provincial, and local elites, becomes apparent.[18] Even though provincial and national elites might see county-level and subcounty elites in the same light, from the perspective of the China beyond county seats there remained significant political and social differences between two networks of elites. One is a squirearchy of men and their families with a countywide reputation. The other network, less distinguished but still important, is a rural elite.[19] Among this elite were village leaders, men who were disadvantaged in the world of township local self-government, with populations ranging up to 50,000. And in education, expensive new-style schools, once envisioned by the Constitutional Commission as the source for councillors,[20] were established only in county seats and the largest market towns. The rural elite highlighted by Zhao Erxun had few opportunities to participate in these new ventures, but these commoners and degree-holders, who may have been no more than rich peasants or small landlords to borrow labels in use from the 1920s on, were distinct from the masses and far from powerless.

What happened to this neglected rural elite once sought by Zhao Erxun? Their fate after the fall of the Qing still remains unclear. But the accommodationist, if authoritarian, approach of Zhao Erxun that sought their participation has not been typical of the twentieth century, when the Confucian disdain for the social practices of rural populations was joined with the ethos of modernizers who echoed the centralism of Beijing in the late Qing and yearned to control ever greater shares of local resources. These men were eager to advance policies of fiscal and symbolic appropriation; rural communities became objects of state control.[21]

Zhao Erxun brooded little about popular sovereignty, but he did think it was important for the state to establish cordial relations with the leaders of identifiable local communities. His state-making goals were less disruptive than the characteristic nineteenth century agenda in Europe: penetrating society, regulating social relationships, extracting resources, and specifying the way in which resources still under local control should be used. But his would be an approach little used in the twentieth century; neither the Qing local self-government regulations nor the ones that followed exemplified this approach. Instead, the building of a wall between rural and urban China began. In time the spheres became incommensurable, a fact that contributed much to China's misery.[22]

Constitutionalism left most of China's rural elite out of the equation, along with other elites. In market towns and county seats, one sectional elite was recognized by both friends and foes of the policy as dominating (some said monopolizing) local self-government: the gentry-managers. The imperial regulations had privileged this group, partly in hopes of curbing it by specifying its powers, focussing public opinion on its actions, and increasing the supervisory functions of local magistrates. In some cases gentry-managers evaded these curbs and simply used the centrally mandated and defined institutions for their own ends.[23] By turning self-government reforms from an inclusive local affair to exclusive sectionalism, these men helped doom the program. They antagonized the powerless in the countryside as well as other sections within elite society in both urban and rural areas. The first studies of the local self-government reforms, which were constrained by limited sources, focussed on a few election results, but the historical significance is to be found in the process, especially the ill-fated attempt to reshape society without reference to its corporate character. The leaders of familiar gentry bureaus and offices, newly established chambers of commerce and education societies, the heads of both old-style and new-style educational hierarchies, advocates of constitutionalism and local self-government, and the county magistrate did figure into the equation. But gentry-managers were entrenched and had the advantage. For example, in Sichuan's Mian department the magistrate established an advisory assembly of elites called the Public Welfare Assembly (Gongyi jiyihui) that first met on 19 September 1909. Representatives *(hui-yuan)* were to be sent from various sections of the elite: education intendants, new-style school administrators and teachers, gentry-managers of bureaus and offices, *baojia* leaders, leaders of chambers of commerce and education societies, and electors for the provincial assembly. But it was temporarily to be composed only of gentry-managers since it would be difficult to hold elections.[24]

These lines of division were prefigured in Prefect Li Shuen's conflict in 1908 with gentry-managers of a rural militia in Binzhou who, he charged, were "ignorant rustics" unaware of the meaning of self-government.[25] The Fengtian essayist cited above wrote that the gentry-managers of rural affairs *(xiang shendong)* were "so stupid that nothing was accomplished."[26] In March 1910 the Fengtian office published an essay that portrayed self-government as a way to eliminate this incompetence as well as corruption. Beginning with a discussion of secret balloting and its role in protecting persons from being bullied, the Fengtian managers of self-government implementation tried to explain the concept of representation and that the elected councils were important because the councillors would be responsible for local administration.[27]

The explanation about the usefulness of secret ballots echoed similar concerns Zhao Erxun had expressed in Shanxi in 1903 when he argued that since consensual selection processes could still be abused by local tyrants, the magistrate must protect local society by selecting *shezhang* from lists of nominated candidates. In Fengtian in 1910, Western-style elections, not state authority, were seen as the way to achieve this goal. But the pessimistic metropolitan official Hu Sijing informed the court early in 1910:

> I am concerned about extending to local elites *(difang shenshi)* the
> power of self-government. The good have no one to back them up
> and their influence is isolated. The plan is that capable persons will
> be elected to serve on councils, but this rarely happens. The cun-
> ning gentry and evil supervisors *(diaoshen liejian)* continue to treat
> their areas wrongly and take the people as their fish and meat.
> . . . The tigers and wolves in the mountains are innumerable.[28]

A year later on 28 August 1911, the Shanghai newspaper *Shibao*
published a vituperative attack:

> Local self-government is that which comes the closest to the
> people. For the last two years it has been in preparation, but what
> have been the accomplishments of these official actions? . . .
> Alas, "self-government" is "self-chaos." . . . The personnel of
> self-government are not the most talented and knowledgeable per-
> sons, but rather the old managers of the countryside *(xiangli)*. It's
> easy to have a name; but it's hard to have the reality of local self-
> government.

(Four years earlier Meng Zhaochang, well connected in Jiangsu elite
society, was certain that the electoral process itself would check the
power of the "old gentry-managers.") The conservative metropolitan
official Hu Sijing and the private newspaper *Shibao*, seen by some
as the most progressive publication in Shanghai,[29] were expressing
virtually identical positions. Jiangsu elites and Beijing bureaucrats,
from their urban perches, had found a common foe in the countryside. Provincial elites and metropolitan bureaucrats could join together, rhetorically at least, in an attack on gentry-managers. The
real issue, they thought, was the division of power between Beijing
and the provinces.

This attack from Beijing and Shanghai on gentry-managers was
serious—and ironic, for it was the self-government regulations
drafted in and promulgated from Beijing that had equated the responsibilities of the new councils, and their fiscal base, with the
projects and public funds customarily managed by gentry-managers
*(shendong)*. Moreover, these men were among those recommended
to magistrates by Beijing to implement the first stages of the electoral program.

Few in Beijing seemed concerned about the corporatism of local society and how the regulations, in such a context, might easily spark a divisive intra-elite struggle for power. Whereas in early 1907 two young officials in the Ministry of Interior had discussed ways to reach gentry-managers *(shendong)*, local notables *(shenqi)*, and leaders of educational societies and chambers of commerce, the court's call in 1909 was for one local self-government council in administrative seats, towns, and townships that would be responsible for all aspects of local administration not handled by the county yamen. But all too often local councils registered the voices of only one section of the elite: gentry members of the county elite. In contrast to the display of cooperation by merchant, degree-holding, gentry, and educational elites in Tianjin during the drafting of the election regulations in 1906–1907, the electoral process in 1909–1911 was marred by factionalism. In a case from southern Jiangsu, merchants battled election managers for the right to vote. Factionalism within the degree-holding county elite, adumbrated in the haughtiness of the Chengdu City Council, also appears in a struggle waged by *shengyuan* and self-government activists with a *juren* in Fujian. Both the Jiangsu and Fujian cases will be described in detail. The regulations did not anticipate the jurisdictional battles involving previously established educational societies, chambers of commerce, and self-government schools that continued to exist, and more important, had institutional patrons in Beijing.

In Huichang, where more than a third of the group of men qualified to vote in provincial assembly elections were not degree-holders, an important and significant section in society was identified by wealth alone and was not part of the "gentry-manager" elite.[30] Did the Huichang councillors represent them?

Analysis of the few extant lists points to dominance by degree-holders but, as the Huichang data suggest, it must have come at the expense of other segments of the population notable for their "movable wealth" such as merchants and artisans. These commercial interests were neither inconsiderable nor indistinct. Two decades after the Huichang magistrate filed his report the young revolutionary Mao Zedong investigated the market-town economy in nearby

Xunwu county and discovered extensive and influential commercial interests with roots in the late Qing.[31] Mao's concern in 1930 was revolutionary; here the question is historical: To what degree was this commercial elite allowed to participate?

Although the regulations promulgated by Beijing made room for all sections of the elite, in practice merchants were discriminated against as a result of the tax-payment qualification, the same requirement that tended to keep some rural elites from voting, as we saw in Hubei and Shandong. China's merchants faced serious obstacles to their participation even though they were often important figures in local society. Their low profile in the land-tax system hurt them. Moreover, even if the *lijin* tax was accepted, sojourning merchants remained outsiders for years, even generations, after their arrival in a particular area. And when non-native merchants retired, they might return home and still retain ownership of their commercial property.

Some of these problems were apparent in Suzhou prefecture's Shengze town in Wujiang county, where elections scheduled to take place on 11 January and 14 January 1911[32] had to be delayed because of vociferous opposition, apparent since mid-1910, by silk merchants[33] who complained to the Ministry of Agriculture, Industry, and Commerce that they were systematically being kept off electoral rolls. A copy of this petition by the Shengze Chamber of Commerce (Shangwu fenhui) was forwarded to the Ministry of Interior on 27 November 1910.[34] But the ministry already knew; a month earlier the Shengze chamber had telegraphed their complaint to it directly with a reminder of the ministry's ruling that had been sent to the governors of Hunan and Jiangxi.[35] The Shengze merchants were well informed; both telegrams are in the ministry's *Collected Explications*. (On 10 August 1910 the ministry had sent one to Changsha declaring the *lijin* tax to be an acceptable category of tax payment. A similar response was sent to Nanchang two weeks later after receipt of a complaint from the Jiujiang Chamber of Commerce [Jiujiang shanghui]).[36]

But the Ministry of Interior learned in the Shengze petition that the provincial self-government office in Suzhou continued to flout its rulings. The Shengze merchants claimed they were being ignored and had told local officials without effect that they must protect merchant power.[37] Correspondence among the principals continued without achieving a resolution, although the Ministry of Interior informed the Ministry of Agriculture, Industry, and Commerce on 17 December 1910 that authorities in Suzhou had been told again to accept the *lijin* tax.[38] But the Suzhou authorities, who agreed in theory, said that *lijin* tax records for individual persons did not exist.[39] The Ministry of Interior wearily told authorities in Suzhou in a telegram of 23 January 1911 to implement the regulations according to local conditions.[40]

The Shengze merchants, however, were indefatigable. They had forced the scheduled elections to be delayed; now they wanted in. A recapitulation from the head of the Shengze Chamber of Commerce, Wang Sijing, was received at the Ministry of Interior on 25 January 1911; he mentioned that the gentryman *(shenmin)* Shen Rongzhao was the cause of the controversy. There was no response but the Ministry of Interior continued discussing this case with the Ministry of Agriculture, Industry, and Commerce, without resolution, until at least 17 April 1911.[41]

These were severe intra-elite rivalries and administrative conflicts. Merchants in Shengze town, self-government managers in the town and in the Wujiang county seat, provincial officials in Suzhou, and at least two groups of metropolitan bureaucrats became embroiled in a year-long dispute.

Suzhou had told Beijing that a disaffected minority of merchants in Shengze was at fault; elsewhere in southern Jiangsu councils had been established without controversy in all administrative seats and about a dozen towns and townships without reliance upon the *lijin* tax.[42] But Suzhou was not the last court of appeal for the Shengze merchants, who communicated directly with two metropolitan bureaus, both of which were supportive. Nevertheless, the Ministry of Interior was unable once again to bend the will of provincial authorities. Suzhou officials had already defied the ministry by allowing council elections to take place ahead of schedule. The reform managers in Wujiang county and Shengze town were no more pliable.

Unyielding self-government officials in Suzhou and stubborn managers in Wujiang and Shengze exposed the weaknesses of the new metropolitan ministries and the dangers of opening new lines of communication with Beijing. Bureaucrats in the capital were receiving one complaining telegram after another from merchants in Jiangsu, Hunan, and Jiangxi; and yet their responses were routed, in accord with precedent, through provincial and local yamen. In the Shengze case, merchants sought metropolitan pressure to resolve their local disputes with Jiangsu officialdom, a group that had been challenging Beijing on self-government policy since early 1907. In that, Jiangsu's merchants could take only cold comfort. Beijing, in this case at least, had to rely on propaganda channels like *Zhengzhi guanbao* and publications like *Collected Explications* to make its will at least known, if not effective. And its will was known and known quickly, as we have seen, for Shengze elites quoted recent Ministry of Interior telegrams as justification for their arguments. Shengze merchants saw Beijing's policy contravened flagrantly by one section of the local elite.[43]

Rural elites and merchants could be outside the fold; it was not only Bland's illiterate masses who were being overlooked. Previous scholarship on the local self-government initiatives in the late Qing stressed the equivalence of the self-government elite and local elites.[44] The only section able to participate easily in the reforms was the part that held degrees. Teraki Tokuko's study demonstrated the dominance of degree-holders in Hubei council elections in 1909–1911. Teraki and, later, Su Yunfeng, analyzed namelists of council and board members for eleven councils in Hubei's prefectural seats. Of 1,340 council members, there were 860 degree-holders and 295 also held official rank. The executive board members included 265 degree-holders and 125 who also were rank-holders out of a total of 430. Merchants and graduates of new-style schools were almost invisible: there were only seven men identified as merchants and thirty-two as graduates.[45]

The dominance of degree-holders in the councils replicated the range of faces in classes at local self-government schools. This had been true in pre-1909 prototypes established in Tianjin and Chengdu and remained so after May 1909, when the Ministry of Interior finally promulgated its school regulations. Most students in the few extant class rosters from provincial schools in the capitals of Henan, Hunan, and Shandong were degree-holders. Of the 205 names of Henan students attending classes in 1909, about 90 percent were degree-holders. In Hunan a report filed on 6 June 1910 included detailed information on 226 students, all but ten of whom were degree-holders. Among all Hunan students twenty-five had received a new-style education, including three who had studied in Japan. A 2 March 1909 report from Shandong listed 216 names, all but three of whom were degree-holders. Seven *juren* and one returned student from Japan also were on this Shandong list. School rosters at the subprovincial level were similar. For example, a self-government school for students from Ji'nan prefecture in Shandong included, in early 1909, 153 men, 140 of whom were degree-holders.[46]

These specific details come from a much larger phenomenon that provides important insight into the self-government reforms. Because much electoral activity was lost in the confusion and turmoil at the end of 1911, some of the surest surviving signs of the energy and significance of the reforms can be found only in the activity associated with self-government schools. In Table 1 (see Chapter Six) aggregated statistics from all provinces record over seven thousand students who had graduated from provincial self-government schools. At the county level there were over one thousand schools with about forty-seven thousand students. There is no reason to suspect that the namelists just mentioned from Henan, Hunan, and Shandong are not representative.

But there was still a potential for conflict. It is easy to mistake similar status markers like degrees with common interests. Degree-holders in late imperial China may have been bound by the common experience of participating in the examination system, but much separated *jinshi* from *tongsheng* at the extremes and even *juren* from *shengyuan* toward the middle. There were significant differences within the degree-holding elite, as the Shengze case, with its implications of a split between an urban county elite and a rural elite, suggests. There could also be generational splits. A well-documented case from Fujian appears to incorporate all these reasons—degree level, residence, and age—that contributed to tensions within this elite.

By the end of 1910 in Fujian a total of 516 men had graduated from the Fujian Provincial Local Self-government School in Fuzhou. Throughout Fujian there were seventy-seven other such schools (sixty-one of which were established by officials) that had already graduated about four thousand students.[47] One of these schools, headed by the Fujian Law School graduate Yang Xiangeng, had been established on 20 September 1909. His school had sixty-nine students and three teachers in early 1911,[48] when he made a complaint that would eventually reach Beijing about a local council in Zhangpu county.[49] Yang Xiangeng's antagonist, Yang Shipeng, was an influential *juren* in Fotan, a market town ten miles from Zhangpu city along the coast of Fujian.

According to a joint petition submitted by Yang Xiangeng, two graduates of a self-government school, and three *shengyuan*, a self-government council was established in late 1910 in Fotan. Yang Shipeng had sold, for five or ten yuan, positions on the council. Besides this perversion of the electoral process, the persons who bought these seats should have been disqualified on the grounds of illiteracy, lack of payment of taxes, opium addiction, ownership of a brothel, youth, and gambling. Furthermore, the petitioners charged, Yang Shipeng used yamen functionaries to make "investigations" in preparation for council elections. Yang used the council, which met in a local temple (a venue that was suggested in the regulations), as a court of law (a function that was not). Yang's foes attached a manuscript copy of an article that had been published in *Fujian ribao* in the fall of 1906 exposing some of his misdeeds; the petitioners wanted to prove that Yang Shipeng was a local despot *(wuduan)*.

Honor, as well as power, was at stake in this struggle. Five of the six petitioners, as well as their target and his associates, had the same surname. Yang Xiangeng and his allies had been worried since at least 1906 that Yang Shipeng's corruption was tarnishing the reputation of their lineage. In 1910 the focus shifted to Yang's local "council," when they petitioned the prefect for redress, goading him by repeating Yang Shipeng's boast that he was beyond the reach or concern of the government. But these officials had done nothing.

The struggle for control of the institutions and rhetoric of local self-government commenced in Fujian as different elite sections in Zhangpu county mobilized. Yang Shipeng's resources were considerable. He was a *juren*, had connections with yamen functionaries, and had been overseas, probably to Southeast Asia. But Yang Shipeng was neither so despotic nor so arrogant that he did not think it expedient, even necessary, to appropriate Beijing's newest rhetorical and institutional flourish, elected local self-government councils, for his purposes. Moreover, Yang went through the motions of petitioning the county magistrate for permission to establish a council.

Other members of Zhangpu's degree-holding elite were appalled when this petition was approved. They too gathered resources in order to check Yang Shipeng and protect their interpretation of local self-government, which was being propounded in recently established law and self-government schools. These men understood what Beijing's "local self-government" meant, but they were unable to persuade the prefect in Zhangzhou to back them. Nevertheless, their grievance, like the Shengze merchants', reached all the way to Beijing.

Yang Shipeng personified the specter raised by Hu Sijing and *Shibao;* he was not the only local tyrant given to corruption. How could they be defeated? Should Beijing encourage local initiatives and autonomous action and depend on public opinion and local democracy to curb excesses? Or should China's state structure be expanded to market towns and villages by creating, as the court had asked Yuan Shikai and Zhao Erxun in 1906, a new position of permanent authority outside county seats? In the starkest terms: Should the state extend its reach or should its subjects become empowered citizens?

Many young reform-minded men in China thought the electoral process, with its ballots, boxes, and tallies, could conjure away despots and bullies. They believed in the power of people joined in hatred of tyranny. But Yang Shipeng's adversaries had not been so serene. They turned away from society and toward the state in hopes of finding a powerful enough ally to fight their local nemesis. Others shared their frustration and dispair.[50] Even well-organized and wealthy merchants could fail to find a seat at the table. But both groups were emboldened enough to try, and therein lies one aspect of the historical significance of the late Qing self-government reforms.

What did the reforms mean in the late Qing? In Fujian's Zhangpu county the answers in action given by Yang Shipeng and Yang Xiangeng begin to define the range. Councillors in Chengdu and merchants in Shengze have provided two more examples. All actions were framed by the imperial regulations promulgated in 1909–1910 that began the sequence of activities summarized in the statistical profile presented in Chapter Six. But even before promulgation numerous activists had made their mark in 1902–1908. "Local self-government" inspired actions in counties, provincial capitals, and Beijing by officials and nonofficials alike. Huang Zunxian, Zhao Erxun, Wu Tingxie, Yuan Shikai, Jin Bangping, Songyu, Li Shuen, and Meng Zhaochang are just a few of the men that moved China. The objects of their activities are more anonymous: subcounty *xiangshe* bodies in Shanxi, rural and urban elites in Zhili, militia organizers in Jilin, gentry-managers, and the empirewide readership of a constitutionalist private press and new-style government gazettes.

From the Neo-Confucian cadences used by Huang Zunxian in his Changsha lecture in 1898 to the supercilious references to a failed policy in the pages of *Shibao* in August 1911, the compound *zizhi* at the end of the Qing dynasty encompassed a wide range of meaning. Fatefully, with the promulgation of the 1909 regulations, the government projected an explicit meaning on the compound: a program defined, granted, and defended from Beijing. At first metropolitan officials had talked about granting "self-government" to "enlightened" persons in economically developed areas, a vanguard that would lead the rest of China. But many of those being portrayed as benighted became convinced that they and their ancestors had been practicing self-government for years, generations, even centuries. They needed neither a patent nor an election. Yang Shipeng fits this category, but more positive representatives of local activism could too. Theorists and practitioners of China's statecraft tradition, with its strain of cameralism and trust in local initiative, could be sure about their prerogatives and contemptuous of an overreaching state.

They could have much in common with England's anti-centralist Toulmin Smith or the burghers of Middle Germany in the middle of the nineteenth century, who were able to resist ambitious Prussian centralizers until 1870.[51] Whether an advocate of local autonomy looked to England or to Middle Germany, to Jefferson's ward republics, or to China's own tradition of administrative cameralism, there was plenty of ammunition to aim at a state eager to use self-government as a tool of centralism.

Unfortunately, this ammunition, which was available to everyone, when reinforced by customary privileges, created formidable adversaries of state power in local society. Yang Shipeng's power play and the obstructionism of leaders in Jiangsu's Shengze town, for example, sharply limited the participation of other members of the elite in self-government reforms, even in the face of Beijing's opposition. What had gone wrong?

Beijing's policy makers had promulgated a set of regulations that refused to acknowledge the corporatist structure of local society. It was not much of a secret. Elites in 1906 had celebrated the constitutionalism edict in gatherings that stressed their distinctive contributions to society. A year later regulation drafters in Sichuan, Jiangsu, and Anhui insisted that representation should first be cast in functional terms. Even Beijing, until the self-government regulations were announced, had implicitly recognized this reality, with patents granted to chambers of commerce, educational and agricultural societies, and gentry societies and bureaus. All of these could be referred to as different types of self-government organizations *(zizhi tuanti)*. But after January 1909 these understandings were swept aside. One was an elector, not a gentry-manager, teacher, or merchant. As had happened in 1906, all sections of the elite expected to have a voice, but all too often too few were heard in local arenas. The search for citizens confronted problems of prejudice against merchants and inconvenience or disqualification when it came to rural elites. This was extremely divisive. Complaints often had to go all the way to

Beijing, as was the case with the Shengze merchants and Zhangpu *shengyuan* and self-government students, before anyone paid attention. But many more were silenced altogether and could vent their frustration only in mute rage. The tax riots, attacks on census-takers, and burning of self-government offices that have come to symbolize self-government's failure need to be studied anew for clues about the identity of the protagonists. How many merchants, disaffected degree-holders, and influential commoners joined overburdened peasants in battle against monopolistic gentry-managers in self-government offices and councils?

There had been other policy options under discussion before 1909 that sought to reach out to rural China in a different way. Zhao Erxun's Shanxi program courted rural elites and the society they led because he was convinced China's regeneration had to begin there. But Zhao, being a skeptic, trusted neither magistrates, rural leaders, nor a Western-style electoral process. He was convinced that elections and councils were no panacea for China's administrative crisis and insisted that the state mediate political relationships in local arenas. Remarkably, given the competition of foreign models imported by returned students, Zhao's ideas had staying power; only in mid-1908 was his authoritarian approach finally abandoned. But Beijing had come close to putting its weight behind a program that would have selected subcounty managers through a government testing program. The old statecraft figure of *xiangguan* was revived and in Fengtian, at least, these "rural officials" were selected.[52] Not even three years had passed since the examination system had been abolished; in every county there were still thousands of educated commoners still wondering about the shape of a new and unfamiliar world, who would have been candidates. But policy makers at the Ministry of Interior were completing their draft of self-government regulations, which placed these administrative responsibilities on councils elected by enfranchised citizens casting ballots in Western-style elections. The old *xiangguan* approach seemed inappropriate in the new age of constitutionalism. Officials in Beijing thought it would be redundant and confusing to have a government testing program for *xiangguan* and elections for council members. The die was cast as Beijing cancelled plans for the testing program.[53]

Had all sections of the elite been able to participate in the reforms in both urban and rural arenas and had Beijing's ministries resisted the temptations of a strain of administrative centralization that served only to encourage local factional struggles, these Qing reforms might have had a chance to succeed. But in that part of the failure assignable to structural conflicts can be found the very supports of a program that would have turned intra-elite tensions and metropolitan demands into strengths.

In between the state-enhancing authoritarian solution identified with officials like Zhao Erxun and the person-oriented exercise in local democracy championed by returned students like Jin Bangping, Wu Xingrang, and Meng Zhaochang, was a road neither taken nor explored. Within the Western experience then under study in China was a corporate approach to constitutionalism that privileged neither person nor state. Given the structure of local elites' activism in late-Qing China, combined with a state bent on administrative centralization that concentrated power at the top but was unable to effect its will at the local level, a corporatist solution to China's crisis begged to be considered.

As both the Shengze and Zhangpu case demonstrate, and others as well,[54] significant sections of the local elite still depended upon state mediation of local political and administrative conflicts. The corporatist solution to the challenge of representation would have encouraged local elites to continue power-sharing arrangements and to practice consensual politics and would have been matched at the metropolitan level by a similar array of functionally specific ministries at the apex of a pyramid with a base in local society.

Instead, Beijing sought to create citizens unencumbered by functional identities. Moreover, policy makers ignored the warnings of men like Hu Sijing and opened the way, without a check in sight, for local tyrants to readorn their old despotisms in the garb of constitutionalism's new rhetoric. With the examination system gone, elections easily corrupted, and much of elite society effectively disenfranchised, the imperial state had rendered itself impotent in local society. The administrative centralization popular among returned students and their patrons in Beijing would have to wait.

Just as the consequences of those decisions extended beyond the Qing, so too did the late imperial search for citizens impart a legacy to the rest of the twentieth century. The search began in earnest with the local self-government program, which put the resources of the state at the disposal of men eager to convey their message far beyond the walls of administrative seats. The prototype of this effort in Tianjin was followed by others in later years. In Fengtian, for example, an essayist whose work was published by the provincial local self-government preparation office assured his audience in early 1910 that citizens *(gongmin)* of a constitutional state would be created through the process of Western-style elections, the open discussion of local affairs, and the execution of council decisions.[55] The elector *(xuanmin)* defined in the imperial regulations and the citizen discussed by the Fengtian essayist were literate males twenty-five *sui* or older who had paid at least two yuan a year in taxes. This concept of citizenship and political participation put China in a league, on paper at least, with Japan and many Western countries, for in 1909 the limitation of the franchise to property-holding males was the norm.[56]

This search, however fraught with dangers and difficulties and failures, was historically significant. Even though local patterns of dominance proved resilient, the imperial reforms did challenge this power. And the concept of citizenship being popularized, however difficult it was to fathom in a local arena given to corporatism, began to blur the boundaries among functionally defined "circles." The right to political participation was now defined by Chinese nationality, sex, age, residence, and wealth. The rhetoric of local self-government defined local citizenship much more inclusively and individually than the circle mentality ever had. The question was: How could the state's new universal definition affect political environments where local citizenship, as much as it existed, had been defined functionally? For example, even though the merchants in Shengze found solidarity in their old circle mentality, they were demanding a citizenship marker defined in Beijing that granted no meaning to their common bond. How could this not influence familiar self-conceptions of political identity? The state's project and the new yearning of individual persons for citizenship, however faintly understood, would continue long after the Qing became part of history.

Had Beijing opted for the middle position between local democracy and administrative centralization, the one defined by the practices of local corporatism, it would have been able to exert more influence at the local level. But it failed to; and once problems became evident, solutions were few and unappealing. Surrender and further attempts at centralization were all that were left. In Beijing and the provinces the flag of administrative centralization was raised in a war cry directed at local elites.

The perfect symbol of such a state was provided by the Jiangxi Provincial Local Self-government Preparation Office when it printed an imposing placard four feet square for distribution to all subordinate authorities. One of these broadsheets was included in a packet of documents from Jiangxi that arrived at the Ministry of Interior early in 1911. The placard, which was written in classical Chinese and intended for electors and councillors, expressed the concerns of provincial authorities: the reforms were being subverted by men who were cloaking private gain in the language of the public good. A reminder, in the form of a quotation of the entire section in the regulations entitled "The Scope of Local Self-government," followed. Responsibilities included, readers were reminded, education, sanitation, commerce and industry, social welfare, road construction and bridge building, and other public enterprises.

Jiangxi officials restated, to make sure there was no room for misunderstanding, the last thought in the reprinted regulations: final authority rested with Beijing; councils must always defer to national administrative prerogatives.[57] At the same time that a petition movement for an early convocation of a national parliament was tending to reunite local self-government and constitutionalism, they were trying to limit the scope of self-government to the narrowest degree possible. They feared corruption; perhaps they also sensed the ebbing of their own authority. Not for them the argument made in 1855 by Lothar Bucher, the German expatriate in London, in which he anticipated a political revolution in consciousness when expansive local initiatives were conjoined with the centralizing policies of a state still eager to accommodate and encourage local communities. For Bucher it would be this new political consciousness, rather than a heavy-handed national administration, that would bind individual person and state. But the Jiangxi placard had merely expressed the familiar statecraft distinction between public good and private gain.

Jiangxi officials in Nanchang had reminded magistrates and local elites alike of the centralization of administration being sought by Beijing. Councils were being established in the county seats where these placards appeared late in 1910[58] and in the countryside beyond. But provincial assemblymen alone had had a say in selecting members for the proto-parliament in Beijing and some counties could not even boast an assemblyman.

In the past degree-holders had been tied to the center through the examination system. At the beginning of the constitutional age some had thought electoral processes and a pyramid of elected bodies would replicate these ties. Instead, the reforms divided society and the rhetoric of centralization was trammelled by intra-elite factionalism and undone by the abandonment of rural China. The imperial regulations and their implementation compounded this defeat by allowing only a select group to participate in the self-government reforms. By ignoring the local corporatism that often typified the way elites got things done in their communities, this central policy split local society into contending factions that vied for Beijing's attention. And even the small slice of elite society that was able to win seats on councils soon realized that the building blocks for the shaky foundation of constitutional government's pyramid of representative assemblies were provincial assemblies, not their councils. Moreover, local self-government, far from encompassing a political revolution in thought about the connection between state and society, was limited to mundane and petty local administration. Caught between authoritarianism and democracy the Qing dynasty bequeathed its dissonant legacy to Yuan Shikai, a man who had contributed much to the program and its problems. Even Yuan, who was freed of many of the burdens of the old regime, proved unequal to the task of harmonizing the strains. With Yuan's death in 1916 the final fade, the search was transformed as China's new citizens and the expired Qing's old subjects, still bound together by the will to gain a place in the world, struggled to find the state that would answer their dreams.

*Appendices*
*Abbreviations Used in the Notes*
*and Bibliography*
*Notes*
*Select Bibliography*
*Character List*
*Index*

# LATE-QING GOVERNMENT GAZETTES AND
# SERIAL COMPILATIONS

Qing officials at the county, provincial, and metropolitan levels sponsored numerous publications that have been overlooked or underemphasized in surveys of late-Qing publishing history and descriptions of historical sources. (See *XHGMSQ*, V, 579–589, for a short discussion of late-Qing government gazettes and a list of forty-nine titles.) In Chapter Five I introduce and assess the significance of these sources; Appendix A lists over one hundred titles of general gazettes, specialized gazettes, and serial compilations issued by government offices. Many aspects of the late-Qing reform agenda, including administrative, educational, economic, and military reforms, as well as developments in fields like foreign affairs, culture, law, and religion can be documented with material contained in these sources. Much of my data on Tianjin, presented in Chapter Two, came from *Fazheng guanhua bao* and *Tianjin zizhi ju wenjian luyao*. *Beiyang guanbao*, *Chengdu ribao*, and *Jilin guanbao* provided information on policies and events in Zhili, Sichuan, and Jilin respectively as well as recording policy implementation throughout China. *Zhengzhi guanbao*, the national gazette published in Beijing from 1907 to 1911, was the source for most of the provincial reports listed in Appendix B.

In order to facilitate research based on these sources, I have recorded which libraries and archives held titles that I surveyed. These are indicated by abbreviations keyed to institutions in the United States, China, and Japan. Reference works that give location and publication data (*QGZW*), publication data and tables of contents (*ZGJD*), and publication data (*XHGMSQ*, V) are so indicated. Descriptive essays about selected titles are also indicated (*XHGMSQ*,

II, III, and IV). Finally, the existence of a small number of titles could be determined only by passing references in both published and archival sources (*CDRB, JLZYJ, ZYCS*, Ge Gongzhen, Fang Hanqi, Shen Huaiyu, MZB, XZBCG, Zhao Papers). See Bibliography for full citations and Appendix B for references to provincial reports, e.g. "Fengtian No. 6".

Key to Abbreviations

| | |
|---|---|
| BNL | Beijing National Library |
| BUL | Beijing (Peking) University Library |
| *CDRB* | *Chengdu ribao* |
| CUL | Columbia University Library |
| Fang | Fang Hanqi, *Zhongguo jindai baokan shi* |
| Ge | Ge Gongzhen, *Zhongguo baoxue shi* |
| IMH | Institute of Modern History Library (Beijing) |
| *JLZYJ* | *Jilin ziyiju diyiniandu baogaoshu* |
| MZB | No. 1 Historical Archives (Beijing), Min-zheng bu dang'an |
| NPM | National Palace Museum (Taibei) |
| PUL | People's University Library |
| *QGZW* | *Quanguo zhongwen qikan lianhe mulu, 1833–1949* |
| Shen | Shen Huaiyu, "Qingmo difang zizhi zhi mengya, 1898–1908" |
| TB | Toyo bunko (Tokyo) |
| UC | University of California Library (Berkeley) |
| *XHGMSQ* | *Xinhai geming shiqi qikan jieshao* |
| XZBCG | No. 1 Historical Archives (Beijing), Xian-zheng bianchaguan dang'an |
| *ZGJD* | *Zhongguo jindai qikan bianmu huilu* |
| Zhao Papers | No. 1 Historical Archives (Beijing), Zhao Er-xun dang'an |
| *ZYCS* | *Zhengyi congshu* |

Anhui
  *Anhui guanbao* (*QGZW*, p. 443; *XHGMSQ*, V, 583)
  *Anhui xuewu zazhi* (cited in XZBCG, 38)

Fengtian
*Fengtian guanbao* (QGZW, p. 706)
*Fengtian zizhi chouban fangfa* (QGZW, p. 706)
*Zizhi baihua bao* (cited in Shen, p. 298)
*Zizhi zazhi* (cited in MZB, 172 and Fengtian No. 6)

Fujian
*Fujian fazheng zazhi* (ZGJD, II, 2435)
*Fujian guanbao* (XHGMSQ, V, 588)
*Fujian jiaoyu bao* (cited in XZBCG, 36)
*Fujian jiaoyu guanbao* (QGZW, p. 1192; XHGMSQ, V, 586)
*Fujian nonggongshang guanbao* (ZGJD, I, 2797)

Gansu
*Gansu guanbao* (formerly *Longyou bao*) (QGZW, p. 295; XHGMSQ, V, 588)
*Gansu jiaoyu guanbao* (QGZW, p. 297; XHGMSQ, V, 587)

Guangdong
*Guangdong gongbao* (QGZW, p. 16; XHGMSQ, V, 583)
*Guangdong xianzheng choubeichu baogaoshu* (NPM)
*Guangdong ziyiju choubanchu baogaoshu* (cited in XZBCG, 28)
*LiangGuang guanbao* (XHGMSQ, V, 589)
*Shunde gongbao* (QGZW, p. 1117; XHGMSQ, V, 589; BUL)

Guangxi
*Guangxi guanbao* (QGZW, p. 30; XHGMSQ, V, 585; BUL)
*Guangxi jiaoyu guanbao* (cited in XZBCG, 36)
*Guanhua bao* (cited in Ge, p. 149)

Guizhou
*Guizhou guanbao* (QGZW, p. 1107; XHGMSQ, V, 587)
*Guizhou jiaoyu guanbao* (QGZW, p. 1110; XHGMSQ, V, 589)
*Zizhi baihua bao* (cited in Guizhou No. 1)

Heilongjiang
*Heilongjiang gongbao* (NPM)
*Heilongjiang guanbao* (QGZW, p. 1104; XHGMSQ, V, 589)
*Heilongjiang ziyiju choubanchu baogaoshu* (cited in JLZYJ, *gongdu* 68b)

Henan
*Henan guanbao* (QGZW, p. 675; XHGMSQ, V, 585)
*Henan jiaoyu guanbao* (XHGMSQ, V, 585)
*Henan quansheng ziyiju choubanchu baogaoshu* (NPM)

*Henan zizhi bao* (QGZW, p. 675; IMH)
*Yusheng zhongwai guanbao* (cited in Ge, p. 64)

Hubei
   *Hankou ribao* (cited in Ge, p. 64)
   *Hubei guanbao* (QGZW, p. 1069; XHGMSQ, V, 583; PUL)
   *Hubei shangwu bao* (QGZW, p. 1072; XHGMSQ, V, 580; ZGJD, I, 1006)
   *Hubei xuebao* (QGZW, p. 1069; ZGJD, II, 777, 3392; XHGMSQ, II, 152)
   *LiangHu guanbao* (XHGMSQ, V, 585)

Hunan
   *Changsha difang zizhi baihua bao* (QGZW, p. 398)
   *Changsha ribao* (formerly *Hunan guanbao*) (cited in Fang, p. 605)
   *Hunan difang zizhi baihua bao* (QGZW, p. 1075; ZGJD, II, 2863)
   *Hunan guanbao* (QGZW, p. 1076; XHGMSQ, V, 582)
   *Hunan jiaoyu guanbao* (QGZW, p. 1080)
   *Hunan tongsu yanshuobao* (ZGJD, II, 1097)

Jiangsu
   *Jiangnan shangwu bao* (QGZW, p. 437; XHGMSQ, II, 34; XHGMSQ, V, 581; ZGJD, II, 19)
   *Jiangning shiye zazhi* (ZGJD, II, 2940)
   *Jiangsu zizhi gongbao* (QGZW, p. 431; XHGMSQ, V, 587)
   *Nanyang bingshi zazhi* (QGZW, p. 858; ZGJD, II, 1930)
   *Nanyang guanbao* (QGZW, p. 858; XHGMSQ, V, 583)
   *Nanyang shang bao* (formerly *Nanyang shangwu bao*) (QGZW, p. 860; ZGJD, II, 2881)
   *Nanyang shangwu bao* (QGZW, p. 860; XHGMSQ, V, 584; ZGJD, II, 1909)

Jiangxi
   *Jiangxi difang zizhi choubanchu baogaoshu* (cited in XZBCG, 12)
   *Jiangxi guanbao* (QGZW, p. 424; XHGMSQ, V, 582; CUL; BNL)
   *Jiangxi riri guanbao* (cited in Ge, p. 64)
   *Jiangxi xuewu guanbao* (XHGMSQ, V, 587)

Jilin
   *Jilin baihua bao* (QGZW, p. 478; XHGMSQ, II, 548)
   *Jilin diaochaju wenbao* (PUL)
   *Jilin guanbao* (QGZW, p. 478; XHGMSQ, V, 587; TB)
   *Jilin jiaoyu guanbao* (XHGMSQ, V, 586)
   *Jilin quansheng difang zizhi choubanchu baogaoshu* (BNL)

*Jilin sifa guanbao* (*QGZW*, p. 478; *XHGMSQ*, V, 588)
*Jilin ziyiju choubanchu baogaoshu* (BNL; TB)
*Zizhi xunbao* (formerly *Gongmin bao* and *Zizhi ribao*) (cited in Jilin No. 5)

Shaanxi
  *Shaanxi guanbao* (*QGZW*, p. 748; *XHGMSQ*, V, 585)
  *Shaanxi jiaoyu guanbao* (*QGZW*, p. 752; *XHGMSQ*, V, 588)
  *Taibao* (formerly *Taizhong guanbao*) (*QGZW*, p. 938; *XHGMSQ*, V, 582)

Shandong
  *Shandong guanbao* (*QGZW*, p. 95; *XHGMSQ*, V, 584)
  *Shandong quansheng difang zizhi choubanchu baogaoshu* (MZB, 181)
  *Zizhi bao* (IMH)

Shanxi
  *Jinbao* (cited in *ZYCS* 2 (GX29): *neizheng tongji* 3:14b)
  *Shanxi baihua yanshuobao* (cited in Zhao Papers, Box 33)
  *Shanxi jiaoyu guanbao* (cited in XZBCG, 36)
  *Zizhi gongbao* (cited in Shanxi No. 3)

Sichuan
  *[Chengdu] Baihua bao* (cited in *CDRB*, GX34/8/16)
  *Chengdu ribao* (*XHGMSQ*, IV, 94; TB)
  *Sichuan jiaoyu guanbao* (formerly *Sichuan xuebao*) (*QGZW*, p. 389, 393; *ZGJD*, II, 1615; *XHGMSQ*, II, 300; *XHGMSQ*, V, 585)
  *Shubao* (*ZGJD*, II, 1116, 2929; *XHGMSQ*, I, 346)
  *Sichuan guanbao* (*QGZW*, p. 388; *XHGMSQ*, III, 220; *XHGMSQ*, V, 583; BUL; PUL)
  *Sichuan ziyiju choubanchu baogaoshu* (PUL)

Yunnan
  *Yunnan jiaoyu guanbao* (*QGZW*, p. 157)
  *Yunnan zhengzhi guanbao* (cited in XZBCG, 36)
  *Yunnan ziyiju choubanchu baogaoshu* (PUL)
  *Zizhi baihua bao* (cited in Yunnan No. 2)

Zhejiang
  *Zhejiang difang zizhi choubanchu wenbao* (IMH)
  *Zhejiang guanbao* (*QGZW*, p. 909; *XHGMSQ*, V, 586)
  *Zhejiang jiaoyu guanbao* (*QGZW*, p. 917; *XHGMSQ*, V, 586; *ZGJD*, II, 2445)
  *Zhejiang jinyan guanbao* (*QGZW*, p. 917; *XHGMSQ*, V, 586)
  *Zhejiang ziyiju choubanchu baogaoshu* (IMH)

Zhili

    Beijing

*Jiaotong guanbao* (QGZW, p. 454; *XHGMSQ*, V, 586; *ZGJD*, II, 2667)

*Neige guanbao* (*XHGMSQ*, V, 587)

*Shangwu guanbao* (QGZW, p. 985; *XHGMSQ*, V, 584; *ZGJD*, II, 1764)

*Xuebu guanbao* (QGZW, p. 700; *ZGJD*, II, 1849)

*Zhengzhi guanbao* (merged with *Neige guanbao* in 1911) (QGZW, p. 837; *XHGMSQ*, V, 585)

    Tianjin

*Beiyang baihua bao* (UC)

*Beiyang bingshi zazhi* (*ZGJD*, II, 2920)

*Beiyang fazheng xuebao* (QGZW, p. 370; *ZGJD*, II, 1997)

*Beiyang guanbao* (*XHGMSQ*, V, 581; PUL)

*Beiyang guanhua bao* (QGZW, p. 371; *XHGMSQ*, V, 581)

*Beiyang xuebao* (QGZW, p. 371; *ZGJD*, II, 1743)

*Beiyang zhengxue xunbao* (formerly *Beiyang fazheng xuebao*) (QGZW, p. 371; *ZGJD*, II, 3085)

*Fazheng guanhua bao* (UC)

*Tianjin zizhi ju wenjian luyao* (PUL)

*Zhili jiaoyu guanbao* (formerly *Zhili jiaoyu zazhi*) (QGZW, p. 737; *ZGJD*, II, 1433)

*Zhili ziyiju choubanchu wenjian luyao* (BNL)

# PROVINCIAL AND METROPOLITAN REPORTS ON CONSTITUTIONAL REFORMS, 1909–1911

The outline of local self-government policy implementation presented in Table 1 was based on information in a prescribed series of provincial and metropolitan summaries that also included data on provincial assembly elections, census-taking, taxation, budgets, education, courts, and police forces. In drawing up the following table, I used the schedule of reporting periods outlined in a directive from the Constitutional Commission, issued in January 1909. See *QMCB*, I, 69–71. For each province, I attempted to locate the reports called for in the directive, beginning with the first reports (Column 1) for the final months of GX34 (1908). I located most of these reports in *Zhengzhi guanbao* (which merged with *Neige guanbao* in August 1911) and have provided citations in this table. For example, the summary from Anhui for the first reporting period (Anhui No. 1) can be found in the *Zhengzhi guanbao* issue published on XT1/int.2/28, which is the date given in Column 1. All lunar dates below refer to the particular issue of *Zhengzhi guanbao* that contains the specified report. By the end of 1911 provincial governors were to have submitted six of these reports. The table shows, for example, that Anhui officials had reported on all but the sixth reporting period, which covered the first half of XT3 (1911). Governors usually identified their reports with a phrase like "circumstances of preparing for constitutional government" and sometimes specified the reporting period according to the Nine-Year Plan announced in 1908. (See *QMCB*, I, 61–67. Year 1 in this plan corresponded to the final months of GX34; Year 2 to XT1.) Other governors numbered their reports sequentially; the Anhui reports, for example, are identified as first, second, third, fourth, and fifth. The correspondences be-

| | No. 1 | No. 2 | No. 3 | No. 4 | No. 5 | No. 6 |
|---|---|---|---|---|---|---|
| Anhui | XT1/int.2/28 | XT1/9/30 | XT2/3/22 | XT2/9/19 | C-422 | NA |
| Fengtian | XT1/int.2/22 | XT1/9/2 | XT2/3/9 | XT2/9/5 | XT3/3/6 | XT3/9/17 |
| Fujian | XT1/3/22 | XT1/8/26 | XT2/4/4 | XT2/10/19 | XT3/4/7 | XT3/9/13 |
| Gansu | XT1/3/16 | D-10 | XT2/6/4 | C-365 | XT3/5/7 | NA |
| Guangdong | XT1/int.2/26 | XT1/10/4 | XT2/3/17 | XT2/9/28 | XT3/4/8 | NA |
| Guangxi | XT1/int.2/19 | XT1/9/28 | XT2/4/9 | XT2/10/12 | XT3/3/28 | D-10 |
| Guizhou | XT1/int.2/29 | C-318 | XT2/3/21 | XT2/10/2 | XT3/4/16 | NA |
| Heilongjiang | XT1/int.2/18 | XT1/9/17 | XT2/3/15 | XT2/9/18 | C-427 | XT3/10/8 |
| Henan | XT1/int.2/18 | XT1/9/7 | XT2/3/10 | XT2/10/6 | C-423 | XT3/10/2 |
| Hubei | XT1/int.2/27 | F-01010 | XT2/3/20 | XT2/9/11 | XT3/3/30 | NA |
| Hunan | XT1/int.2/19 | XT1/9/7 | XT2/3/16 | A-789 | XT3/3/28 | XT3/8/24 |
| Jiangsu-Ning | XT1/3/3 | B-15;44b | XT2/3/22 | XT2/10/29 | XT3/4/10 | NA |
| Jiangsu-Su | XT1/3/3 | XT1/9/29 | XT2/4/2 | XT2/9/17 | XT3/3/15 | XT3/9/17 |
| Jiangxi | XT1/int.2/21 | C-326 | XT2/3/14 | XT2/9/18 | XT3/3/20 | XT3/9/2 |
| Jilin | XT1/int.2/23 | C-320 | XT2/3/18 | XT2/9/15 | XT3/3/14 | XT3/10/10 |
| Shaanxi | XT1/int.2/14 | XT1/8/13 | XT2/2/13 | XT2/9/4 | C-414 | XT3/7/11 |
| Shandong | XT1/2/18 | XT1/9/14 | XT2/3/1 | XT2/8/25 | XT3/3/11 | XT3/9/13 |
| Shanxi | NA | XT1/9/1 | XT2/3/10 | XT2/9/14 | C-428 | NA |
| Sichuan | XT1/int.2/28 | XT1/10/6 | XT2/3/24 | XT2/10/17 | XT3/2/9 | NA |
| Sichuan (supplement) | — | — | — | — | XT3/4/7 | — |
| Xinjiang | XT1/4/27 | XT1/10/18 | XT2/4/5 | XT2/10/22 | XT3/4/19 | NA |
| Yunnan | XT1/3/9 | XT1/11/7 | XT2/5/8 | A-801 | XT3/5/9 | NA |
| Zhejiang | XT1/int.2/22 | C-331 | XT2/3/7 | XT2/9/25 | XT3/3/5 | XT3/9/4 |
| Zhili | XT1/int.2/17 | XT1/8/29 | XT2/2/29 | XT2/8/22 | XT3/2/11 | XT3/8/13 |
| Rehe | C-309 | XT1/9/20 | XT2/4/6 | C-384 | XT3/3/25 | XT3/8/12 |
| Shuntian | NA | NA | XT2/3/21 | NA | XT3/3/20 | E-167 |

| Constitutional Commission | XT1/5/3 | XT1/11/2 | XT2/5/4 | XT2/11/5 | XT3/5/3 | NA |
|---|---|---|---|---|---|---|
| Const'al Comm. (supplement) | — | — | — | — | XT3/6/2 | — |
| Ministry of Interior | NA | XT1/10/9 | XT2/3/14 | XT2/10/13 | XT3/3/30 | NA |

### Key

A    *Qingmo choubei lixian dang'an shiliao*, p. no.
B    Duanfang, *Duan Zhongmin gong zougao, juan*:p. no.
C    No. 1 Historical Archives, Beijing, Xianzheng zhuanti, Document no.
D    No. 1 Historical Archives, Beijing, Xianzheng bianchaguan dang'an, Box no.
E    No. 1 Historical Archives, Beijing, Minzheng bu dang'an, File no.
F    National Palace Museum, Taibei, Gongzhong dang, Accession no.

tween the sequentially numbered reports and reporting period in the Nine-Year Plan are as follows:

First report (GX34)                          Year 1
Second report (XT1/1–XT1/6)                  Year 2, first period
Third report (XT1/7–XT1/12)                  Year 2, second period
Fourth report (XT2/1–XT2/6)                  Year 3, first period
Fifth report (XT2/7–XT2/12)                  Year 3, second period
Sixth report (XT3/1–XT3/int.6)               Year 4, first period

I was unable to find thirty-six reports in *Zhengzhi guanbao;* nineteen of the missing ones were found in other published or archival sources. Those locations are identified by a letter keyed to the list of sources below. Reports that I have been unable to locate are indicated by NA (not available).

See *QMCB*, II, 758–820 for punctuated versions of seventeen provincial reports.

# The Jiading County Council Members

| | Residence | Biographical Data |
|---|---|---|
| Chen Chuande | Qianmentang | A vice-president of the council; coeditor of the *Jiading xian xuzhi*. |
| Chen Qingrong | Lutang | Also an executive board alternate. |
| Gao Rongdi | Xuxing | — |
| Gu Rui | Jiading city | A representative in 1909 to the first Jiangsu Provincial Assembly (*Jiading xian xuzhi*, 6.3b; subsequently *JDXXZ*); in 1911 elected to the council, and subsequently elected to the executive board. |
| Hou Zhaoxi | Luduqiao | — |
| Huang Baochen | Shigang | — |
| Huang Shizuo | Ximen | *Juren* in 1903 (*JDXXZ*, 10.3); initial efforts to organize local self-government blocked by provincial authorities; selected by the Jiading magistrate to participate in self-government preparation for the county in 1910 (*JDXXZ*, 6.4); had official posts connected with educational affairs in 1905–1907 (*JDXXZ*, 7.4); a coeditor of *Jiading xian xuzhi*. |

|                | Residence      | Biographical Data                                                                                                                                                                                                                                              |
| -------------- | -------------- | --------------------------------------------------------------------------------------------------------------------------------------------------------------------------------------------------------------------------------------------------------------- |
| Huang Shouheng | Ximen          | An executive board member; organized a militia during late 1911 (*JDXXZ, juan mo* 1–2b); in November 1911 became vice president in charge of financial affairs in the county administration (*JDXXZ, juan mo* 1).                                                 |
| Jin Wenluan    | Huangdu        | *Suigong* degree in 1904 (*JDXXZ,* 10.3).                                                                                                                                                                                                                       |
| Li Chaozhen    | Fanqiao        | —                                                                                                                                                                                                                                                              |
| Li Chunhua     | Caowangmiao    | —                                                                                                                                                                                                                                                              |
| Li Rukun       | Zhenshengtang  | Refused to serve on the county council; *suigong* degree in 1892; served as a Commissioner of Education in Shanyang county (in the northern Jiangsu prefectural seat of Huaian).                                                                                 |
| Lu Hongzhao    | Jiwangmiao     | An executive board alternate.                                                                                                                                                                                                                                   |
| Mao Jingxue    | Wangxianqiao   | President of the council.                                                                                                                                                                                                                                       |
| Qian Ding      | Chendian       | —                                                                                                                                                                                                                                                              |
| Qian Jun       | Waigang        | —                                                                                                                                                                                                                                                              |
| Wang Songming  | Guangfu        | —                                                                                                                                                                                                                                                              |
| Wu Yanze       | Malu           | An executive board alternate.                                                                                                                                                                                                                                   |
| Xia Yueao      | Huangdu        | An executive board member; probably related to Xia Yue, a *juren* (1884) from Huangdu elected to the provincial assembly in 1909 (*JDXXZ,* 10.2b and 6.3b).                                                                                                      |
| Xu Chaogui     | Nanxiang       | An executive board alternate.                                                                                                                                                                                                                                   |
| Xu Yuanzhu     | Chengqiao      | —                                                                                                                                                                                                                                                              |
| Ye Yueding     | Zhenshengtang  | —                                                                                                                                                                                                                                                              |

| | Residence | Biographical Data |
|---|---|---|
| Yu Zhengai | Gelong | — |
| Zhang Jiarui | Xiaohongmiao | Active in self-government in his native place (*JDXXZ*, 6.25; 13.6b). |
| Zhang Shixiong | Xuxing | — |

*Source:* All data derived from *Jiading xian xuzhi,* much of which comes from the county council table (*JDXXZ*, 6.15b–16b).

# Abbreviations Used in the Notes and Select Bibliography

| | |
|---|---|
| *DFZZ* | *Dongfang zazhi* |
| *GXZY* | *Guangxu zhengyao* |
| MZB | Minzheng bu dang'an (Ministry of Interior Archives), No. 1 Historical Archives, Beijing |
| *PDPOC* | Brunnert, H. S., and V. V. Hagelstrom, *Present Day Political Organization of China* |
| *QMCB* | *Qingmo choubei lixian dang'an shiliao* |
| *SMMS* | *Shinmatsu minsho Chūgoku kanshin jinmeiroku* |
| *STSB* | *Shuntian shibao* |
| XZBCG | Xianzheng bianchaguan dang'an (Constitutional Commission Archives), No. 1 Historical Archives, Beijing |
| *ZGJD* | *Zhongguo jindai qikan bianmu huilu* |
| Zhao Papers | Zhao Erxun, Zhao Erxun dang'an, No. 1 Historical Archives, Beijing. |
| *ZYCS* | *Zhengyi congshu* |
| *ZZGB* | *Zhengzhi guanbao* |

# Notes

INTRODUCTION: THE IDEA OF LOCAL SELF-GOVERNMENT IN THE
AGE OF REVOLUTION

1. See Young, pp. 148–152. Young's survey, with specific discussion of Hunan, Guangxi, Shandong, Zhejiang, and Guizhou, was based on contemporary sources like British diplomatic reporting and the *North China Herald*. For the abolition of the Shanghai City Council see Elvin, "The Gentry Democracy in Chinese Shanghai, 1905–1914," p. 59. For a copy of the 1914 regulations see *DFZZ* 12.5:*faling* (1915).

2. In government documents "upper-level" self-government refers to county councils and "lower-level" self-government to administrative seat, town, and township councils. There were revolutionaries in the late Qing advocating provincial independence movements who used the concept of *zizhi*, as would those active in the federalist movement of the 1920s. See Arthur Waldron, "Warlordism Versus Federalism: The Revival of a Debate?," *China Quarterly*, no. 121 (March 1990):116–128. See also Ling Yu-long, "The Doctrine of Democracy and Human Rights," in *Sun Yat-sen's Doctrine in the Modern World*, ed. Chu-yuan Cheng (Boulder: Westview Press, 1989), pp. 175–200.

3. Cao Rulin, p. 59.

4. Other editions published in Zhejiang in 1898 and Shanghai in 1901 followed. See Wang Xiaoqiu, pp. 182–187; and Guo Tingyi, p. 988. See also Noriko Kamachi, pp. 53–54 and 214–215. Kamachi notes that Huang's work remained the definitive Chinese account of early Meiji Japan even after the 1911 Revolution.

5. See Kuhn, "Local Self-government," pp. 270–271. The audience figure of three hundred can be found in Sung Wook Shin, p. 381n7.

Jocelyn Chen (p. 26), who also discusses this speech, dates it to the opening session of the Nanxue hui held on 21 February 1898. Huang Zunxian's speech can be found in Liang Qichao, *Wuxu zhengbian ji* (An account of the coup in 1898) (n.p.: n.d.), 8:11–13b.

6. Rankin, *Elite Activism*, p. 349n165. For a survey of relevant essays written by Chinese thinkers in 1830–1907, with an emphasis on the pre-1900 period, see Shen Huaiyu, "Qingmo xiyang difang zizhi sixiang de shuru" (The importation of the Western idea of local self-government at the end of the Qing), *Zhongyang yanjiuyuan jindaishi yanjiusuo jikan* (Bulletin of the Institute of Modern History, Academia Sinica), no. 8 (1979):159–182. Zhang Luxiang, a staunch Neo-Confucian and Ming loyalist wrote, in 1669, a treatise on "self" compounds, arguing that the self can be an "active and sufficient agent." *Liangzhi* (intuitive knowledge), conscience, divinity, or Confucian authority was not needed. Zhang begins his treatise with one hundred *zi* (self) compounds (a verb prefixed by *zi*), including "self-governing" *(zizhi)*. See Wu Pei-yi, *The Confucian's Progress: Autobiographical Writings in Traditional China* (Princeton: Princeton University Press, 1990), p. 221. For a discussion of "Neo-Confucian individualism" see de Bary, pp. 43–46.

7. Sung Wook Shin, p. 311.

8. Kwong, pp. 124–126.

9. The Guangxu Emperor issued a wide range of reform edicts which, if implemented, would have affected many aspects of life in China: education, political recruitment, administrative structure, and social practice to name a few. But the range of proposals was well within the boundaries of reform established during the self-strengthening era. By placing the reform edicts in this broader context, recent scholarship has recast Kang and Liang in this drama, making their roles less central than previous scholarship had suggested. See Kwong, pp. 169–174. See also Bays, p. 47.

10. My copy of this work, found in 1984 in a bookstore in Canton, appears to have been purchased in Chengdu, Sichuan, in 1902.

11. Jian Bozan et al., *Wuxu bianfa* (Shanghai: Renmin chubanshe, 1957), II, 200.

12. Philip Kuhn discusses Kang's essay in "Local Self-government," pp. 272–275. Kang Youwei's "Citizen Self-government" was published in 1902.

13. Nai Xuan, pp. 1–8. *Jiangsu* was published in Tokyo in 1903–1908 under the auspices of the Jiangsu tongxiang hui. See Ge Gongzhen,

p. 221; and *Xinhai geming qianshinianjian shilun xuanji,* I, 968. For the Zhejiang essay see *Zhejiang chao,* no. 2 (GX29/2): *sheshou* 1–12.

14. Yang Dusheng's essay is reprinted in *Xinhai geming qianshinianjian shilun xuanji,* I, 612–648. For biographical information, see ibid., I, 969.

15. The 1905 *Nanfang ribao* article is in *DFZZ* 2:*neiwu* 216–218 (GX31). For Philip Kuhn's discussion of this article, see his "Late Ch'ing Views of the Polity," p. 4.

16. See Zhao Erxun memorial GX28/10/28. See also Zhao Papers, Box 32. For a survey of the contents of the Zhao Erxun Papers (Zhao Erxun dang'an) in the No. 1 Historical Archives, Beijing, see Li Pengnian.

I will refer to most edicts *(shangyu),* imperial rescripts *(zhi),* court letters *(tingji),* memorials *(zouzhe),* attachments *(pian),* directives *(zha),* telegrams *(dianbao),* petitions *(cheng, bing),* endorsements *(pi),* regulations *(zhangcheng),* and implementation schedules *(qingdan)* by the date of the document according to the Chinese lunar calendar. A chronological list of these documents, accompanied by a citation, can be found in the Bibliography. The first number in each date refers to the particular year in the reign periods of the Guangxu Emperor (GX: 1875–1908) and the Xuantong Emperor (XT: 1909–1911). The second and third numbers in each date refer to the month and day according to the Chinese lunar calendar. "Inter." stands for the "intercalary" months occasionally inserted in the lunar calendar in order to ensure that this calendar year was as long as a solar year.

17. See Zhao Papers, Box 55. *Hunan tongsu yanshuobao* was a trimonthly first published in May 1903.

18. See Guo Tingyi, p. 1011; and Li Kan and Gong Shuduo.

19. See Min Tu-ki, pp. 89–136. See also Kuhn, "Local Self-government"; Rankin, *Elite Activism;* and Lojewski. John E. Schrecker, *The Chinese Revolution in Historical Perspective* (New York: Praeger, 1991) emphasizes *fengjian* theory.

20. *DFZZ* 3.5:*neiwu* 111–121 (GX32).

21. See *Oxford English Dictionary,* 2nd ed. (Oxford: Clarendon Press, 1989), XIV, 922. For the reference to Jefferson's use of the term in 1820, see his letter to John Holmes, 22 April 1820, in *The Life and Selected Writings of Thomas Jefferson,* ed. and intro. Adrienne Koch and William Peden (New York: The Modern Library [Random House], 1944), p. 699. See also Jefferson's letter of 2 February 1816 to Joseph C. Cabell, where he enumerates the separate and non-

overlapping duties of the national government, state governments, counties, and wards. See ibid., pp. 660–662.

22. Redlich, II, 238n1. Redlich is quoting from a short work on English government Vincke published in 1815.

23. Gneist, *English Constitution*, II, 352.

24. Maltbie, p. 70.

25. Tocqueville, pp. 256–257. The italicized "self-government" can be found in Alexis de Tocqueville, *L'Ancien régime et la révolution* (Paris: Calmann-Lévy, 1887), p. 379. For a discussion of the contemporary situation in Russia see Pearson.

26. Lothar Bucher, *Der Parlamentarismus wie er ist* (Berlin: Verlag von Franz Dunker, 1855), p. 231. I thank Prof. Victor Bers for clarifying this passage for me.

27. Gneist, *English Constitution*, II, 643–645; and Gneist, *Englische Verfassungsgeschichte* (The history of the English constitution) (Berlin: Verlag von Julius Springer, 1882), pp. 350–353.

28. This is especially apparent in Gneist's 1871 work *Selfgovernment: Communalverfassung und Verwaltungsgerichte in England*, in which the final two chapters describe "*obrigkeitlichen* self-government" and "*wirtschaftlichen Selbstverwaltung.*"

29. See Steiner, pp. 21–54. Richard Staubitz, who has written on Yamagata's reforms, argues that the core of Gneist's ideas, as transmitted to Japan by Mosse, was expressed in a system of local self-government in which "the state would grant autonomous control to the community over affairs of interest and concern to the local community alone and the right publicly to elect local officials." See Staubitz, p. 111. For a contemporary account of Yamagata's efforts see John Wigmore's essays in *Nation*, 3 July 1890, pp. 8–10 and 10 July 1890, pp. 25–27. Another useful introduction to Meiji reforms in local administration and constitutional reform can be found in Ishii, pp. 408–437.

30. Cited in Syed, p. 54.

31. Ibid., pp. 53–75.

32. One student of the problem, Milo Maltbie, a University Fellow in Administrative Law at Columbia, wrote in 1897, "The spheres of the national and commonwealth governments were delimited by the Civil War, and the delimitation then reached has been recognized by subsequent legislation. The relation of commonwealth and local governments now demands our attention, and a solution of the problem becomes more urgent as each year passes. The origin of the problem is comparatively recent." See Maltbie, p. 13.

33. It proved difficult to gain support for new-style schools and per-

suade people to leave behind the conventions of the old examination system. More than three years after the abolition edict was issued Sichuan authorities had to remind readers of the official provincial gazette that degrees would only be granted to those persons who had graduated from new-style schools. See *Chengdu ribao*, XT1/2/15. A memorial and set of regulations from the Ministry of Education had been issued in August 1908 that specified the fees required of these graduates, ranging from twenty-four taels for a *jinshi* degree to two taels for a *shengyuan* degree. See *Kindai Chūgoku kyoiku shi shiryo: Shinmatsu hen* (Documents on the history of education in modern China: Late Qing), ed. Taga Akigoro (Tokyo: Nihon gakujutsu shinkō kai, 1972), p. 501. See also *STSB*, GX34/8/15, p. 7 on the promulgation of these regulations.

34. "County" will refer, generally, to *xian* (county) as well as *zhou* (department) and *ting* (subprefecture).

35. Although the *jiansheng* degree referred literally to a degree held by a student at the Imperial Academy in Beijing, very few holders of this degree actually studied there. In fact, the *jiansheng* degree was usually purchased by commoners. Chang Chung-li estimates that approximately 534,000 men had held the *jiansheng* degree at any one time in the post-Taiping period. A larger number—Chang gives a figure of 910,000—began their careers with the *shengyuan* degree awarded to successful civil service examination candidates. See Chang Chung-li, pp. 5, 19, and 102–111. For Chang's estimate on the number of *tongsheng* see p. 92. For an extended discussion on the so-called *sheng[yuan]jian[sheng]* stratum see Min Tu-ki, pp. 21–49.

36. See, for example, Shen Jiaben memorial GX31/6/12.


### 1. ZHAO ERXUN'S SEARCH FOR LOCAL LEADERS IN SHANXI

1. On 29 August 1905 Yuan Shikai's provincial gazette *Beiyang guanbao* published a memorial by Shen Jiaben in which Zhao Erxun's *xiangshe* reform regulations and local self-government institutions in other countries are presented as useful models for local administrative reforms. See Shen Jiaben memorial GX31/6/12. At the end of his Shanxi tenure Zhao issued an order *(yu)* to the people of Shanxi in which he described his *xiangshe* reform and other new policies and institutions, all of which, he said, were intended to establish the basis for local self-government *(difang zizhi)*. See Zhao Papers, Box 32.

2. Richard, pp. 299–302.

3. Boorman, I, 141; *Donghua lu*, GX24/5/24; and Guo Tingyi, pp. 1031, 1162, and 1166.

4. Directive GX28/9/21. This directive, which accompanied *baojia* reform regulations adapted by Zhao from those he drafted during his tenure in Anhui in 1894–1898, was sent to prefectures, counties, and *xiang* on 22 October 1902. The directive can be found in a manuscript copy of a provincial yamen record book that gives the texts of directives *(zha)* and regulations *(zhangcheng)* sent down from 9 September 1902 to 6 January 1903.

5. Directive GX28/11/11.

6. Directive GX28/12/8.

7. Ibid. Zhao also felt part of the problem was cultural. Insufficient education in Shanxi, which Zhao pointed out was far removed from China's more developed coastal areas and the Yangtze River valley, had contributed to a situation in which most of the people— whether scholars or peasants—held opinions that were narrow and bigoted. See Directive GX28/11/11.

8. Directive GX28/12/8.

9. Directive GX28/9/21. Zhao Erxun, according to his associate Wu Tingxie, had been interested primarily in rewarding competent *baojia* leaders. See Wu Tingxie petition GX28/12/8. Zhao turned a familiar practice into explicit policy. For example, earlier in the year a *baojia* leader in a village in the southern Shanxi county of Yicheng had been presented a tablet by the magistrate for his "untiring and courageous service." See Hsiao Kung-ch'uan, *Rural China*, p. 584n180.

10. Chang Chung-li, p. 68.

11. Zhang Zhidong memorial GX8/12/16.

12. Wu Tingxie, p. 53; and Boorman, III, 456. Wu was not breaking China's law of avoidance, which barred officials from serving at home, because he was a native of Jiangsu technically. His father, who had been an official, spent his career in Shanxi. Wu Tingxie's petition for the *xiangshe* reform, the regulations, and Zhao Erxun's 6 January 1903 (GX28/12/8) directive to subprovincial authorities can be found in Zhao Papers, Box 31. A published version of these three documents can be found in *Zhengyi congshu* 2:*neizheng tongji* 2:10–12b (GX29). In an autobiography Wu Tingxie claims to have drafted Zhao Erxun's 23 February 1903 (GX29/1/26) memorial on *xiangshe* reform. The importance of this memorial is suggested by Wu's short summary of its contents rather than the usual listing of subject only. See Wu Tingxie, p. 53.

13. Hsiao Kung-ch'uan discusses the position of the rural constable in

a section on the metamorphoses of the *xiangyue* lecture system. He remarks that the system began to assume *baojia* functions in the mid-Qing, becoming an instrument of police control. See his *Rural China*, p. 202.

14. Regulations GX28/12/8, Article 2. The published version of this article omits the *shou* in *sheshou*, a mistake that obscures the important contrast between *sheshou* and *gongzheng* apparent in the archival version.

15. See *[Huangchao] Jingshi wenbian*, 18:17–20.

16. See Feng Guifen. Philip Kuhn discusses this essay in *Rebellion and Its Enemies*, pp. 214–215 and in "Local Self-government," pp. 266–267. K. C. Liu has also discussed Feng's essay in Fairbank, ed., *The Cambridge History of China*, X, 487–488. An extended analysis of "Fuxiang zhiyi," although it is not referred to by name, can be found in Lojewski, pp. 150–156.

17. See Rankin, *Elite Activism*, p. 185.

18. See Sun Yirang.

19. For an authoritative description of English local administration see Redlich. For a critique of Gneist's understanding of English "self-government" see Redlich, II, 380–418.

20. Directive GX28/12/8. Zhao referred to the justice of the peace with the phrase *xianzhi difang guan* (literally, local official of a county).

21. Hsiao Kung-ch'uan, *Rural China*, pp. 271–275.

22. See Redlich, I, 203–205. Redlich argued that the changes in 1888 were fundamental: "The last entrenchment of class government had been stormed; the principles of representative democracy had now been extended over the whole field of English administration." See Redlich, I, 203.

23. Regulations GX28/12/8, Articles 7 and 8.

24. These topics were the focus of a series of directives and regulations issued from Zhao's provincial yamen that were preserved in manuscript form. See Zhao Papers, Box 31. The post–Boxer reform program, the so-called New Policies *(xinzheng)*, in its earliest stages was conceived primarily in a yamen like Zhao's. A comprehensive summary of the first round of reform proposals was made in late 1901 by Zhang Zhidong with the assistance of Liu Kunyi in three memorials that addressed education, administration, and economic and military affairs. See Ayers, pp. 203–204, for the background to the drafting of these memorials and a brief summation. The first memorial, concerning education, is discussed in detail on pp. 205–216. For partial translations from each memorial see Ssu-yu Teng and John K. Fairbank, *China's Response to the West: A Documen-*

*tary Survey, 1839–1923* (New York: Atheneum, 1963), pp. 197–205. For discussions of reform efforts from late 1898 through 1902, see Bays, pp. 54–57, 71, and 101–111.

25. The specifications for *shezhang* jurisdictions differ in the regulations and in Zhao's memorial that describes his program. In the regulations Zhao focussed on the number of villages under one *shezhang*, prescribing ten as the limit. See Regulations GX28/12/8, Article 2. But in his memorial Zhao emphasized population as the determining factor. Villages with at least one hundred families needed one *shezhang*; smaller villages should be grouped together with larger villages that were nearby. See Zhao Erxun memorial GX29/1/26.

26. For a discussion on family size in late imperial China see Ho Ping-ti, pp. 50–57.

27. Regulations GX28/12/8, Article 3.

28. Zhao Erxun memorial GX29/1/26.

29. Regulations GX28/12/8, Article 4.

30. Available evidence suggests that this was a moderate amount of land, slightly less than the average size of farm holdings in this part of China at the turn of the century. See John Lossing Buck, *Land Utilization in China: A study of 16,786 farms in 168 localities, and 38,256 farm families in twenty-two provinces in China, 1929–1933* (1937; reprint, New York: The Council on Economic and Cultural Affairs, 1956), p. 58.

31. Regulations GX28/12/8, Article 3. Zhao's selection method resembled customary practices. One of the leading authorities in the study of rural China, Hsiao Kung-ch'uan, describes the process of selecting village leaders as a process in which the official leaders of the village were "usually appointed by local officials upon recommendation of the rural inhabitants concerned." Hsiao distinguishes these "official leaders," who "were in reality subadministrative government agents" from "unofficial leaders" who were "prominent and effective village gentry or scholars, who were also heads of families with appreciable influence." See his *Rural China*, pp. 267 and 274. Elsewhere Hsiao mentions Arthur Smith's observations about the way in which Shandong subcounty leaders received the approval of local magistrates (p. 554). A specific example comes from a prefecture in Guizhou, where *baojia* leaders were selected by a village's gentry and elders, and subsequently investigated by the yamen. If this investigation went well, the new *baojia* head was invited to the county yamen and treated with special courtesy. A similar process was used in Shaanxi. See ibid., pp. 59 and 584n179.

32. Regulations GX28/12/8, Articles 1, 4, and 7.

33. Feng Guifen, 1:13.
34. For a discussion of the eight ways to gain an entrée to officialdom, four of which were related to the examination system, see *PDPOC*, entries 954–962.
35. Regulations GX28/12/8, Article 9. See Allee for examples of similar practices in late nineteenth-century Taiwan. Kuhn cites a mid–nineteenth-century administrative handbook from Guangdong that mentions wooden seals of authority *(chuoji)* in a section on *tuanlian* regulations. See *Rebellion and Its Enemies*, p. 59n34.
36. Wu Tingxie had told Zhao that two degree-holders in two southern Shanxi counties, for example, had been instrumental in eliminating opium addiction and in raising the educational level of the people. These contemporary local examples, combined with the precedent of local elite leadership of militia units during the Taiping Rebellion and the distant example of rural private academies established in the Song dynasty that rivalled government-sponsored urban academies, suggested that it was both necessary, feasible, and proper to find cultivated leadership at the subcounty level. See Wu Tingxie petition GX28/12/8.
37. Regulations GX28/12/8, Article 5.
38. Directive GX28/12/8.
39. Ibid. Like Zhao Erxun, Zhang Zhidong's first post as a governor was in Shanxi. Zhang was dismayed, after his arrival in 1882, with corruption among Shanxi officials. His vigorous reform efforts ended with his transfer to Guangdong in 1884. See Hummel, I, 28.
40. Directive GX28/11/11.
41. Zhao Erxun memorial GX28/10/28; and Zhao Papers, Box 31. The Shanxi provincial record book includes a directive sent out on 29 November 1902 that mentions the memorial submitted on 16 November. Another entry states that thirty copies of Zhao's memorial were sent to the Bureau of Government Affairs.
42. See Kwang-ching Liu, "Nineteenth-Century China," pp. 108–113. Liu's arguments counter those advanced by scholars like Franz Michael and Stanley Spector, who argued that provincial governors like Zeng Guofan, Li Hongzhang, and Zuo Zongtang rose to power and prominence in regional contexts at the expense of central power and authority. Franz Michael writes, "Regionalism, as we like to call this development, must therefore not be interpreted narrowly as a provincialism with a local patriotism hostile to outsiders. The leaders of these new bureaucratic organizations that grew within the imperial bureaucracy could be shifted from one province to another without losing control of their organizations, which they took with

them, and without even losing their military power, since their armies remained loyal to them." See Franz Michael, "Introduction: Regionalism in Nineteenth-Century China," in Stanley Spector, *Li Hung-chang and the Huai Army: A Study in Nineteenth-Century Chinese Regionalism* (Seattle: University of Washington Press, 1964), pp. xl–xli.

43. John Locke, "An Essay Concerning the True Original, Extent and End of Civil Government," in *Two Treatises of Government* (London: J. M. Dent & Sons, Ltd., 1924), Sec. 219.

44. See Wang Zutong memorial GX29/3/6 and Bureau of Government Affairs memorial GX29/6. In addition to the coverage Zhao's reforms received in the Shanghai journal *Zhengyi tongbao*, Zhao's *xiangshe* memorial was included in an issue of a national government gazette called *Dibao*. See Zhao Papers, Box 36. Yun Yuding, who noted his approval of Zhao's reforms in a diary entry dated 26 February 1903, was disappointed that Zhao was being transferred to Hunan. Yun, a *jinshi* recipient in 1889, was especially heartened by Zhao's close attention to domestic affairs at a time when everyone seemed preoccupied with foreign relations. See "Chengzhai riji," entry for GX29/1/29. This manuscript is held by Beijing University Library.

45. Shen Jiaben memorial GX31/6/12.

46. Bureau of Government Affairs memorial GX31/7/12. A short entry in *DFZZ* 2.10:*zazu* 73 (GX31) notes a 24 September 1905 request by the Bureau of Government Affairs to fill *xiangguan* posts at the county level with persons possessing official rank.

47. Yuan Shikai was actually Zhili's governor-general *(zongdu)*, a title he would hold until 1907. By then most governors-general were concurrently governors *(xunfu)* of the provinces their yamen were located in. Only those in Chengdu, Tianjin, Nanjing, and Shenyang lacked the second title. In Sichuan and Zhili there was no governor, in Jiangsu the governor's yamen was in Suzhou, and in Shenyang both the governor-general of the three Manchurian provinces and the governor of Fengtian could be found (at least until 1910, when that governorship was abolished). In the text, for stylistic reasons, governors-general will be referred to as governors unless clarity or force of argument requires otherwise. And only for the governors-general in Sichuan, Zhili, Jiangsu, and Fengtian (until 1910) is this, technically, incorrect. All others were also governors. Those men who were governors alone were nominally subordinate to their corresponding governor-general, but both groups of officials had direct

access to the court and metropolitan ministries and they were expected to work collegially when their responsibilities overlapped. In 1907 the governors-general in Chengdu, Tianjin, Nanjing, and Shenyang were joined by five governors-general who were concurrently governors in Lanzhou, Fuzhou, Wuchang, Canton, and Kunming. The fifteen men who were governors alone were stationed in Ji'nan, Taiyuan, Kaifeng, Suzhou, Anqing, Xi'an, Hangzhou, Nanchang, Changsha, Guilin, Guiyang, Urumqi, Shenyang, Jilin city, and Qiqihar. See Fu Zongmao, *Qingdai dufu zhidu* (The system of governors-general and governors in the Qing dynasty) (Taibei: Guoli zhengzhi daxue, 1963), pp. 31–41 and p. 42 Table 3. I thank Prof. R. Kent Guy for bringing this book to my attention. See also Raymond W. Chu and William G. Saywell, *Career Patterns in the Ch'ing Dynasty: The Office of Governor-general* (Ann Arbor: Center for Chinese Studies, The University of Michigan, 1984), pp. 1–12.

48. Zhao Erxun used the term *xiangguan* in his directive on reforming *xiangshe* in Shanxi. See Directive GX28/12/8. He also used *xiangguan* in the attachment to his memorial describing his reforms. See Zhao Erxun attachment GX29/1/26.

49. Gu Yuan memorial GX32/4/6. Gu Yuan's boards of advisors sound similar to a practice in Hubei recounted by a late-Qing magistrate. Jin Zhanlin said a county was divided into four sections administered by bureaus (*ju*). The staff of each bureau assisted a board of twelve counsellors, selected from the local population, that attended to civil affairs. See Hayes, p. 174. Gu Yuan's proposal differs from this practice in Hubei in that each *xiangzhang*, presumably based in the county seat, was advised by a number of boards whose members would live outside the county seat.

50. Gu Yuan memorial GX32/4/6. Gu Yuan does not mention Gu Yanwu by name. Gu Yuan's statement was: "When there are many minor officials, the realm will be ordered (*zhi*)." Gu Yanwu, in an essay concerning village-level officials, wrote: "From ancient times until the present, when there are many minor officials the age is prosperous." See *[Huangchao] Jingshi wenbian*, 18:19. In an essay on subcounty administrative reform Feng Guifen also quoted this line. See Feng Guifen, 1:12 for his quotation of Gu Yanwu.

51. MacKinnon, p. 154.

52. *Japan Weekly Mail*, 19 August 1905, p. 193.

53. Bureau of Government Affairs memorial GX32/5/24.

54. *Tianjin zizhi ju wenjian luyao, Chubian*, 1a–b.

## 2. YUAN SHIKAI'S FOREIGN MODEL FOR CHINA

1. There were reports that about two thousand persons had gathered on 4 July 1907 merely to watch the opening of the ballot boxes and the vote counting. See Shen Huaiyu, pp. 307–308. There has been little work done on self-government efforts in Tianjin. These efforts were mentioned by Cameron, pp. 111–112; Elvin, "Gentry Democracy," p. 60n42; Fincher, p. 43; and MacKinnon, p. 138. In each case, the few details cited came from *Foreign Relations of the United States, North China Herald,* or *Dongfang zazhi.* Shen Huaiyu's research, the most comprehensive to date, is based on *Beiyang gongdu leizuan* and supplemented with two reports in *Shuntian shibao* on the elections. See Shen Huaiyu, pp. 305–308. Shen Huaiyu also emphasized the accomplishments of self-government reforms in Shanghai, where, in contrast to Tianjin, merchants rather than returned students from Japan played the leading role. The Shanghai electoral procedure called for Shanghai's various elite activists, primarily merchants, to submit a list of seventy-six names to the local official, who then selected thirty-three men to serve on the council board. See ibid., pp. 318 and 300. Fincher (p. 41) points out that the Shanghai initiative did not require the compilation of electoral rolls. Elvin notes that the Shanghai initiative really was an example of an "early modern urban government [that] sprang directly from a fusion of previously existing institutions: the assembly of county gentry gathered to advise the magistrate, the gentry-run charitable formation, the late traditional merchant guild, and the local government board with a specialized function." See Elvin, "The Administration of Shanghai," p. 239. Thus the Shanghai council and board is a culmination of trends while the Tianjin initiative represents a striking, new departure. The Shanghai initiative was more than a fusion of familiar forms and practices, for it too drew on the advice of returned students; but the weight of familiar practice and the state was heavier in Shanghai than in Tianjin.
2. For a look at urban administration in Tianjin from 1850 to 1903, see Chen Ke, pp. 54–77.
3. James Ragsdale to W. W. Rockhill, 4 June 1907 (Despatch no. 675), Records of the Peking Legation of the Department of State, Record Group 84, *Despatches from Tientsin, 1907,* National Archives.
4. *North China Herald,* 29 September 1905.
5. *STSB,* GX32/6/23, p. 5. See also Guo Tingyi, p. 1257 and Li Zongyi. Both Guo Tingyi and Li Zongyi misidentify this as a memorial. The National Palace Museum's (Taibei) copy of the Grand

Council's record book of all memorials, *Suishou dengji*, does not reflect any memorial from Yuan Shikai on this topic nor can it be found in published collections of Yuan's memorials like *Rongan dizi ji* and *Yuan Shikai zouyi*. I thank Prof. Beatrice Bartlett for bringing *Suishou dengji* to my attention.

6. Yuan Shikai memorial GX33/6/19. This memorial is not included in *Yuan Shikai zouyi*.

7. Li Zongyi, p. 132.

8. *Fazheng guanhua bao*, no. 1 (GX32/8):6b–7.

9. Ibid., 8b–9.

10. Ibid.

11. *STSB*, GX32/8/1.

12. Edict GX32/7/13. See also Sun E-tu Zen, pp. 251–269. Zhang Yufa highlights the pre-1906 discussions on constitutional government with Liang Qichao's April 1899 essay in *Qingyi bao* comparing different constitutional systems, Zhang Jian's 1901 essay on reform ("Bianfa pingyi"), Kang Youwei's 1902 essay on self-government ("Gongmin zizhi") published in *Xinmin congbao*, and two books on constitutional government published in Shanghai in 1902. See Zhang Yufa, *Qingji de lixian tuanti*, pp. 300–305. See also Meienberger, pp. 22–25. For a survey of government documents dating from 1905–1906 see Min Tu-ki, pp. 140–150. For a sample of the debate among officials in September and October 1906 on topics like constitutional government and local self-government see *QMCB*, I, 386–462.

    For the despatches by the U.S. Legation in Beijing on the September 1906 edict, see *Foreign Relations of the United States* (1906), p. 350. A thirteen-page narrative by an American official in China on constitutional reforms through November 1906 can be found in Peking Legation to Department of State, 16 November 1906 (Despatch no. 452), General Records of the Department of State, Record Group 59, National Archives, Numerical and Minor Files of the Department of State (1906–1910), Microfilm Series 862, Roll number 171.

13. Duanfang and Dai Hongci memorial GX32/7/6.

14. I surveyed over one hundred issues, each of which ran to eight pages, that were published between February 1905 and January 1906. For an example of *Beiyang guanbao*'s role as a source, take the essay "On Local Self-government as the Basis for Establishing Constitutional Government." This was published in *Beiyang guanbao* on 29 November 1906 and reprinted in *Dongfang zazhi* (vol. 4, no. 1) on 9 March 1907.

15. The format in *Beiyang guanbao* was similar to other gazettes I surveyed, which include *Sichuan guanbao, Jiangxi guanbao, Jilin guanbao, Guangxi guanbao, Heilongjiang gongbao,* and *Zhejiang guanbao,* as well as the subprovincial gazettes *Shunde gongbao* (Guangdong) and *Chengdu ribao* (Sichuan).

16. For Zhao Binglin's proposal of 15 December 1906 for a national gazette see Zhao Binglin memorial GX32/10/30. Ge Gongzhen's section on government gazettes (pp. 63–78) contains most of the documentation for these policy discussions. Additional documents can be found in *[Da Qing Guangxu] Xin faling,* 13:20–24 and *QMCB,* II, 1059–1073. For the date of the first issue of *Beiyang guanbao* see Lai Xinxia, ed., *Tianjin jindai shi* (A modern history of Tianjin) (Tianjin: Nankai daxue chubanshe, 1987), p. 345.

17. A Zhejiang censor submitted a memorial on 7 October 1906 that included a long quotation from the Duanfang memorial that had itself been quoted in an article about reorganization plans that had run in the 3 October 1906 issue of *Beiyang guanbao.* For the censor's memorial see *QMCB,* I, 426–429.

18. Zhao Papers, Box 33.

19. But Cen's successor, Xiliang, reportedly cancelled all subscriptions to the reform-oriented gazette published by Yuan Shikai. The anonymous correspondent of an item in the *North China Herald* interpreted Xiliang's action as a "marked snub to the powerful satrap" Yuan Shikai. See *North China Herald,* 7 May 1903. It is unclear if Xiliang's order was obeyed, but there was less need for this import from the north in 1904, when the gazette *Sichuan guanbao* was first published. However, *Beiyang guanbao* was not forgotten in distant Sichuan. Several years later, in the 8 March 1909 issue of the Sichuan government gazette *Chengdu ribao,* it was reported that *Beiyang guanbao* was a daily publication focussing on reform efforts in north China.

20. Duanfang was in Japan on behalf of the Qing government. A member of his suite, Xiong Xiling, was able to contact a fellow provincial in Tokyo, Yang Du, who in turn had access to Liang. Xiong, like Liang, had been part of the reform circle active in Hunan in 1897–1898. See He Hanwen and Du Maizhi, eds., *Yang Du zhuan* (A biography of Yang Du) (Changsha: Renmin chubanshe, 1979), p. 43. Yang Du was one of twenty Hunan students at Hosei University who had petitioned Duanfang in 1905 for 3,000 yuan from the Hunan treasury to support their efforts to publish, for distribution in Hunan, one thousand copies of *Hunan fazheng yanjiulu*

(Memoirs of legal studies by Hunan [students]). See *Qingdai dang'an shiliao congbian,* no. 14 (1990):279–281.

21. See Court letter GX31/12/21, Telegram GX32/inter.4/20; and Guo Tingyi, p. 1254. Bays (p. 198) mentions Zhang Zhidong's unease in using these men as officials. Earlier, in 1903, Zhang Zhidong had proposed rewarding students who had studied overseas. See *ZYCS* 2:*zhengshu* 6:50b–51b. (GX29).

22. *Tianjin zizhi ju wenjian luyao, Chubian,* pp. 5a–b. This is the first of a two-volume collection of documents compiled by the Tianjin Self-government Bureau from its founding in August 1906 through about March 1907. Among the better-known members were Lin Kunxiang, Sun Songling, Qi Shukai, and Yan Fengge. See individual entries in *SMMS,* pp. 246, 350, 648, and 737.

23. See Li Zongyi, p. 134n1; *STSB,* GX33/8/26; Yuan Shikai memorial GX30/8/18; Edict GX31/6/12; Yuan Shikai attachment GX31/6/26; and Rankin, *Early Chinese Revolutionaries,* p. 248n14.

24. Yuan memorial GX31/6/20. During the summer of 1905 it had been reported that Yuan had selected seventy-three students to study in Japan and had also sent sixty-eight men to study Japanese approaches to local government. This report combines information on both short-term and long-term visits to Japan. See *Japan Weekly Mail,* 29 July 1905, p. 108 and 19 August 1905, p. 193.

25. Reynolds, p. 115. See also Jansen.

26. Bays, pp. 120–123; and *North China Herald,* 21 July 1905, p. 142.

27. See Ye Longyan, pp. 107–108. For a discussion of the post-1905 examinations, see Zhang Yufa, *Qingji de lixian tuanti,* pp. 81–83.

28. According to the regulations for accelerated courses in law and administration, students who were neither officials nor expectant officials were required to be 20 *sui* or older. See Ye Longyan, p. 91.

29. Yuan memorial GX33/2. In his March 1907 report Yuan states that fifty men had graduated from the accelerated course at Hosei and had returned to China. These graduates included bureau members Qi Shukai and Yan Fengge. These efforts continued. In early 1907 the Self-government Bureau and Tianjin educational officials put out plans to send local leaders to Japan to study local self-government. See *Beiyang gongdu leizuan,* 1:16b–17. Similarly, in late 1906 and early 1907, provincial efforts to send people to Japan were being planned. See *Beiyang gongdu leizuan,* 1:17b–18b.

30. See Sanetō Keishū, p. 50; and Ye Longyan, p. 95. In 1906 Ume Kenjirō, the president of Hosei University, travelled to China, where his discussions with Zhang Zhidong and Yuan Shikai

prompted him to close admissions to the accelerated classes at Hosei and establish a new three-year preparatory course that would be followed by matriculation in the regular program of study. See Ye Longyan, p. 94. For figures on the Chinese student population in the summer of 1905, see *Japan Weekly Mail*, 1 July 1905, p. 9, where it states that 296 of the 433 students at institutions of higher learning were attending classes at Hosei University. There were 456 students at military schools and 1110 students at major preparatory schools.

31. The age limit of 45 *sui* was specified in the regulations for Zhili Law School. Even this limit would be exceeded in some provinces. In Hubei, for example, the age distribution for sixty-seven students listed in a report on the government's Hubei Law School was: 12 (20–29 *sui*), 28 (30–39 *sui*), 19 (40–49 *sui*), 8 (50–59 *sui*). See XZBCG, Box 52.

32. See Ye Longyan, p. 154. A short description of the Zhili Law School is available in *Beiyang guanbao*, GX31/8/14, pp. 3b–4. By November 1905 the first class had graduated. See *Beiyang guanbao*, GX31/10/15, pp. 3–5 and GX31/10/17, p. 3b.

33. For a copy of the Japanese regulations see *Hōrei zenshu: Meiji nen-kan* (Meiji 21:1) *hōritsu*, pp. 1–60.

34. *Tianjin zizhi ju wenjian luyao, Chubian*, pp. 23a–b and 25a–b.

35. Ibid., pp. 27–28b; Yuan Shikai memorial GX33/7/22.

36. For Zhang Boling, see Boorman, I, 100–105; for Wang Xianbin and Ning Shifu, see MacKinnon, pp. 166 and 168.

37. Wu Xingrang was a native of Wu county, in southern Jiangsu. See ZGJD, II, 3085. His interest in self-government went back to his Japan days. Wu's essay "Difang zizhi zhi yanjiu" (A study of local self-government) was published in *Beiyang fazheng xuebao* (Bei-yang law and administration journal), no. 12 (January 1907) and his translation of his Japanese law professor's lectures on the Japan model was published in eight installments between September 1906 and March 1907.

38. This description of the drafting process is based on Articles 5 and 6 in the regulations governing the procedures of the self-government committee, an essay by bureau member Wu Xingrang on self-gov-ernment, and an item in *Fazheng guanhua bao*. See *Tianjin zizhi ju wenjian luyao, Chubian*, pp. 25a–b; Wu Xingrang, p. 1; and *Fa-zheng guanhua bao*, no. 7 (GX33/2):4. An item in the 23 February 1907 issue of *Shuntian shibao* states that the self-government com-mittee had completed its deliberations and Tianjin Prefect Ling Fu-

peng and others had petitioned Yuan and presented the complete draft of the regulations. See *STSB*, GX33/1/11.

39. A final version of the regulations and Yuan's approval is in *Beiyang gongdu leizuan*, 1:6b–13. The versions in *DFZZ* 4:*neiwu* 208–222 (GX33) and *ZYCS* 6:*neizheng tongji* 2:5b–16b (GX33), are not final. A translation of the regulations was submitted by the U. S. Legation in Beijing to Washington. See Peking Legation to Department of State, 9 August 1907 (Report no. 690), General Records of the Department of State, Record Group 59, National Archives, Numerical and Minor Files of the Department of State (1906–1910), Microfilm Series 862, Roll Number 171.

40. *Guangdong difang zizhi yanjiulu*, no. 1 (GX33/11/20): *xu*.

41. This description of the self-government school is based on the petition from the Tianjin Prefect Ling Fupeng and "others" (probably the self-government bureau), the school rules, a report (probably by the self-government bureau) filed after classes had begun, and namelists of teachers and students. See *Tianjin zizhi ju wenjian luyao, Chubian*, pp. 10a–b, 13–14, 16a–b, and 17–19b, respectively. See also *Beiyang gongdu leizuan*, 1:13a–b. Although classes were originally held at the normal school, the school was moved to the South Gate Lecture Hall because it was closer to the dorm used by the students. See *Tianjin zizhi ju wenjian luyao, Chubian*, p. 16.

42. These lecture halls and their activities were to be supervised by county education offices *(quanxue suo)*. By 1907 there were 135 of these lecture halls established throughout Zhili. See MacKinnon, pp. 147–148. For the 13 May 1906 national regulations see *[Da Qing Guangxu] Xin faling*, 7 (*jiaoyu* 3):92b–95.

43. *Tianjin zizhi ju wenjian luyao, Chubian*, pp. 10b–12b.

44. *Fazheng guanhua bao*, no. 1–3 (GX32/8–10).

45. Ibid., no. 2 (GX32/9):10b.

46. See Tanaka Issei, *Shindai chihō geki shiryo shu* (Collections of materials in the regional drama of the Qing) (Tokyo: Toyo bunka kenkyujo, 1968), II, 9–12. See also Alexander Woodside, "Some Mid-Qing Theorists of Popular Schools: Their Innovations, Inhibitions, and Attitudes Toward the Poor," *Modern China* 9.1 (January 1983): 33 for a discussion on connections between local opera, religious festivals, and education.

47. Thirteen issues of *Fazheng guanhua bao*, which was published at least until October 1909, are available at the University of California at Berkeley.

48. *Beiyang fazheng xuebao*, edited by Wu Xingrang, was published

every ten days from September 1906 to November 1910. See *ZGJD*,
II, 1997–2026, for a listing of the table of contents of each issue.

49. *Fazheng guanhua bao*, no. 3 (GX32/10):2.
50. Sanetō Keishū, p. 50.
51. *Fazheng guanhua bao*, no. 3 (GX32/10):2.
52. *Tianjin zizhi ju wenjian luyao, Chubian*, p. 20.
53. *Fazheng guanhua bao*, no. 3 (GX32/10):10–14b.
54. Ibid., no. 1–3 (GX32/8–10).
55. Ibid., no. 3 (GX32/10):4.
56. *Tianjin zizhi ju wenjian luyao, Erbian*, p. 1.
57. *Tianjin zizhi ju wenjian luyao, Chubian*, p. 10.
58. In Jin Bangping's opening remarks to the bureau he explicitly
    placed the Tianjin reforms in the context of borrowing from the
    West. At the same time he emphasized the elitist nature of reform
    planning: "In the past the tide of civilization came from East to
    West. Now it comes from West to East. . . . You should act in
    accord with what is best for an area. . . . We all have an extremely
    great responsibility. . . . We are the well-known and respected
    people of the area." See *Fazheng guanhua bao*, no. 1 (GX32/8):8–9.
59. *DFZZ* 3:*neiwu* 274–275 (GX32). For a convenient summary of
    early planning efforts concerning investigation and training see Zhao
    Erxun memorial GX33/3/18.
60. Shen Huaiyu, p. 297 citing *Shuntian shibao*, GX33/1/10.
61. Shen Huaiyu, p. 298.


### 3. LOCAL ELITES IN CORPORATISM'S REALM

1. Edict GX32/7/13.
2. *STSB*, GX32/8/2 and GX32/8/5.
3. *STSB*, GX32/8/1.
4. *STSB*, GX32/11/17. These councils, which were prohibited from
   dealing with the affairs of individual persons or litigation, were
   called for in all provinces except Yunnan, Guizhou, Shanxi,
   Shaanxi, and Gansu.
5. Ibid., GX33/6/11.
6. See Memorial and Regulations GX33/5/27.
7. See W. W. Rockhill to U.S. State Department, 9 August 1907, in
   *Foreign Relations of the United States* (1907), p. 189. A circular
   mentioned in a draft by the Ministry of Interior dated 30 August
   1907 called for emulation of the Tianjin model. Sun Pei mentioned
   this in his response to a report from Fujian concerning local initiatives in self-government. See MZB, 196. The Ministry of Interior

Archives (Minzheng bu dang'an) are held by the No. 1 Historical Archives of China in Beijing. When I used these materials in 1983 the documents were still in their original Qing dynasty folders. Most of these folders contained series of correspondence between Beijing and the provinces. These folders had been placed within printed wrappers when the materials were being organized in Nanjing. Beatrice S. Bartlett notes that the National Palace Museum's Archives Bureau began shipping materials from Beijing to Shanghai in 1933. In late 1936 the collection was moved to a new museum building in Nanjing. See Beatrice S. Bartlett, "The Ch'ing Central Government Archives: Provenance and Peregrinations," *Committee on East Asian Libraries Bulletin*, no. 63:29 (October 1980). The file numbers I use in the endnotes (e.g., MZB, 1) to identify documents are taken from these wrappers. All of these files are part of a larger group of documents referred to, by the Nanjing curators, as General Category No. 1509 (*jiguan daihao* 1509). I will make no reference to the numbering of these documents made by Ministry of Interior personnel in the late Qing. Most of the files used in this study were compiled by the Local Self-government Section (Difang zizhi ke) of the Ministry of Interior.

For a brief listing of the categories of materials in these archives see Zheng Li, p. 79.

8. *STSB*, GX33/8/12.
9. Edict GX33/9/13.
10. Ministry of Interior directive GX34/7/17. Partial copies of this directive can also be found in *DFZZ* 5:*jizai* 114–115 (GX34) and in *STSB*, GX34/8/22.
11. *DFZZ* 5:*jizai* 115 (GX34).
12. Zhang Yufa, pp. 90–143.
13. Regulations GX29/11/24.
14. Regulations GX32/6/8. Regulations for agricultural societies were promulgated on 20 October 1907. See Regulations GX33/9/14.
15. In January 1908 a publication in Guangdong identified the Tianjin Self-government School and the Shanghai society as the two most noteworthy initiatives. Others in Fujian, Jilin, and Hubei were mentioned. See *Guangdong difang zizhi yanjiulu*, no. 1 (GX33/11/20): *xu.*
16. Zhang Yufa, pp. 90–98.
17. Shen Huaiyu, p. 317. Shen's list is incomplete in part because she did not use archival sources and published provincial gazettes and also because she did not include various initiatives occurring between August 1908, when the Ministry of Interior completed its

draft of local self-government regulations, and January 1909, when imperially sanctioned regulations were promulgated. These omissions include various subprovincial initiatives in Shandong, Henan, Shanxi, and Guangdong. See issues of *STSB*, GX34/8/28, GX34/7/23, GX34/8/8, and GX34/7/13 respectively. Although Shen begins her survey with two local initiatives associated with the Hunan reform movement of 1897–1898, and includes a county-level initiative in Shanxi in 1903, a multicounty effort in Fengtian in 1904, and the municipal administrative reforms in Shanghai in 1905–1908 that have been studied by Mark Elvin, most of her article concerns initiatives taken in 1906–1908 in the "age of constitutionalism."

18. *Chengdu ribao*, GX34/8/16.
19. Ibid., GX34/11/28.
20. Ibid., GX34/11/23.
21. Ibid., GX34/11/6.
22. Yet one more addition to Shen Huaiyu's survey based on this kind of source is a local initiative in Zhejiang. See *Chengdu ribao*, GX34/9/6.
23. Those counties in which local self-government organizations were definitely established by September 1907 include Jiading, Yangzhou, Changshu, Zhaowen, Suzhou, and Wu. The figures in the text are based on surveys made by Wang Shuhuai and Shen Huaiyu; I have counted only those organizations with "self-government" in the title. Joint counties forming one organization are counted as two counties. By January 1908 Taicang, Zhenyang, Baoshan, Jiangning, Ganyu, Wujin, and Yanghu had local self-government organizations. See Shen Huaiyu, p. 304; and Wang Shuhuai, p. 314.
24. *Jiading xian xuzhi*, 6.4.
25. For a Sichuan initiative in Chengkou see Zhao Papers, Box 275. Hubei initiatives included one far from the capital, about 145 miles upriver on the Han at Nanzhang county, where there were self-government educational activities as well as one in Yun county, far away in Hubei's northwest corner. See Hubei No. 3. (See Appendix B for citation convention.) Initiatives in Fujian in 1907 included planning for a local self-government investigation and study society in Xiamen. See MZB, 196.
26. For the Yunnan Self-government Bureau and school see MZB, 207. For the regulations for the Heilongjiang Self-government Study Society established by July 1908 see MZB, 177. For the Guangdong self-government school see MZB, 202.
27. Albert Pontius to W. W. Rockhill, 5 September 1906 (Despatch no. 599), Records of the Peking Legation of the Department of State,

Record Group 84, *Despatches from Tientsin, 1906*, National Archives. *Jingbao* was probably the basis for a report filed shortly after the bureau's founding by the American vice and deputy consul in charge at the American Consulate in Tianjin. The establishment of the Tianjin bureau was reported in *DFZZ* 3.11:*neiwu* 238 (GX32).

28. MZB, 189.1.
29. *SMMS*, p. 577; and MZB, 189.1.
30. *SMMS*, p. 702; and *Ming-Qing jinshi timing beilu suoyin* (An index to the names of Ming-Qing *jinshi* registered on stelae) (Shanghai: Guoji chubanshe, 1980), p. 2660.
31. A prospective member needed to be introduced by at least two members (a requirement that could only have taken effect after the original membership was established); register his name, age, residence, and occupation; and pay a membership fee of one yuan initially, and two yuan annually. The only people specifically prohibited from participating were those disqualified for one of the following reasons: residence in another country, being younger than twenty *sui*, displaying poor comportment, possessing a bad reputation, or having a criminal record. See MZB, 189.1.
32. Ibid.
33. *SMMS*, p. 34, entry for Wang Tongyu, and p. 702, entry for Jiang Bingzhang.
34. Dennerline (pp. 75–77) notes that sometimes, but rarely, these rural landlords left their villages and became officials.
35. MZB, 189.1.
36. Documents associated with the Jiangsu Law School in Suzhou, the school at which Fei Tinghuang and another self-government society colleague were instructors, suggest some of the context of the Suzhou initiative. According to information in *Jiangsu fazheng xuetang xuean* (Jiangsu law school principles of instruction) classes met from eight in the morning until three in the afternoon in hourly sessions, breaking an hour for lunch. There were three six-week sessions which were deemed sufficient to cover the entire curriculum. Administration was taught in the fifth week of the second session from eight until noon each day. Another source has an extensive section on the administration lectures given at this school, running to about 200 pages. The Japanese influence is clear. In the opening remarks to a set of lectures on municipal administration, a brief overview of the history of administrative reform in the early Meiji is given. At the end of these remarks reference is made to the city and town codes of 1888, saying that this is the system being

explained. See *Jiangsu fazheng xuetang jiangyi*, 37:84b. Over fifty pages of these lecture notes refer to Japanese examples of municipal administration. For information on Fei Tinghuang's colleague, who also had studied at Hosei University, see *SMMS*, p. 490, entry for Lu Bingzhang.

37. Polachek; Wang Yeh-chien. A more positive interpretation of this devolution of power to local elites informs the work of Kuhn and Rankin.

38. MZB, 189.1.

39. Ibid.

40. Wang Shuhuai.

41. *Jilin gongshu zhengshu, minzheng si* 7. See also Shen Huaiyu, p. 298.

42. Zhang Pengyuan, p. 211. See also *SMMS*, p. 266; and Meng Dong-feng, "Xinhai geming qianhou de Songyu" (Songyu around the time of the 1911 Revolution), *Bowuguan yanjiu* (Museum studies) 1984.3.

43. *Jilin gongshu zhengshu, minzheng si* 8. Unlike the Tianjin initiative, which was begun at the request and on the authority of Yuan Shi-kai, the Jilin society, like its Suzhou counterpart, was a voluntary organization. In accordance with the regulations, natives of Jilin, as well as natives of other provinces residing in Jilin, could participate in the society as long as they agreed with its goals. Members were divided into three categories determined on the basis of financial support to the society: ordinary members, who paid one yuan upon joining the society, and three yuan annually; special members, who fulfilled these dues requirements plus paid a subscription of ten yuan or more; and honorary members selected by the community *(youzhong gongju)* who joined the society without financial obliga-tions. See MZB, 174.

44. Ibid. Five of the twelve returned students were lower degree-hold-ers. Finally, on the basis of name alone, less than half of this group of fifty leaders appear to be Manchu.

45. Ibid.

46. Songyu's abilities, displayed in self-government, education, com-merce, and journalism, have been cited by Zhang Pengyuan as evi-dence of his progressive attitude. See *SMMS*, p. 266; and Zhang Pengyuan, p. 211.

47. *Jilin gongshu zhengshu, minzheng si* 8.

48. MZB, 174.

49. For the participation of the self-government society in tax collec-tion, in cooperation with the Chamber of Commerce, see *Chengdu*

*ribao*, GX34/11/17, pp. 2–3; for Songyu and the railroad issue, see *Chengdu ribao*, GX34/10/5; and Zhang Pengyuan, p. 211; for the abolition of the self-government society see *Jilin guanbao*, GX34.1:*tebie yaojian* 1–2b; and Guo Tingyi, p. 1315; for a photo of the monument to Zhu Jiabao see *Jilin guanbao*, XT1.19.

50. MZB, 174.

51. Ibid., 165.

52. Another example of an elite-dominated initiative comes from Canton. The Guangdong Local Self-government Study Society (Guangdong difang zizhi yanjiushe), a voluntary association whose members numbered 159 when it was established late in 1907, included 153 men who were identified as degree-holders or holders of official rank (active or expectant). Returned students from Japan (e.g., Zhang Shutang, a Panyu native who had studied law in Japan) were members of the society. Zhang was a lecturer at a local law school as were other persons whose essays were published in the society's journal. The self-government association was founded by Liang Qinggui, a *gongsheng* from Shunde who was also a law school lecturer. In addition to essays on the Japan model for local self-government, readers were introduced to the Tianjin model. See *Guangdong difang zizhi yanjiulu*, no. 1 (GX33/11/20) and no. 3 (GX34/3/10).

53. MZB, 165.

54. Ibid.; see also *DFZZ* 3.7:*zazu* 36 (GX32) concerning the 2 July 1906 founding of this society.

55. MZB, 165. For the society's regulations see also *ZYCS* 5:*neizheng tongji* 3:5–6 (GX32).

56. A prospective member had to be at least twenty-five *sui*, literate, not engaged in improper occupations, of a good reputation, and not a foreigner. See MZB, 165.

57. *PDPOC*, entry 920.

58. MZB, 165.

59. Ibid.

60. Ibid.

61. This extensive network of merchant and official participants in Beijing bears comparison to those discussed in David Strand's work on later decades in Beijing urban history and also echoes themes discussed by William Rowe in his work on Hankou.

62. The list combines the category of "old gentry elite" and "discrete functional elites" discussed by Esherick and Rankin (p. 335). Schoppa (pp. 43–46) argues that "functional elites" were important elements in self-government reforms. I differ from these scholars in

the meaning I attach to "gentry." My use of "gentry," "gentrymen," and "gentryman" is based on the ways in which terms like *shen, shendong,* and *shi* are used in late-Qing texts. I follow convention in translating *shendong* as "gentry-manager." Less conventionally, I use "gentry" and its cognates to refer to local men with power or prestige recognized by local yamen or the Ministry of Personnel (Li bu) in Beijing. Leaders of gentry bureaus, retired officials, officials who had returned home for mourning rituals, expectant officials, and possessors of official rank were all gentrymen *(shen).* Most of these men also possessed examination degrees granted by the Ministry of Ritual (Li bu). But many more degree-holders had no connection with either the local yamen or the Ministry of Personnel. I see this group *(shi),* in terms of power and prestige, as distinct from the gentry *(shen).* When officials called for students to come to provincial capitals to fill seats in local self-government schools, they sought *shishen,* which I take to mean degree-holders and gentrymen. This conclusion is based on analysis of lists of students in Henan, Hunan, Jilin, and Shandong. See sources cited at Chapter Seven, note 46.

63. See Sichuan regulations GX34/9/26; and, for the Mian department assembly, see *Chengdu ribao,* XT1/11/8, pp. 1–2, Article 4.

64. Zhao Papers, Box 280.

65. Ibid.

66. Regulations GX33/12/4, Article 12.

67. XZBCG, Box 25.

68. MZB, 189.2. The Ministry of Interior copy is in a file dated 13 January 1908. For the published versions of the fifty-seven–article provincial *ziyiju* regulations and the fifty-five–article county council regulations see *ZYCS* 6:*neizheng tongji* 4:13b–25b (GX33).

69. This high tide of nineteenth-century corporatist thought, which extended until 1918, was overcome by new currents, coming out of the ruins of post–World War I Germany, Italy, and later, Spain, that sought to reduce all politics to functional groups, partly in hopes of diminishing the conditions and perspectives leading to class struggle. See Landauer, p. 36. But neo-corporatism of the post–World War II period, associated with liberal democratic regimes, has been distinguished from the authoritarian corporatism of Italy, Germany, and Spain in 1918–1945. Neo-corporatism, while emphasizing the importance of hierarchically-organized bodies of "voluntary" associations like labor unions representing and negotiating the interests of their members with the state (interest intermediation),

has room for an "electoral channel" in which men and women participate in political parties and elect representatives to national parliaments. For neo-corporatists, the electoral channel and interest intermediation combine to create complementary forms of representation keyed to both individual persons and groups. See *Patterns of Corporatist Policy-making,* eds. Gerhard Lehmbruch and Philippe C. Schmitter (London: Sage Publications, 1982), p. 9. The "concept of 'corporatism' was first developed by French theorists referring to a quite restricted concept of 'corporatism', namely, a functional association comparable to the estates and guilds of the Ancien Régime." See ibid., p. 28n1. A basic formulation of "corporatism" by Philippe C. Schmitter can be found in *Trends Toward Corporatist Intermediation,* eds. Philippe C. Schmitter and Gerhard Lehmbruch (London: Sage Publications, 1979), pp. 7–52.

70. One of the first to make this argument was Johann Fichte. See Landauer, p. 9.
71. Ibid., p. 20.

## 4. THE CENTER READIES ITS ARSENAL

1. Hao Chang, p. 155.
2. Ibid., p. 156.
3. Ibid., p. 100.
4. *Zhongguo jindaishi cidian,* p. 376.
5. Shen Huaiyu, "Qingmo xiyang difang zizhi sixiang de shuru" (The importation of the Western idea of local self-government at the end of the Qing), *Zhongyang yanjiuyuan jindaishi yanjiusuo jikan,* no. 8 (1979):178–179; and Min Tu-ki, p. 142.
6. Cameron, pp. 105–107.
7. Edict GX32/9/20. For the Board of Police (Xunjing bu) regulations see *GXZY* 31:90–92. For an overview of the institutional structure of the ministry, see Zhu Xianhua.
8. MZB, 132.
9. Walker, pp. 146–147.
10. Ibid., p. 147. Although the rulers of the Germanic states claimed the prerogative to legislate in fine detail economic, social, cultural, and religious life, implementation was only possible through the cooperation of local elites. Marc Raeff argues, "Given the technological limitations of the time, the central administration *sensu strictu* was unable to take effective care of everything and never really expected to; of necessity its instruments had to be local, re-

gional, and estate institutions. It sufficed that the central power held
the initiative and coordinated the performance, which enabled it to
set the overall direction of the dynamic development." See Marc
Raeff, *The Well-ordered Police State: Social and Institutional
Change through Law in the Germanies and Russia, 1600–1800*
(New Haven: Yale University Press, 1983), p. 154.

11. The phrase is Cheng Yi's. See *A Source Book in Chinese Philosophy*,
tr. and comp. Wing-tsit Chan (Princeton: Princeton University
Press, 1963), pp. 544 and 550. This Neo-Confucian concept informed Qian Mu's attempt to understand China's troubled passage
into the twentieth century. He insisted that China's local diversities
were merely epiphenomenal. But there was a unity that, while existing only in the mind, was the essence of Chinese culture. See
Dennerline, p. 9.

12. Yamagata Aritomo, Japan's architect of local self-government in the
1880s, wrote a preface to the Japanese translation of J. R. Seeley's
*Life and Times of Stein* (Cambridge: At the University Press, 1878)
that was published in 1887. The chapter on "Municipal Reform"
(Ibid., II, 223–247) was printed and distributed to Ministry of Interior officials in Tokyo. See Staubitz, p. 68.

13. Walker, pp. 21–33, 210–216, and 261–267.

14. Ibid., pp. 109–110.

15. Applegate, pp. 1–19.

16. MZB, 85; and Fang Zhaoying, p. 5. Sun arrived in Tokyo around
August 1901.

17. MZB, 132.

18. Ibid.

19. Ibid.

20. Constitutional Commission memorial GX34/4/26.

21. Meng Zhaochang's comments can be found in *Difang zizhi zhi
gangyao, xu* 2–3.

22. Wu Xingrang.

23. Ministry of Interior officials reviewed Meng's booklet favorably.
See MZB, 189.2. On 16 October 1907 the ministry's Local Self-
government Section had received a letter from society president
Zheng Xiaoxu and twenty-one others in which books on local self-
government such as *Difang xingzheng zhidu* (Systems of local administration), *Difang zizhi zhi gangyao*, and *Gongmin bidu* (What
every citizen should read), were introduced. The letter from Shanghai was written shortly after an edict of 30 September 1907—cited
in the society's letter—was issued that stressed the ministry's re-

sponsibility for drafting local self-government regulations. In the draft of an endorsement composed by a ministry staff member, who noted the strong influence of the Japan model in these books, provincial officials were urged to ensure that copies be sent to counties for use in local self-government societies *(zizhi yanjiu hui)* and lecture societies *(jiangxi hui)*. This endorsement draft was approved by ministry president Shanqi who added that these useful books were well done. See ibid. For a published version of Zheng Xiaoxu's letter see *Zhonghua Minguo dang'an ziliao huibian* (Compilations of documents from the archives of the Republic of China), no. 1 (1979):100–102.

24. MZB, 1.
25. Regulations GX33/5/27, Article 33. Cameron (p. 109) is mistaken in arguing that Article 33 was not implicitly approved in the edict of 7 July 1907. A draft of these regulations had been circulating since early in 1907. For example, a copy was published in *DFZZ* 4.8:*neiwu* 410–414 (GX33) and *ZYCS* 6:*neizheng tongji* 1:5–8b (GX33). The Peking Legation of the Department of State forwarded a copy to Washington based on a translation from the 3 March 1907 edition of *Tianjin riri xinwen* (Tianjin daily news). See Peking Legation to Department of State, 28 March 1907 (Report no. 592), General Records of the Department of State, Record Group 59, National Archives, Numerical and Minor Files of the Department of State (1906–1910), Microfilm Series 862, Roll Number 171.

   For a translation of the 7 July 1907 regulations and memorial see *Foreign Relations of the United States* (1907), pp. 181–189.
26. MZB, 132.
27. Ibid.
28. *STSB*, GX33/6/19.
29. Ibid., GX33/6/25.
30. Ibid., GX33/7/7. After four ministry officials were assigned to the bureau, regulations were drafted and explained in selected areas of Beijing in August. See ibid., GX33/7/13, 19, 21, 22, and 23. Guo Tingyi (p. 1286) gives the founding date of the Beijing Self-government Bureau as 3 September 1907, but the report on Shanqi assigning four Ministry of Interior members to head the bureau was published on 21 August. Regulations had been written and propagation efforts begun in the week prior to 3 September.
31. Bureau of Government Affairs memorial GX33/8; and Yuan Shikai memorial GX33/6/19.
32. Yuan Shikai memorial GX33/7/22. But it is a telling detail that the

rescript attached to this second memorial did not request the ministry to respond.

33. For the assistance Shanqi rendered to Westerners during the Boxer uprising see Richard, pp. 314–315. See also Hummel, I, 281.

34. *STSB*, GX33/5/20, GX33/6/7, 19, 25.

35. Ibid., GX33/7/26.

36. The Bureau of Government Affairs had intended, according to later press reports, to present its recommendation on Yuan's memorial on 18 September 1907. See ibid., GX33/8/13. The Grand Council, which would have conveyed these recommendations to the court, was reported, in the 18 September issue of *Shuntian shibao,* to have instructed the Ministry of Interior to issue the self-government telegram. See ibid., GX33/8/12. See also Bureau of Government Affairs memorial GX33/8.

37. MZB, 189.1.

38. Ibid.

39. Edict GX33/8/23; and *STSB*, GX33/8/24. The topics of the edict were similar to those discussed by Yuan Shikai in his memorial of 28 July, which dealt with a national consultative assembly, local self-government, and education, as well as the focus of the Bureau of Government Affairs in its response to Yuan's memorial. The bureau had emphasized the interrelated and fundamental importance of these reforms in establishing a basis for constitutional government. See Bureau of Government Affairs memorial GX33/8. But even though this edict reflects Yuan's influence, the court responded to the Ministry of Interior's demand to control policy making for local self-government. Neither Yuan Shikai nor the Bureau of Government Affairs made this proposal; they had called for provisional efforts in local self-government to be attempted in provincial capitals, treaty ports, and flourishing areas.

40. Regulations GX33/5/27, Article 33.

41. *PDPOC,* entry 150.

42. Memorial GX33/7/5. For a list of the personnel of the Constitutional Commission see Liu Ruxi, pp. 34–59. Returned students holding staff positions included Cao Rulin, Zhang Zongxiang, and Wang Rongbao. The censor Zhao Binglin, one of Yuan's adversaries, stated that these three men had ties to Yuan Shikai. See Zhao Binglin, 12:3b. Over half of the persons in the important statistical and compilation bureaus of the commission were returned students. See Liu Ruxi, pp. 37–49.

43. *STSB*, GX33/8/26.

44. The Empress Dowager granted an audience to Shanqi in June 1907

and the Guangxu Emperor did the same in October. See ibid., GX33/5/20 and GX33/9/11.

45. Shanqi's negotiations in early 1908 with Liang Qichao and Kang Youwei about their opposition to Yuan Shikai enhanced this reputation. See Guo Tingyi, pp. 1167, 1290, and 1301.

46. Although Yuan's foes forced him from office in early 1909, several reform-minded officials with ties to Yuan remained members of the commission. These included Yan Xiu, Shen Jiaben, Jin Bangping, Zhang Yilin, and Lao Naixuan. Stephen MacKinnon mentions the connection between Yuan Shikai, and Yan Xiu and Shen Jiaben, in a table listing the leadership of Beijing ministries for September 1907 through November 1908. See MacKinnon, pp. 191–194.

47. Standard documentary collections like *Donghua lu* and *Guangxu zhengyao* do not contain any references to deliberations between August 1908 and January 1909. There are, however, numerous references in the Sichuan gazette *Chengdu ribao* in these months. See, for example, the issues for GX34/7/17, 28; GX34/8/6, 16, 25; GX34/9/7, 12, 13, 22; and GX34/10/23. These issues carried relevant stories reprinted from various gazettes and newspapers, including *Gonglun xinbao*, *Dongsansheng ribao*, *Shangbao*, and *Zhongwai ribao*.

48. Cameron, p. 113.

49. See Wu Tingxie, p. 53. Wu also mentions that he was involved in the compilation of *Guangxu zhengyao*, a collection of memorials and edicts intended to aid government officials in sorting out the myriad institutional and administrative changes of the late nineteenth and early twentieth centuries. This source includes the Ministry of Interior memorial discussed in the text.

50. Min Tu-ki, p. 142.

51. Ministry of Interior memorial GX33/2/13. The draft of this memorial was signed by Lu Zongyu, a returned student heading the Administration Department of the Ministry of Interior, on 24 February 1907. This draft copy notes that a rescript was received on 6 March 1907. See MZB, 162. This date, although corresponding to the lunar month under which this memorial is placed in *Guangxu zhengyao*, differs from the date given in the *Donghua lu* entry (26 March 1907). Xiao Yishan includes a long quotation from this memorial in *Qingdai tongshi* (A comprehensive history of the Qing) (Beijing: Zhonghua shuju, 1986) IV, 1459–1460, but does not discuss it.

52. Ministry of Interior memorial GX33/2/13.

53. The posts, in order listed, were: 1) *xiangzheng*, *xiangqi* and *lizheng*,

2) *zhaizhang* and *weizhang,* 3) *tuanzong* and *lianzong,* 4) *gong-zheng* and *gongzhi,* 5) *zhendong* and *cundong,* 6) *sheshou* and *huishou.*

54. The memorial gives the measurement "one hundred tens of li *(bai shi li).*" Ch'ü T'ung-tsu (p. 2) states that measurements of counties were given in terms of length added to width at the widest point, with *xian* ranging in size from a hundred li to several hundred li. This does not seem to be the method used in describing the size of subcounty areas under the control of unofficial leaders mentioned in this memorial.

55. Sun E-Tu Zen; and *QMCB,* I, 43.

56. *Zhongguo jindaishi cidian,* p. 363.

57. Memorial GX32/10/7. Important information on the data gathered and processed by this commission is available in manuscript form in an Investigation Commission record book held by the No. 1 Historical Archives in Beijing containing about one hundred entries. See XZBCG, Box 94. Thirty different categories of abstracts *(tiyao)* of some of this translated material were published in ZZGB, beginning in October 1907. For a description of this effort see also ZZGB, GX34/2/1, p. 24. For a discussion of the Japanese codes of 1888 and 1890 see ibid., GX33/9/21, 22.

By early 1908 some of this material was available in book form: an advertisement announcing thirteen titles can be found in the 9 April 1908 issue of ZZGB. This translation effort continued into 1907 and 1908. The Constitutional Commission, the agency responsible for publishing ZZGB, also had its own translation office. See PDPOC, entry 156.

58. See Constitutional Commission memorial and regulations GX34/12/27. A translation of the regulations is in *Foreign Relations of the United States* (1909), pp. 136–144.

59. The Japanese codes of 1888 are in *Hōrei zenshu: Meiji nenkan* (Meiji 21:1) *hōritsu,* pp. 1–60. A translation appears in McLaren, pp. 367–404. This Japanese influence at the national level echoed the importance of the Japan model on the Tianjin Self-government Bureau's approach to local self-government. A Republican-era reference to the Japanese influence on these late Qing reforms can be found in Yang Shouqi's essay comparing Chinese and Japanese regulations on local self-government in a collection of statecraft essays. He says the basis for the 1909 regulations was the Japanese regulations for local administration promulgated in 1888. See Yang Shouqi.

60. Zhao Papers, Box 267.

### 5. PROVINCIAL OFFICIALS CHANNEL ELITE ACTIVISM

1. Ministry of Interior directive GX34/7/17.
2. Because of the ad-hoc nature of institutions associated with the New Policies, it was possible to maneuver around the law of avoidance, which barred officials from serving in their native provinces. In the July 1907 provincial reorganization principles it stated that the yamen officials responsible for the local economy should be selected from among local elites. Regulations GX33/5/27.
3. *STSB,* GX32/12/3.
4. Ibid., GX32/12/20. For surveys of the late 1906 reorganization see Fincher, pp. 69–76; Cameron, pp. 103–110; Meienberger, pp. 48–55; Bays, pp. 200–202; and Borthwick, pp. 73–78. One premise behind the emphasis in general on administrative reorganization was that China's state structure *(guanzhi)* had to be put in order prior to the election of local councils, provincial assemblies, and a parliament, since the purpose of these bodies was to assist, not replace, state authorities.
5. *STSB,* GX33/2/21 and GX33/2/28.
6. MacKinnon, pp. 77–89 and 180–182.
7. Regulations GX33/5/27.
8. Duanfang memorial GX33/7/18.
9. Hummel, II, 780–781.
10. Zhao Papers, Box 329. One example of interest in Sichuan concerning self-government policy: In July 1908 two *juren* from Chongqing prefecture studying at the Sichuan Provincial Self-government School in Chengdu, Yin Mingze and Zhou Xuyi, asked Zhao Erxun to send graduates from the school to give lectures in their home counties. See Petition GX34/6/6.
11. Fincher argues that events in Sichuan, specifically the establishment of a provincial local self-government school, are prototypical examples of how provinces were beginning to challenge and defy Beijing's authority. It is difficult to see anything in Zhao's stance that was challenging Beijing. Fincher also notes (p. 105): "Zhao Erxun's use of Hubei organizations rather than central regulations as his model in preparing for self-government [in Sichuan] illustrates the difficulty the central government faced in setting a norm for the provinces." In fact, when Zhao was governor in Hubei he established the Hubei Provincial Self-government Bureau in accordance with the Tianjin model, just as Beijing had requested. See Zhao Papers, Box 216; and Shen Huaiyu, p. 313.

    This provincialism bears comparison with the type of regionalism

K. C. Liu insists was displayed by governors like Li Hongzhang in the mid-nineteenth century. Liu's student Stephen MacKinnon, in his study of Yuan Shikai, extends this argument to the final years of the dynasty. MacKinnon argues that Yuan remained loyal to Beijing and that even late-Qing innovations like new armies were managed by Beijing in ways that checked provincial autonomy. See MacKinnon, pp. 135–136 and 222–224. This perspective is supported by archival evidence about the late-Qing reforms managed by Zhao Erxun. In Sichuan, for example, Zhao and his brother Zhao Erfeng, the previous Sichuan governor, may have gone beyond the policies sanctioned by Beijing, but the fundamental reason for their initiatives was to keep local activism directed along paths acceptable to imperial authority. There is no evidence that Sichuan authorities were trying to deceive, let alone defy, Beijing. On 15 June 1908, five days after Governor Zhao Erxun had taken over the seals of office, the regulations and a report about the Sichuan Provincial Self-government School were sent to Beijing. One set of these documents, which included regulations for the Chengdu Prefecture Self-government Bureau, was sent to the emperor, another set was sent to the Ministry of Interior. The ministry received its copies on 10 July 1908. See MZB, 205. The report, without the regulations, can be found in *ZZGB*, GX34/6/11. For Zhao Erxun's arrival in Chengdu, see Adshead, p. 83.

12. A proposal made by the Ministry of Interior in April 1908 anticipated the day when the drafting of the local self-government regulations would be completed. The Local Self-government Section at the ministry, recognizing the need for local action, knew that information had to be disseminated first. Citing the examples of foreign countries, in which study societies were often formed in periods of preparation for new policies, provincial officials were requested, based on local conditions, to establish local self-government schools at the provincial capital. Students from every county in the province were to be sent to the school to study local self-government systems of foreign countries and also to study law. Afterward they were to return to their counties and establish lecture halls *(jiangxi suo)*. See MZB, 162.

13. *Chengdu ribao,* GX34/9/13; and *SMMS*, p. 256.

14. *SMMS*, p. 644.

15. Lu Hsun [Lu Xun], *A Brief History of Chinese Fiction* (Peking: Foreign Languages Press, 1959), pp. 372–388.

16. *DFZZ* 5.3:*neiwu* 163–167 (GX34).

17. XZBCG, Box 50; and XZBCG, Box 44.
18. See Min Tu-ki, pp. 155–157.
19. *Guangdong xianzheng choubeichu baogaoshu*, no. 1, xianzheng 1–2b.
20. *Henan quansheng ziyiju choubanchu diyici baogaoshu*, pp. 56–57b and 62–63b. This description of election managers was taken from Guangxi No. 1 (see Appendix B).
21. Zhang Zhidong telegram GX32/11/18.
22. Provincial governors and even county magistrates had been establishing "bureaus" for decades, appointing expectant officials and even degree-holders to bureaus instituted to aid, in a quasi-official manner, administration. An old China hand of the nineteenth century, William Frederick Mayers, saw these deputies *(weiyuan)* as being engaged in a "variety of forms of temporary employment, in connection with the judicial or revenue administration or upon special missions." See Mayers, p. 127; and *PDPOC*, entry 859. See also Perdue, pp. 193–196. Marianne Bastid has argued that these positions allowed experts on developments and institutions outside China's borders to be incorporated in the bureaucracy. These men were charged with specific tasks related to their areas of expertise. Bastid traced this to the era of the Taiping Rebellion, when provincial officials formed private advisory boards to deal with suppression efforts and with foreigners. The use of *weiyuan* was pioneered by Li Hongzhang, Zeng Guofan, and Zhang Zhidong. Often these deputies were active in specialized bureaus or agencies with specific responsibilities, such as administering the lijin tax, managing arsenals, or undertaking industrial enterprises. The significance of these bureaus *(ju)* and the deputies *(weiyuan)* who staffed them, according to Bastid, was that they made "room for a degree of expertise in administration" and served "as a principal channel between the old scholar elite and a new professional elite." See Bastid-Bruguiere, p. 560. See also Elvin, "The Administration of Shanghai," pp. 245–246; and Fincher, p. 139. Esherick and Rankin, in their summary of recent scholarship, conclude that since the late sixteenth century "local elites gradually established a public sphere for their activities in philanthropy, education, local defense, water control, public works, fiscal affairs and, in the twentieth century, in professional associations, journalism, political organization, economic development, and local self-government." See Esherick and Rankin, p. 340. See also Rankin, "The Origins of a Chinese Public Sphere."

23. Shi Fujin memorial GX32/12/12.
24. For a list of the forty-two members of the commission see *Xinhai geming*, IV, 18.
25. Telegram GX32/9/19.
26. Zhang Zhidong telegram GX32/11/18. For Zhang the men in bureaus and offices were neither arrogant nor did they arrogate the powers of government. See also Bays, pp. 200–202.
27. *Fazheng guanhua bao*, no. 13 (GX33/8):18a–b.
28. Edict GX33/9/13; and Min Tu-ki, pp. 153–154. See Chapter Three above for a discussion of Anhui's attempt in 1907 to establish a *ziyiju*.
29. A memorial from Anhui in early 1909 discussed the Constitutional Commission's request that the consultative bureaus *(ziyiju)* be restyled provincial assembly preparation offices *(ziyiju choubanchu)*. See ZZGB, GX34/12/20. For studies of provincial assemblies see Zhang Pengyuan; Fincher; and Min Tu-ki, pp. 137–179. For Beijing's regulations see Constitutional Commission memorial and regulations GX34/6/24.
30. One scholar of the Qing provincial assemblies, Zhang Pengyuan, identified almost one hundred returned students, and suspects there were more, among the rosters of assemblymen. Every assembly, except the ones in Jilin, Heilongjiang, and Gansu, had at least one returned student. See Zhang Pengyuan, pp. 28 and 248–320. Zhang (p. 13) gives a total of 1,643 assemblymen that were called for in the election regulations.
31. Ministry of Foreign Affairs memorial GX29/7/19.
32. Ge Gongzhen, p. 74.
33. Ge Gongzhen (p. 64) gives these titles: *Anhui guanbao, Hubei guanbao,* and *Jiangxi guanbao.* Planning for the Shanxi gazette *Jinbao* began on 4 August 1902 according to a directive from the provincial yamen dated 10 December 1902. See Zhao Papers, Box 31. See Appendix A for additional references as well as citations for *Hunan guanbao, Nanyang guanbao, Sichuan guanbao, Guangdong gongbao, Shandong guanbao, Guangxi guanbao,* and *Henan guanbao.*
34. Ge Gongzhen, p. 67. These metropolitan gazettes were *Shangwu guanbao* and *Xuebu guanbao.* For a listing of the table of contents of these gazettes, both of which have been reprinted, see ZGJD, II, 1764–1831 and 1849–1908.
35. See Appendix A for titles of the self-government gazettes and compilations issued by government authorities in Fengtian, Guizhou, Henan, Hunan, Jiangsu, Jiangxi, Jilin, Shandong, Shanxi, Yunnan,

Zhejiang, and Zhili. The Jilin self-government gazette *Zizhi ribao* was published in runs, reportedly, of approximately 1,500 copies. Distribution figures during the fall of 1909 include thirty copies sent to other publications throughout China, eighty-four to individual persons, forty-eight to Fengtian, fifty to Heilongjiang, and five hundred eighty to Jilin. See *Jilin quansheng difang zizhi choubanchu diyici baogaoshu*, no. 1. In addition to the specialized gazettes concerning local self-government discussed above, there were provincial publications focussing on topics like education or commerce. For an indication of the type of information to be found in these publications, see the table of contents for specialized gazettes issued by provincial authorities in Sichuan, Zhili, and Jiangsu in *ZGJD*, II, 1615–1669, 1743–1753, and 1909–1929. None of the general provincial gazettes are included in this reference work. For a discussion of the gazette for Sichuan, *Sichuan guanbao*, see *Xinhai geming shiqi qikan jieshao*, III, 220–226.

36. A precursor to *Hunan guanbao* was the short-lived *Xiangbao*, published daily from March to October in 1898. Edited by Tan Sitong and Tang Caichang in Changsha, *Xiangbao* was published by the Nanxue hui. See *ZGJD*, I, 1079–1100 for a brief introduction and the table of contents of each issue.

37. See Chen Tianhua, *Chen Tianhua ji* (Works of Chen Tianhua) (Changsha: Hunan renmin chubanshe, 1958), pp. 14–18. Chen's distaste for *Hunan guanbao* should be interpreted on at least two levels. Chen is arguing that a government-sponsored publication could never achieve the proper goals of a private newspaper. But Chen's diatribe is also part of an ongoing political struggle pitting Chen and his fellow Hunan expatriates against powerful conservatives in Hunan like Wang Xianqian and Ye Dehui, both of whom were mentioned in this critique.

38. See Zhang Pengyuan, *Zhongguo xiandaihua de quyu yanjiu: Hunan sheng, 1860–1916* (A regional study of modernization in China: Hunan province, 1860–1916) (Taibei: Zhongyang yanjiuyuan jindaishi yanjiusuo, 1983), pp. 318–319; Charlton M. Lewis, *Prologue to the Chinese Revolution: The Transformation of Ideas and Institutions in Hunan Province, 1891–1907* (Cambridge: East Asian Research Center, Harvard University, 1976), pp. 145–146; Zhang Jinglu, pp. 425–426. A British consular report filed in 1906 stated that ownership of the paper was in the hands of the provincial government.

39. The gazettes published in Beijing were referred to by a number of titles and usually rendered in English as *Peking Gazette*. See Ocko.

40. Britton, pp. 89 and 109. Andrew Nathan, in his interpretation of the evolution of government gazette publishing, describes government attitudes toward gazettes that changed from disapproval to approval. Nathan argues that the government's attitude toward gazettes moved from disdain in 1851, when the Xianfeng Emperor rejected a proposal for a government gazette, "to official sponsorship and finally to reliance upon gazettes to give force to the law." See Nathan, p. 1292. For a slightly different version of this essay see Leo Ou-fan Lee and Andrew Nathan.
41. Ge Gongzhen, p. 74; Fang Hanqi, p. 605.
42. Nathan has speculated that the "pro-reform officials and organizations which sponsored the gazettes apparently hoped to entrench themselves against political opposition from conservatives by creating a constituency for their reform programs both throughout the bureaucracy and also among the attentive public." See Nathan, p. 1292.
43. Ye Longyan, p. 154. The regulations for the Zhili Law School were recommended as a model on 26 June 1906. See Ye Longyan, p. 55; and Guo Tingyi, p. 1254.
44. The Jiangsu Law School (Susheng fazheng xuetang) was established in early 1906 but soon experienced fiscal problems. Zhang Jian, acting as a member of the Provincial Educational Association (Zong xuehui), asked the governor-general in late summer to allow the educational association to establish a lecture hall on law and administration (*fazheng jiangxi suo*), so that nonofficials could have access to some of these new ideas. See *DFZZ* 3.7:*jiaoyu* 175 (GX32); and *STSB*, GX32/7/10 and GX32/7/25.
45. See Ye Longyan, pp. 60, 393–394. As late as 16 December 1907 the Constitutional Commission was still urging provinces without schools to establish them within three months. See ibid., p. 60.
46. For a report on the opening of the school, with a list of students grouped by prefecture, see *Chengdu ribao*, GX34/9/13, pp. 3–4.
47. Memorial GX33/1/20. See also Zhang Dafu, "Qingmo 'Weixin bianfa' zai Chengdu" (The late-Qing reform movement in Chengdu), *Chengdu wenshi ziliao xuanji* (Selections of historical and cultural materials concerning Chengdu), no. 4:109 (1983). The government monopoly on law schools in Chengdu would not last long. For example, two privately run law schools were established in Chengdu in 1910. These schools included returned students from Japan among their founders. See ibid., p. 113. According to the Sichuan newspaper *Shubao*, by 1911 there were eleven private law schools in Chengdu, with between one hundred and six hundred

students each. I thank Ms. Kristin Stapleton for sharing this research finding with me.

48. Zhao Papers, Box 468.

49. Regulations GX34/5/17. According to Wang Di, there were fourteen, twenty-two, and thirty-five Sichuanese students at Hosei University in 1904, 1905, and 1906, respectively. See Wang Di, p. 83. My thanks to Ms. Kristin Stapleton for bringing this article to my attention, as well as for kindly furnishing a copy.

50. *SMMS*, pp. 256 and 644.

51. The ages of these persons are available, with the median age of the students from the self-government school older than those students from the law school. All but six of the law school students were under the age of 40 *sui*, whereas sixteen of the sixty self-government school students were over the age of 40 *sui*. See *Sichuan ziyiju choubanchu diyici baogaoshu*, pp. 35–43.

52. Regulations GX34/9/26.

53. Hubei No. 1 (see Appendix B). According to an item from *Zhongwai ribao*, the schools for nurturing citizens were established to train people to staff local criminal justice institutions. See *Chengdu ribao*, GX34/11/15, p. 2. However, an item in *Chengdu ribao*, XT1/1/20, p. 3, reprinted from *Xinglun ribao*, states that this school, which was opened June 1908 with students from Wuchang and Hanyang, was composed of students who were expected to return to rural areas *(xiangcun)* after their graduation to give lectures, make investigations, and attend to self-government organizations *(zizhi tuanti)*. See Su Yunfeng, p. 333 for enrollment figures.

54. Shen Huaiyu, pp. 313–314. For the regulations see Zhao Papers, Box 216.

55. Hubei No. 1 (see Appendix B); *Macheng xianzhi xubian*, 9.8b–9.

56. *Jilin xingsheng Binzhou fu zhengshu, yibian*, p. 10.

57. Ibid., *dingbian*, pp. 9–10. See also *SMMS*, p. 168.

58. *Nongan xian baogaoshu*, p. 72.

59. *Jilin xingsheng Binzhou fu zhengshu, yibian*, p. 10.

60. See ibid., pp. 10 and 189; ibid., *dingbian*, p. 1. Sometime in April or May a call went out for one or two students to be sent from each of the twenty districts *(qu)*. A month later these students began their studies. Eight months later, thirty-nine students and eight auditors took the final exams.

61. See *Jilin xingsheng Binzhou fu zhengshu, yibian*, pp. 38–40.

62. Ibid., *bingbian*, p. 61.

63. See, for example, Cen Chunxuan memorial GX33/4/13. See also Min Tu-ki, pp. 137–153.

64. Zhang's perspective could be found at the lowest levels of the administrative structure. In the 1891 gazetteer for Baling county, in northeastern Hunan, the militia bureau was given as an example of official supervision and gentry management *(guandu shenban)*. See Kuhn, *Rebellion and Its Enemies*, p. 62.
65. Regulations GX34/12/27, Article 5, Section 8.

## 6. LOCAL COUNCILS IN CHINA

1. Fincher, pp. 104 and 109–116; Cameron, p. 124.
2. The local self-government regulations drafted by the Ministry of Interior were reviewed by the Constitutional Commission, but during implementation, the Ministry of Interior was the responsible agency in Beijing. A record book of documents that were sent out in 1910 by the Constitutional Commission identifies each of the 617 documents by a subject category. Only thirteen documents concerned self-government. Of those, all but one (to Shandong) were sent on to the Ministry of Interior or other metropolitan offices. See XZBCG, Box 100. In general the Constitutional Commission deferred to the Ministry of Interior except in cases involving both provincial assemblies and local self-government organizations and in cases where an implementation schedule was being revised. See, for example, *Jilin guanbao,* XT2.12:*guandian lei* 3–4b, where a query about electoral requirements from Shandong to the Constitutional Commission was forwarded for action to the Ministry of Interior.
3. Ministry of Interior implementation schedule XT1/inter.2/23. The Constitutional Commission's original schedule was promulgated in August 1908. See Edict and implementation schedule GX34/8/1.
4. Zhao Erxun memorial XT1/4.
5. National regulations for local self-government schools were promulgated in May 1909. See Regulations XT1/3/16.
6. Jiangsu-Su No. 2 (see Appendix B).
7. MZB, 189.1.
8. ZZGB, XT1/8/13.
9. Jiangsu-Su No. 3 (see Appendix B).
10. Jiangsu-Su No. 4 (see Appendix B).
11. A Ministry of Interior memorial rescripted on 29 January 1911 mentioned memorials from provincial officials in Yunnan, Hubei, Shandong, and Guangxi, who were complaining that it was hard enough to implement the regulations at one level, let alone several. See Ministry of Interior memorial XT 2/12/27.

12. "Fu ting zhou xian difang zizhi zhangcheng" (Regulations for local self-government in prefectures, subprefectures, departments, and counties). See Regulations XT1/12/27.

13. Sun Baoqi memorial XT2/5/6.

14. This information is drawn from a document submitted by the governor of Guangxi, dated 19 May 1911, to the Ministry of Interior, which includes a long quote from the July 1910 directive from the Ministry of Interior. See MZB, 204.

15. Li Jingxi memorial XT2/11/1. A Grand Council copy of the memorial sent to the Ministry of Interior is in MZB, 207. Li Jingxi's copy to the Ministry of Interior is dated 28 October 1910.

16. XZBCG, Box 12.

17. See Wang Jiajian, pp. 211–212. Wang exaggerates the degree of opposition to this proposal. In the *Zhengyi tongbao* report Wang relied upon, four officials were identified as opponents of the proposed reforms, but only the Sichuan governor Xiliang adamantly opposed the idea. See *ZYCS* 6:*zhengzhi tubiao* 1:1–3 (GX33). See also *North China Herald*, 25 January 1907, pp. 175–177. These responses were summarized and forwarded to the court. See Memorial GX33/5/27. For full texts of these telegraphic responses see *STSB*, GX32/11/6, 7, 8, 10, 12, 13, 17, 21, 22, 24, 25, 26, 27, and 28 and GX32/12/2, 3, 4, 5, 6, 7. For an example of how these responses affected policy making in Beijing see a memorandum *(shuotie)* by the Compilation Commission published in *DFZZ* 4.8:*neiwu* 416–423 (GX33).

18. Edict XT2/10/3. See also Fincher, pp. 147–149 and 169–170.

19. Edict XT2/12/17. This revised schedule, submitted along with a memorial rescripted on 17 January 1911, which was not as detailed as the 1908 version, called for the convocation of a parliament in 1913 and continued implementation of local self-government reforms.

20. Ministry of Interior memorial XT2/12/27.

21. Ibid; MZB, 132.

22. XZBCG, Box 13. A similar argument had been made in Tianjin during preparations in 1906–1907 for council elections. Bureau member Wu Xingrang thought there was sufficient precedent in the funding of local charities and public projects. But Wu realized that fiscal capabilities of counties would influence the scope and speed of reform implementation. See Wu Xingrang, pp. 16–17.

23. Zhu Jiabao memorial XT3/3/18.

24. *Shandong quansheng difang zizhi choubanchu disanci baogaoshu*, pp. 78–81b. The August figures are taken from a manuscript in the library of the Institute of Modern History in Beijing. Based on the

physical characteristics of this document, I suspect that this county-by-county election record was originally sent to the Ministry of Interior. The manuscript is entitled "Shandong sheng Zhangqiu dengchu qishi zhou xian choushe yishihui canshihui chengji biao." See MZB, 181 for references to comparable documents that had been sent to Beijing from Shandong. A summary of the information in this manuscript can be found in Shandong No. 6 (see Appendix B).

25. See Zhili No. 4, No. 5, No. 6 (see Appendix B).
26. Information on these institutional transitions can be found in numerous provincial reports filed in early 1909. See citations in Appendix B for memorials from the first reporting period (GX34/8–GX34/12).
27. *Guangdong xianzheng choubeichu baogaoshu*, no. 2, *minzheng 6–8*.
28. Guangdong No. 3; and Constitutional Commission No. 3 (see Appendix B).
29. Guangdong No. 3 and No. 4 (see Appendix B).
30. A table published in *Guangdong xianzheng choubeichu baogaoshu*, no. 7 summarized eighteen months of activity (1909 and the first half of 1910).
31. Bland, pp. 127–128 and 130. In fact, the returned students who dominated policy making in the Constitutional Commission were not really concerned about the "masses of China." Although they did not, as Bland asserts, draft local self-government regulations—that was the responsibility of the Ministry of Interior—the commission did draft the regulations for the provincial assembly elections that took place in 1909. But they only reviewed and amended the draft of local self-government regulations sent over by the Ministry of Interior in August 1908.
32. Fincher, pp. 17–18. See also pp. 231–232.
33. *PDPOC*, entry 160.
34. Fujian No. 4 (see Appendix B).
35. Beijing, however, did occasionally cashier officials who were dilatory in implementing reform measures. See Constitutional Commission memorial XT2/11/13 and *North China Herald*, 23 December 1910. The Shanghai newspaper chose to accentuate the negative, publishing the list of officials who were being cashiered. The names of the officials, including Li Shuen, praised in this memorial were not, however, included in this translation.
36. A convenient documentary compilation of violence recorded in the late Qing, arranged by province, can be found in *Xinhai geming*, III, 367–536. See also *Xinhai geming qianshinianjian minbian*

*dang'an shiliao.* For a survey of violence in Jiangxi in 1904–1911 see Sheel, pp. 116–126.

37. See Roxann Prazniak, "Tax Protests at Laiyang, Shandong, 1910: Commoner Organization Versus the County Political Elite," *Modern China* 6 (1980):41–71.

38. See Ma.

39. Shandong No. 5 (see Appendix B).

40. Compare Wang Shuhuai, pp. 319–320 with Jiangsu-Ning No. 5 (see Appendix B).

41. See Zhejiang No. 4 and No. 5 (see Appendix B).

42. *North China Herald,* 4 December 1909, p. 525. Keith Schoppa's study of late-Qing initiatives in Zhejiang, based on newspapers like *Shibao* and gazetteers, does not mention any more placenames than do provincial reports. See Schoppa. Newspapers give a better sense of the drama of contested reforms in specific areas, but provincial reports are far better sources for assessing the range of reform initiatives.

43. Constitutional Commission No. 5 (see Appendix B).

44. *North China Herald,* 8 July 1911, p. 96.

45. The investigation teams were dispatched in the spring of 1910 to Heilongjiang, Jilin, Fengtian, Zhili, Shandong, Shanxi, Henan, Hubei, Jiangxi, Anhui, Jiangsu, Zhejiang, Fujian, and Guangdong. See Constitutional Commission memorial XT2/11/13; and Liu Ruxi, p. 196. For the preparations taken by Jilin officials in anticipation of Lu Zongyu's investigation mission, which was reportedly leaving Beijing in June 1910, see *Jilin guanbao,* XT2.12: *gongdu lei* 1a-b and XT2.13: *shishi lei* 1.

46. See MZB, 132. Although Guangxi No. 4 did report the sixty-two figure, Guangxi No. 5 stated that there had been graduating classes in thirty-six schools. Thus, on the basis of internal evidence alone, the "sixty-two" figure becomes suspect. See Appendix B.

47. MZB, 189.2. These namelists of council and board members in administrative seats reached the ministry on 7 January 1911. Over two hundred additional names of men associated with local self-government bodies in ten townships in southern Jiangsu arrived on 21 April 1911.

48. MZB, 132.

49. *Shibao,* XT2/5/24 and XT2/9/17; *DFZZ* 7.1 and 7.2; and Wang Shuhuai, p. 314. Similar correlations between press accounts and provincial reporting can be found elsewhere. Beijing's *Shuntian shibao,* which provides excellent coverage for Zhili, Henan, and Shanxi, also reported on implementation in Shandong, Jilin, Hei-

longjiang, Hunan, Hubei, Jiangsu, and Guangdong. In a survey of issues published between September 1908 and May 1910 I found well over one hundred items about self-government implementation. Coverage of Beijing and Tianjin is especially detailed.

50. *Jiading xian xuzhi*, 6.10–11b. Information on the township name-lists submitted by provincial authorities in Suzhou to the Ministry of Interior also corresponds to records in Jiading's gazetteer. The preparation office established by permission on 10 January 1910 for Ximen township was responsible for actions leading to the council elections that were held by June 1910. The names of the eight council members were included in a namelist that arrived in Beijing on 21 April 1911. See *Jiading xian xuzhi*, 6.10; Jiangsu-Su No. 2 (see Appendix B); Jiangsu-Su No. 4 (see Appendix B); and MZB, 189.2. The editors of the Jiading gazetteer, which was published in 1930, noted, as did provincial and metropolitan officials in 1909–1910, that implementation in Ximen occurred ahead of schedule. See *Jiading xian xuzhi*, 6.4b.

51. *[GuangXuan] YiJing xuzhi*, 5.10.

52. See Elvin, "Gentry Democracy"; Ma; Schoppa; Wang Shuhuai; and Zhang Yufa, "Qingmo minchu de Shandong difang zizhi."

53. Zhang Yufa, "Qingmo minchu de Shandong difang zizhi," pp. 178–180. Zhang was able to document councils in only fourteen administrative seats, four towns, and fourteen townships. In at least one case, Zhang's gazetteer data correspond exactly with information compiled by Shandong officials. In the Shandong Provincial Local Self-government Preparation Office's periodic report for 5 August 1910–29 January 1911 a council in Jinxiang's county seat was noted to have been established in December 1910. See *Shandong quansheng difang zizhi choubanchu disanci baogaoshu*, p. 119.

54. Wang Shuhuai's study of local self-government implementation in Jiangsu relies almost entirely on provincial reports, which he uses without reference to Beijing's skepticism. Although Wang did use gazetteers, he only used them to document county council establishment in nine areas. See Wang Shuhuai, p. 315.

55. *PDPOC*, entry 846. The following figures, for 1910, are given in this source: counties *(xian)*, 1381; departments *(zhou)*, 139; independent departments *(zhili zhou)*, 75; subprefectures *(ting)*, 57; and independent subprefectures *(zhili ting)*, 54.

56. Provincial reporting and metropolitan guidance were disseminated throughout China in government gazettes like *Zhengzhi guanbao* and in private periodicals like *Dongfang zazhi*. For example, provincial officials responded to an 8 April 1910 request by the Ministry of Interior to report on local self-government implementation.

Within a month reports on all parts of China had been received and published in the 7 May 1910 issue of *Zhengzhi guanbao*, which was distributed throughout China. Furthermore, many of these reports were also published in the June 1910 issue of *Dongfang zazhi*, which included forty-three pages of provincial reporting on reform implementation. Information on mapping activities, especially problems concerned with interpretation of the regulations, is discussed in these telegraphic exchanges between provincial authorities and the Ministry of Interior. See *DFZZ* 7.4:*lunshuo* 108–123 (XT2).

57. A similar publication issued by the Constitutional Commission was used extensively by John Fincher in his study of provincial assemblies in *Chinese Democracy* (p. 150n9). I have not been able to estimate the total number of exchanges between the Ministry of Interior and the provinces; the *Collected Explications* contains 295 documents in its 160 pages. This must have been a selection, for we know that the Constitutional Commission, in one four-month period (24 September 1909–11 January 1910), received over one thousand communications from metropolitan bureaus and provincial officials. See XZBCG, Box 100.

58. *Difang zizhi zhangcheng jieshi huichao, dianwen* 31b.

59. Ibid., 31b–35. For copies of two maps for Suihua prefecture, Heilongjiang, see MZB, 177.

60. *Difang zizhi zhangcheng jieshi huichao, dianwen* 19b–20.

61. Ibid., 52b–53. There is some evidence about how these problems were solved. In Heilongjiang's Suihua prefecture three *xiang* located east of the prefectural seat had populations ranging from 32,000 to 44,000; in Fengtian's Chengde county, the head district of Fengtian prefecture, there were twenty-two *xiang* with a median thirty villages *(tun)* per *xiang* and populations ranging from 10,000 to 21,000; in Jiading, near Shanghai in Jiangsu province, the county's thirty-three *xiang* registered population figures between 2,001 and 17,514, with a median of 5,688; and in Sichuan's Taiping county the population of 152,000 persons was divided among the county seat and nine *xiang*. See MZB, 177 and 172; *Jiading xian xuzhi*, 6.6b–8b; and "Sichuan Suiding fu Taiping xian cheng zhen xiang difang zizhi quyu biao" (Table of local self-government districts for the administrative seat, towns, and townships in Taiping county, Suiding prefecture, Sichuan). This Sichuan manuscript is held by the Beijing National Library.

62. Local Self-government Regulations GX34/12/27, Article 3; subsequent references to these regulations will be noted only parenthetically in the text.

63. Schoppa, p. 81.

64. Local Self-government Election Regulations GX34/12/27, Article 81.
65. *Difang zizhi zhangcheng jieshi huichao, dianwen* 29a–b; see also ibid., 42b–43b for an exchange with Jilin.
66. Schoppa, p. 82.
67. Ibid., p. 81.
68. *Jiading xian xuzhi*, 6.3b–4b and 6.10–11b.
69. Eleven other counties beside Wujin and Yanghu in the lower Yangtze shared county seats, an administrative feature instituted in 1724. See Ch'ü T'ung-tsu, p. 201n5. Skinner (p. 344) states that the empirewide number of cities with such joint jurisdictions was twenty-four.
70. *Guofeng bao* 1.5 (XT2):22.
71. *Difang zizhi zhangcheng jieshi huichao, dianwen* 5, 21, and 2a–b.
72. Ibid., 21a–b (XT2/2/24).
73. Ibid., 23b–24.
74. Ibid., 12–13 and 22b–23b.
75. Ibid., 10b–11.
76. *Difang zizhi zhangcheng jieshi huichao, zilei* 6b–7. This recapitulated an exchange that began with Zhao Erxun's query of 20 December 1909 that arrived in Beijing on 15 January 1910. The Ministry of Interior telegraphed its clarification to Chengdu on 22 January 1910. See MZB, 205.
77. *Difang zizhi zhangcheng jieshi huichao, dianwen* 7a–b; 7b–8; and 52b–53.
78. The Zhejiang Local Self-government Preparation Office had discussed the Manchu garrison problem in a 9 August 1909 report to the governor. A Manchu Self-government Society had been established and regulations promulgated in November 1908. In his query to the Ministry of Interior the Mongol governor Zengyun argued that the Manchu population should not become part of the common electorate of Hangzhou. See MZB, 191.
79. MZB, 205.
80. It is beyond the scope of this study to consider the actions of thousands of councils established by late 1911, but Keith Schoppa did attempt such a study for Zhejiang, using gazetteers and newspaper accounts. For Zhejiang's seventy-five counties Schoppa was able to use about a dozen gazetteers. With this data Schoppa made the following observations: In inner-core areas (twenty counties with major cities and towns) episodes differed and the loss of social control varied, but there is evidence that events were linked in part to networks reaching to other parts of China. In the outer three zones

(the remaining fifty-five counties in Schoppa's four categories of inner-core, inner-periphery, outer-core, and outer-periphery), limited data showed that "the revolutionary denouement was the seizure of the local political scene by old-line military types, opportunistic bandits, or obstreperous local militia companies. The other common revolutionary outcome . . . was social chaos that sometimes lasted more than half a year." Schoppa's general observation for all of Zhejiang: "[T]he revolutionary spasms of social disorder and confusion rapidly spent themselves and stimulated only great elite concern for stability and, in cases, the greater solidification of the oligarchical control of county elites." See Schoppa, pp. 151, 153, and 156. For a discussion of local elite strategies in Guizhou during the 1911 Revolution see Edward A. McCord, "Local Military Power and Elite Formation: The Liu Family of Xingyi County, Guizhou," in Esherick and Rankin, pp. 180–184.

81. See Esherick, pp. 177–189 and Fung, pp. 195–210.
82. For Duanfang's death see Hummel, II, 781. For narratives of the 1911 Revolution see Esherick, pp. 189–215; and Fung, pp. 210–229. See also *Xinhai geming shi;* and Wright.
83. *Jiading xian xuzhi,* 6.4, 6.12, and 6.12b.
84. Ibid., 6.12.
85. For a discussion of militia connections to local self-government personnel in Zhejiang see Schoppa, pp. 153–154.
86. *Jiading xian xuzhi, gaige jilue* 1; and *Zhonghua minguo kaiguo wushinian wenxian* (Documents concerning the fifty years since the founding of the Republic of China) (Taibei: Zhonghua minguo kaiguo wushinian wenxian bianzuan weiyuanhui, 1961–1965), II:3, 493–494. This declaration may have spared Jiading from destructive civil war; for that same day a force of forty soldiers from Wusong fort, about fifteen miles from Jiading city, arrived in town. But they merely billeted in the city, and left several days later.
87. *Jiading xian xuzhi, gaige jilue* 2b–3.
88. Liu Ruxi, pp. 34–59; and Boorman, III, 301–302.

### 7. QING POLICY, RURAL CHINA, AND ELITE FACTIONS IN THE AGE OF CONSTITUTIONALISM

1. A description of local administration presented in a memorial by the Ministry of Interior submitted in 1907 placed managers *(dong)* in market towns and villages. See Ministry of Interior memorial GX33/2/13. A few months earlier planners in Tianjin sought gentry-managers in rural areas who influenced local opinion. See Chap-

ter Two, p. 47. Suzhou activists also sought managers who lived outside the city. See Chapter Three, p. 61.

2. See Kuhn, *Rebellion and Its Enemies,* pp. 223–224. Ideas similar to Kuhn's can be found in work by Joseph W. Esherick. His "urban reformist elite" lived in large provincial cities and possessed allies among the local elites in outlying towns and small cities, especially prefectural capitals. This "subordinate reformist elite," then, was part of the "elite revolution" of 1911. See Esherick, pp. 109–110 and 212–215. A "rural elite" is not to be found. Esherick does mention the "local gentry" and how their power increased in the post-1911 period, but he supposes that the activists within the local gentry were "probably members of the urban elite, with rather specific class interests of their own and little contact or sympathy with the peasantry" (p. 251).

3. Min Tu-ki, p. 160.

4. Fincher, p. 111.

5. Min Tu-ki, p. 168.

6. Neither Min Tu-ki nor the other foremost scholars of provincial assemblies, Zhang Pengyuan and John Fincher, found any electoral rolls. See Zhang Pengyuan, pp. 14–17; Fincher, pp. 108–111; and Min Tu-ki, pp. 157–158. Fincher declared that "not even partial rolls of voter or elector names have themselves come to light for any locality except Guangzhou [Canton]." See Fincher, p. 109. The situation would appear even bleaker, for Fincher's claim for the Canton society is incorrect. Fincher states that *Guangdong difang zizhi yanjiushe chouzhenchu baogaoshu* identifies "members of the electorate behind the members of local self-government institutions." See Fincher, p. 250n47. This society had members who were active in the affairs of constitutionalism and local self-government, but it was a private body entirely unrelated to government-sponsored reforms. Fincher argues that the thousands of persons listed "were prepared to contribute funds regularly to the self-government movement" (p. 238). In my reading of the Toyo bunko copy of this document, we have instead a record of contributions for disaster relief in Guangdong, an effort which is glossed in the preface as an example of "local self-government" *(difang zizhi).* See Chapter Three, note 52 for a discussion of the parent Guangdong self-government society's founding in 1907.

7. XZBCG, Box 25. Other rolls for provincial assembly elections can be found in *Shuntian shibao*'s coverage during the spring and summer of 1909. See, for example, the county-by-county listing of per-

sons who participated in the second stage of assembly elections in Jiangsu published in *STSB*, XT1/inter.2/20, 21, 23–28.

8. *Fengtian zizhi chouban fangfa*, no. 1 (XT2/2):13–14b. This was published periodically by the Fengtian Provincial Self-government Preparation Office. The first issue appeared in March 1910. Issues no. 1 (XT2/2) and no. 2 (XT2/8) are available at the Beijing University Library. Issue no. 3 (XT3/2) can be found in MZB, 172.

9. *Jiading xian xuzhi*, 6.1b, 6.15b, 6.8, and 6.12.

10. Zhang Pengyuan, pp. 266–270. Zhang's list of assemblymen used the Qing dynasty county name for Xunwu (Changning).

11. Fincher, p. 128.

12. Illiteracy *(bushi wenzi)* was one of the possible reasons for disqualification mentioned in Article 16 of the 1909 self-government regulations. There were ongoing efforts to address this problem, such as establishing literacy schools for adults. See *QMCB*, II, 1008–1011 for two memorials on this subject. A member of Yuan Shikai's entourage, Lao Naixuan, who became a member of the Constitutional Commission on 4 January 1909, was involved in drafting a memorial in late 1909 that specifically discussed the relationship of literacy, voting qualifications, and local self-government. See Lao Naixuan, *Qing Lao Rensou xiansheng Naixuan ziding nianpu* (Lao Naixuan's chronological autobiography), ed. Wang Yunwu (Taibei: Taiwan shangwu yinshuguan, 1978), p. 43. See also *STSB*, GX34/8/4 and GX34/8/6 for information on Lao's efforts in 1908 to bring China's literacy problems to the attention of the court.

   The government had been taking steps to address this problem since at least 1903, when vernacular *(baihua)* gazettes began to appear. These publications, whose messages were intended to be read by those with moderate reading skills and read aloud to others, became more and more popular in the late Qing. On 2 April 1903 the Shanxi governor approved a request to publish a vernacular gazette that would be entitled *Shanxi baihua yanshuobao*. See Zhao Papers, Box 33. A vernacular gazette in Hunan, entitled *Hunan tongsu yanshuobao*, was first published in May 1903, presumably in Changsha. For the table of contents of seven issues dating from 1903 see *ZGJD*, II, 1097–1102. A copy of the sixth issue, published in July 1903, can be found in Zhao Papers, Box 54. Draft versions of articles for this gazette can be found in Zhao Papers, Box 55. In a major compilation of the tables of contents of periodicals published between 1857 and 1911 there are nineteen titles which include the characters for *baihua*. See the table of contents for periodicals published in 1898, 1901, 1903–1906, 1908, and 1910 in *ZGJD*. For a list of 119 titles of vernacular periodicals published in 1897–1911, see *Xinhai geming shiqi qikan jieshao*, V, 494–538. This provided the foundation, whether acknowledged or not, for the vernacular movement in the early Republican period associated with returned students like Hu Shi.

13. Jin Bangping, discussing this issue in Tianjin in 1906, insisted that a key element in a constitutional government was the participation of all people in governing *(canyu zhengzhi)*. Jin suggested that local self-government would start with the election of subcounty *(xiang)* assemblies. After people became familiar with these new institutions, there would be a basis for a county assembly, and finally a parliament. See *Fazheng guanhua bao*, no. 1 (GX32/8):6–9.

14. Wu Xingrang, pp. 19–20.

15. *Difang zizhi zhangcheng jieshi huichao, dianwen* 49b–50b and 29a–b.

16. For the references to Heilongjiang, Fengtian, and Sichuan see MZB, 177 and 172; and "Sichuan Suiding fu Taiping xian cheng zhen xiang difang zizhi quyu biao." For Jiading see *Jiading xian xuzhi*, 6.8b–10.

17. For the 1910 parliamentary movement see Zhang Pengyuan, pp. 63–104; and Fincher, pp. 147–149. For studies of the railway rights recovery movement in the lower Yangtze see Min Tu-ki, pp. 181–218; and Rankin, *Elite Activism*, pp. 248–298. For data on the movement in Sichuan, see Wei Yingtao, *Sichuan baolu yundong shi* (A history of the protection movement in Sichuan) (Chengdu: Sichuan renmin chubanshe, 1981).

    The provincial activists at the center of Fincher's study, for example, saw their challenge to central authorities as one that was "local." But it is unfair to activists at the county and subcounty levels to subordinate them to provincial activists. These truly local activists could often have other ideas, ones that sometimes caused them to look to the imperial center for support. Clearly, they saw advantages in having a patron in Beijing. This was a strand of activity that Fincher's sources did not allow him to explore.

18. Kuhn, *Rebellion and Its Enemies*, p. 4.

19. Work by Watson, Duara, and Averill in Esherick and Rankin, pp. 239–304 discusses elite power and activities in rural areas. But the remaining essays in this conference volume, entitled *Chinese Local Elites and Patterns of Dominance*, explore the world of county and market-town urban elites defined in terms of degree-holding or functional roles in commerce or local security.

This affects one's reading of past scholarship on the self-government movement. For example, Kuhn's use of "rural elite" interchangeably with "local elite" in separate discussions of how the self-government policy legitimized or formalized customary powers obscures the inherent divisiveness of this policy within local elite society and focusses instead on tensions between center and locality. See Kuhn, *Rebellion and Its Enemies*, p. 217; and "Local Self-government," p. 280.

Even Mao Zedong, the peasant revolutionary, remained focussed on the county elite of Jiangxi's Xunwu county in his most detailed local investigation, which was done in 1930. In his analysis of elite definition and transformation, Mao noted that four of the powerful "Five Tigers" who were being pushed off the political stage by civil war and revolution were Qing degree-holders. See Mao Zedong, p. 142. Two of these men, Pan Mingdian (p. 138) and Peng Zijing (p. 146), were among the more than one hundred noteworthy large and middle landlords profiled by Mao (pp. 132–148).

20. Constitutional Commission memorial GX34/4/26.
21. See Roger R. Thompson, "Twilight of the Gods in the Chinese Countryside: Christians, Confucians, and the Modernizing State, 1861–1911," in *Christianity and China, The Eighteenth Century to the Present: Essays in Religious and Social Change,* ed. by Daniel H. Bays (Stanford: Stanford University Press, forthcoming).
22. Evidence of attempts to breach this wall can be seen in the "to-the-people" movements of the 1920s, when urban-based university students headed for the countryside. See Laurence A. Schneider, *Ku Chieh-kang and China's New History: Nationalism and the Quest for Alternative Traditions* (Berkeley: University of California Press, 1971), pp. 121–187. Recent books on this topic include Hung Chang-tai, *Going to the People: Chinese Intellectuals and Folk Literature, 1918–1937* (Cambridge: Council on East Asian Studies, Harvard University, 1985); and Charles W. Hayford, *To the People: James Yen and Village China* (New York: Columbia University Press, 1990). Helen Siu, in her survey of short stories published as early as 1929 and as late as 1988, observes that Chinese writers who took the countryside as a subject were ill-informed:

> A major issue in the literature on peasants is that a literate elite is writing about an inarticulate peasantry whose world is far from their own but whose lives are interlocked with theirs in multiple ways. In the wake of the May Fourth period, writers indicted the old cultural tradition and the political order by describing what it had meant for the peasants to be victimized. But in treating the unawakened populace as objects of social engineering and them-

selves as the providers of that engineering, the intellectuals failed to bridge the distance between themselves and the peasants. By reifying tradition as an object of attack, they prevented themselves from reflecting on the roots of their claims to authority. [These] works [are] by those who chose to write about peasants as a way of exposing the frailty of power, peasants as objects of abuse. Most of these images of peasants should not be treated as "real." Rather, they disclose the authors' naïveté about village life and popular culture and their distance from rural reality."

See Helen Siu, "Social Responsibility and Self-expression" in her *Furrows: Peasants, Intellectuals, and the State: Stories and Histories from Modern China* (Stanford: Stanford University Press, 1990), p. 23.

23. Kuhn, "Local Self-government," p. 280. Amy Ma, in her study of Chuansha, a county located east of Shanghai, concludes, "It was a case of the same people, using the same funds for the same purposes, such as running orphanages, charity medicine, charity burial, famine relief and waterworks or road construction." Ma, p. 56. Ma points out that the gentry bureau for land reclamation *(shaju)* was restyled the "local self-government office" in the New Policies era. See Ma, pp. 67–68. For a discussion of such bureaus in nineteenth-century Guangdong see Frederic Wakeman, Jr., *Strangers at the Gate: Social Disorder in South China, 1839–1861* (Berkeley: University of California Press, 1966), pp. 152–156.

24. *Chengdu ribao,* XT1/11/8, pp. 1–2 and XT1/11/9, pp. 1–2. See especially articles 4.1, 4.2, and 5.4. The regulations governing this body specify that at any time, when at least three society members opposed the action of a gentry-manager, they could petition the society's leader and open the question for debate.

25. *Jilin xingsheng Binzhou fu zhengshu, yibian,* p. 10 and *bingbian,* p. 61.

26. *Fengtian zizhi chouban fangfa,* no. 1 (XT2/2):15–18b.

27. Ibid., 13–14b.

28. Hu Sijing memorial XT2/5/20. This was a common suspicion in Beijing. Back in 1907, when local self-government policy began to be discussed at the Ministry of Interior, high-ranking officials clearly distrusted local elites. For example, in response to a proposal by Sun Pei and Xu Chengjin to establish self-government study societies *(hui),* one official suggested that the familiar label for subordinate gentry bureaus *(ju)* be used instead. Suspecting the public-mindedness of local elites *(shenshang),* this ministry official argued that all local initiatives should require prior approval by local magistrates. See MZB, 132. Similar suspicions were voiced by censor Wang Zutong and the Bureau of Government Affairs in 1903 in

their responses to Zhao Erxun's *xiangshe* reform program in Shanxi. See Wang Zutong memorial GX29/3/6 and Bureau of Government Affairs memorial GX29/6.

29. John King Fairbank and Kwang-ching Liu, *Modern China: A Bibliographical Guide to Chinese Works, 1898–1937* (Cambridge: Harvard University Press, 1961), p. 505.

30. XZBCG, Box 25. The detailed Huichang data on the degree-holders (198) and commoners (129) eligible to vote in prefectural electoral colleges suggests that the blurring of the line between degree-holders and merchants due to the latter's access to the purchased *jiansheng* had not happened in Huichang. Most degrees were in the *shengyuan* category (165 *fusheng*, 13 *buzeng*, 13 *bulin*, 1 *linsheng*), with 3 *suigong*, 1 *engong*, 1 *bagong*, and 1 *juren* rounding out the rest of the list. None of the remaining 129 persons, most of whom qualified on the basis of property holdings, were identified as *jiansheng*.

31. Mao Zedong, pp. 64–121 *passim*. For a discussion of state-merchant relations in the late imperial period see Mann.

32. MZB, 189.2

33. *Difang zizhi zhangcheng jieshi huichao, dianwen* 104.

34. *Difang zizhi zhangcheng jieshi huichao, zilei* 13b.

35. MZB, 189.2

36. *Difang zizhi zhangcheng jieshi huichao, dianwen* 47b and 48a–b.

37. *Difang zizhi zhangcheng jieshi huichao, zilei* 13b.

38. Ibid., 12b–13b.

39. *Difang zizhi zhangcheng jieshi huichao, dianwen* 62.

40. Ibid., 61b.

41. MZB, 189.2.

42. Ibid.

43. For a socioeconomic analysis of Shengze's elite, with a special focus on elite networks throughout Wujiang county, see Kojima Yoshio, pp. 84–101. In one section of this essay Kojima looks specifically at the conflict between Chamber of Commerce head Wang Sijing and *jiansheng* who had petitioned the magistrate in early 1911 (XT3/?2) to permit a guild *(gongsuo)* to be established. Kojima argues that the chamber was dominated by Guangdong merchants living in Shengze town, merchants who had developed a reputation for opposing rural handicraft workers in the recent past. The petition by the *jiansheng* on behalf of these workers to establish a guild challenged this dominance.

The degree-holders were less advocates of handicraft workers than protectors of their own role in the industry. Lynda Bell has pointed out that a precedent for a gentry-merchant guild established in nearby Wuxi in 1902 can be found in the "culture association" *(wenshe)* established in the 1880s that focussed its efforts on cocoon-marketing activities. See Lynda Bell in Esherick and Rankin, pp. 131–132.

44. Kuhn, *Rebellion and Its Enemies,* p. 217; Kuhn, "Local Self-government under the Republic," p. 280; and Schoppa, p. 200.

45. Teraki Tokuko, pp. 16–17, Tables 1 and 2. In his study of sixteen Zhejiang gazetteers Keith Schoppa identified 532 council members at the administrative seat, town, and township levels for the period 1911–1914. Schoppa argues (p. 200) "that analysis of self-government elites provides reasonably close hypotheses about the nature of important county functional elites in general. . . . The non-self-government functional elites were by every indication men of the same type, with similar backgrounds and scope of functions as self-government elites." The lacunae in Schoppa's sources—gazetteers and newspapers—compromise such sweeping generalizations based on his painstaking compilation of biographical data on council members. Although only an approximate quarter of the men in his sample were explicitly identified as degree-holders, for most of his sample, almost a third, Schoppa only knew that these men were council members. About a fifth of his sample was identified simply as "functional elites." For Schoppa, this category included people who were associated with chambers of commerce, agricultural societies, militias, charities, schools, and public works (pp. 43–46). In core areas Schoppa found that about half of these activists were either council members or were related to council members. In areas distant from Zhejiang's major towns and cities Schoppa found the overlap to be even greater—about 75 percent.

   Although Schoppa's data are useful, he has probably underestimated the percentage of council members who were degree-holders. Since gazetteers often fail to note *jiansheng* or *shengyuan* status, many men in his categories of "functional elites" or "only self-government role known," about half of the total sample, may well have been degree-holders. If so, that would bring Schoppa's figures more in line with the composition of Hubei councils studied by Teraki Tokuko and Su Yunfeng.

46. These namelists can be found in MZB, 179 (Henan); MZB, 199 (Hunan); and MZB, 181 (Shandong). Most of the 226 Hunan students were in their thirties, although there were twenty students in their twenties, thirty-four in their forties, and four in their fifties. See also *Jilin quansheng difang zizhi choubanchu diyici baogaoshu,*

no. 1 for detailed information on a class of seventy-one students at the Jilin Provincial Self-government School. Other namelists, with less complete information, can be found for Fujian, Shaanxi, and Xinjiang. See MZB, 196; MZB, 185; and XZBCG, Box 14, respectively. For information on the thirty students making up the first class at the Suifen Department Self-government School in Jilin see *Jilin quansheng difang zizhi choubanchu diyici baogaoshu*, no. 1.

47. XZBCG, Box 14.
48. Ibid.
49. MZB, 196.
50. See petitions from Sichuan's Fushun county, Jiajiang county, Mei independent department, Kai county, and Chengkou subprefecture in Zhao Papers, Box 476.
51. Walker, p. 405.
52. STSB, GX33/6/26.
53. Constitutional Commission memorial GX34/4/26. Zhao Erxun had anticipated the commission in his address to the Hubei Provincial Self-government Bureau, which he established in January 1908. He referred to his own Shanxi reforms, Gu Yuan's *xiangguan* memorial, and models developed in Japan and Tianjin. Zhao explained the difference between the *xiangguan* and self-government models in terms of numbers: one person vs. a group. See Zhao Papers, Box 216.
54. An example of the contentious nature of local communities can be found in northern Zhejiang. In his *Xiang Lake—Nine Centuries of Chinese Life* (New Haven: Yale University Press, 1989), Keith Schoppa shows how two factions *within* a power structure vied for the attention and the support of local Qing magistrates for various development schemes. In the Hengzhu Dike Case of 1901, Magistrate Qiu supported the faction opposed to Huang Yuanshou's plan to reclaim land from Xiang Lake. This ecologically sound decision was challenged in 1903 and again in 1910, with the same result. Without the strong leadership of local magistrates, according to Schoppa, an ecologically disastrous autonomous social initiative would have gone on unchecked. See ibid., pp. 159–178. The state, then, acted correctly. But the faction led by Huang Yuanshou might certainly have thought, during the 1911 Revolution, that the collapse of the Qing *would* bring with it greater political and economic opportunities. But their local opponents might add, "at the expense of the environment and the public good." Schoppa suggests that local elites could act against the interests of the public good and that the state could defend those interests.

55. *Fengtian zizhi chouban fangfa*, no. 1 (XT2/2):15–18b.
56. Manhood suffrage was not the norm in most European countries, or countries settled by Europeans, until the end of World War I. France had reached this stage several times—in 1793, 1848, and 1875—while Britain's franchise was steadily expanded and universal manhood suffrage was attained in 1918. Prussia had instituted manhood suffrage in 1867. See Stein Rokkan, *Citizens, Elections, Parties: Approaches to the Comparative Study of the Processes of Development* (New York: David McKay Company, 1970), pp. 84–87 and 149–152. In the United States most voting restrictions on white males were lifted between 1800 and 1860. See J. Morgan Kousser, "Suffrage," in *Encyclopedia of American Political History: Studies of the Principal Movements and Ideas,* ed. Jack P. Greene (New York: Charles Scribner's Sons, 1984), III, 1238–1239. For a survey of electoral practices throughout the world at the turn of the twentieth century see Charles Seymour and Donald Paige Frary, *How the World Votes: The Story of Democratic Development in Elections* (Springfield, Mass.: C. A. Nichols Co., 1918), 2 vols. Japan is the only country in East Asia that is granted a chapter in this work.
57. MZB, 195. For the articles quoted from the imperial self-government regulations see Constitutional Commission regulations GX34/12/27, Articles 5–7.
58. For a reference to the posting of official proclamations in Jiangxi in 1909 see Sheel, p. 5.

# Select Bibliography

## DOCUMENTS

The following edicts, decrees, memorials, petitions, directives, regulations, and proclamations are arranged chronologically according to the Chinese lunar calendar for the Guangxu (GX) and Xuantong (XT) reigns. Full bibliographical data on the collections in which they appear are provided below in Archival and Published Sources.

GX8/12/16. Zhang Zhidong memorial. Wen Juntian, *Zhongguo baojia zhidu kao*, pp. 353–356.

GX25/2/14. Zhang Zhidong memorial. *[Huangchao xu] Wenxian tongkao*, p. 9631. Date given in Guo Tingyi, p. 1043.

GX27/3/3. Edict. *GXZY*, 27:8b–11b.

GX28/9/21. Shanxi provincial yamen directive. Zhao Papers, Box 31.

GX28/10/28. Zhao Erxun memorial. Quoted in Bureau of Government Affairs memorial of GX29/2/9. *ZYCS* 2 (GX29): *zhengshu tongji* 2:15b–18.

GX28/11/11. Shanxi provincial yamen directive. Zhao Papers, Box 31.

GX28/12/8. Wu Tingxie petition, Zhao Erxun directive, and *xiangshe* reform regulations. *ZYCS* 2 (GX29): *neizheng tongji* 2:10–11b.

GX29/1/26. Zhao Erxun memorial and attachment. Quoted in Bureau of Government Affairs memorial of GX29/6.

GX29/3/6. Wang Zutong memorial and attachment. Quoted in Bureau of Government Affairs memorial of GX29/5.

GX29/5. Bureau of Government Affairs memorial. *ZYCS* 2 (GX29): *zhengshu tongji* 4:29a–b.

GX29/6. Bureau of Government Affairs memorial. *ZYCS* 2 (GX29): *zhengshu tongji* 4:30–31b.

GX29/7/19. Ministry of Foreign Affairs memorial. *ZYCS* 2 (GX29): *zhengshu tongji* 6:48b–50b.

GX29/11/24. Rescripted memorial and regulations. [*Da Qing Guangxu*] *Xin faling*, 10:30–34b.

GX30/8/18. Yuan Shikai memorial. *DFZZ* 2 (GX31): *zazu* 9.

GX31/6/12. Edict. *GXZY*, 31:50b–51.

GX31/6/12. Shen Jiaben memorial. *ZYCS* 4 (GX31): *zhengshu tongji* 4:2–3.

GX31/6/20. Yuan Shikai memorial. *Donghua lu*, 194:7–8.

GX31/6/26. Yuan Shikai attachment. National Palace Museum. *Suishou dengji*.

GX31/7/12. Bureau of Government Affairs memorial. *ZYCS* 4 (GX31): *zhengshu tongji* 5:1b–2. Date given in the National Palace Museum's copy of *Suishou dengji*.

GX31/12/21. Court letter. *DFZZ* 2 (GX31): *zazu* 10.

GX32/4/6. Gu Yuan memorial. No. 1 Historical Archives. Grand Council Reference Collection of Palace Memorials.

GX32/inter.4/20. Telegram. *DFZZ* 3 (GX32): *zazu* 32.

GX32/5/24. Bureau of Government Affairs memorial. *ZYCS* 5 (GX32): *zhengshu tongji* 5:5–6b.

GX32/6/8. Ministry of Education rescripted memorial and regulations. [*Da Qing Guangxu*] *Xin faling* 7 (*jiaoyu* 3): 95–98.

GX32/7/6. Duanfang and Dai Hongci memorial. *QMCB*, I, 367–383.

GX32/7/13. Edict. *QMCB*, I, 43–44.

GX32/9/19. Compilation Commission telegram. *GXZY*, 32:42–43.

GX32/9/20. Edict. Cited in *PDPOC*, entry 339.

GX32/10/7. Zaize memorial. *ZYCS* 5 (GX32): *zhengshu tongji* 7:7b–8.

GX32/10/30. Zhao Binglin memorial. *QMCB*, II, 1059–1060.

GX32/11/18. Zhang Zhidong telegram. Zhang Zhidong, *Zhang wenxianggong quanji*, 197:19b–20b.

GX32/12/12. Shi Fujin memorial. *QMCB*, I, 488–490.

GX33/1/20. Memorial. National Palace Museum. *Sichuan sheng zougao*.

GX33/2/13. Ministry of Interior memorial. *Donghua lu*, 205:1b–2b; *GXZY*, 33:1a–b; and *DFZZ* 4 (GX33): *neiwu* 158–161.

GX33/2. Yuan Shikai memorial. *Rongan dizi ji*, 4:17b.

GX33/3/18. Zhao Erxun memorial. *QMCB*, II, 716–718.

GX33/4/13. Cen Chunxuan memorial. *QMCB*, I, 497–503. Date is for submission of memorial; rescripted on GX33/4/30.

GX33/4/30. Rescript to Cen Chunxuan's GX33/4/13 memorial. National Palace Museum. *Suishou dengji*.

GX33/5/27. Rescripted memorial and regulations. *QMCB*, I, 503–510.

GX33/6/19. Yuan Shikai memorial. No. 1 Historical Archives. Special Collection of Documents on Constitutional Government, Box 33, Document 144.

GX33/7/5. Edict. *QMCB*, I, 45.

GX33/7/18. Duanfang memorial. *QMCB*, I, 46–47.

GX33/7/22. Yuan Shikai memorial. *QMCB*, II, 719–723.

GX33/8/13. Edict. *QMCB*, II, 606.

GX33/8/23. Edict. *GXZY*, 33:49b.

GX33/8. Bureau of Government Affairs memorial. *ZYCS* 6 (GX33): *zhengshu tongji* 4:8–9b.

GX33/9/13. Edict. *QMCB*, II, 667.

GX33/9/14. Regulations. [*Da Qing Guangxu*] *Xin faling*, 10:41b–43.

GX33/12/4. Feng Xu memorial and Anhui regulations. MZB, 192.

GX34/4/26. *QMCB*, II, 723–724.

GX34/5/17. Sichuan regulations. MZB, 205.

GX34/6/6. Yin Mingze and Zhou Xuyi petition. Zhao Papers, Box 493.

GX34/6/24. Rescripted Constitutional Commission memorial and regulations. *QMCB*, II, 667–683. Does not include election regulations.

GX34/7/17. Ministry of Interior directive. *DFZZ* 5 (GX34): *jizai* 114–115. Date from archival draft in MZB, 162.

GX34/8/1. Edict and Constitutional Commission implementation schedule. *QMCB*, I, 61–68.

GX34/9/26. Sichuan regulations. Zhao Papers, Box 329.

GX34/12/27. Constitutional Commission memorial and regulations. *QMCB*, II, 724–741; and *ZZGB*, GX34/12/28 (election regulations).

XT1/inter.2/23. Ministry of Interior implementation schedule. *ZZGB*, XT1/3/6.

XT1/3/16. Constitutional Commission memorial and regulations. *QMCB*, II, 745–748.

XT1/4. Zhao Erxun memorial. *ZZGB*, XT1/5/2.

XT1/12/27. Constitutional Commission memorial and regulations. *ZZGB*, XT2/1/8.

XT2/5/6. Sun Baoqi memorial. Quoted in Constitutional Commission memorial of XT2/7/20 in *ZZGB*, XT2/7/22.

XT2/5/20. Hu Sijing memorial. *Tuilu shugao*, 2:29–34.

XT2/10/3. Edict. *QMCB*, I, 68–69.

XT2/11/1. Li Jingxi memorial. MZB, 207.

XT2/11/13. Constitutional Commission memorial. *QMCB*, II, 796–800.

XT2/12/17. Edict, Constitutional Commission memorial, and implementation schedule. *QMCB*, I, 88–92.

XT2/12/27. Ministry of Interior memorial. *ZZGB*, XT3/1/16.

XT3/3/18. Zhu Jiabao memorial. XZBCG, 13.

## ARCHIVAL AND PUBLISHED SOURCES

Adshead, S. A. M. *Province and Politics in Late Imperial China: Viceregal Government in Szechwan, 1898–1911*. London: Curzon Press Ltd., 1984.

Allee, Mark A. *Law and Local Society in Late Imperial China: Northern*

*Taiwan in the Nineteenth Century*. Stanford: Stanford University Press, forthcoming.

Applegate, Celia. *A Nation of Provincials: The German Idea of Heimat*. Berkeley: University of California Press, 1990.

Ayers, William. *Chang Chih-tung and Educational Change in China*. Cambridge: Harvard University Press, 1971.

Bastid-Brugiere, Marianne. "Currents of Social Change," in John K. Fairbank and Kwang-ching Liu, eds.

Bays, Daniel H. *China Enters the Twentieth Century: Chang Chih-tung and the Issues of a New Age, 1895–1909*. Ann Arbor: University of Michigan Press, 1978.

*Beiyang gongdu leizuan* 北洋公牘類纂 (A classified collection of documents from the Beiyang yamen). Comp. Gan Houzi 甘厚慈. Beijing: Yisen yinshua, 1907.

*Beiyang guanbao* 北洋官報 (Beiyang gazette). Tianjin.

Bell, Lynda S. "From Comprador to County Magnate: Bourgeois Practice in the Wuxi County Silk Industry," in Joseph W. Esherick and Mary Backus Rankin, eds.

Bland, J. O. P. *Recent Events and Present Policies in China*. London: William Heinemann, 1912.

Boorman, Howard L., ed. *Biographical Dictionary of Republican China*. 5 vols. New York: Columbia University Press, 1967–1979.

Borthwick, Sally. *Education and Social Change in China: The Beginnings of the Modern Era*. Stanford: Hoover Institution Press, 1983.

Britton, Roswell. *The Chinese Periodical Press, 1800–1912*. Shanghai: Kelly and Walsh, 1933.

Brunnert, H. S. and V. V. Hagelstrom. *Present Day Political Organization of China*. Shanghai: Kelly and Walsh, 1912.

Cameron, Meribeth E. *The Reform Movement in China, 1898–1912*. Stanford: Stanford University Press, 1931.

Cao Rulin 曹汝霖. *Yisheng zhi huiyi* 一生之回憶 (Remembering one's life). Hong Kong: Chunqiu zazhi she, 1966.

Chang, Chung-li. *The Chinese Gentry: Studies on Their Role in Nineteenth-century Chinese Society*. Seattle: University of Washington Press, 1955.

Chang, Hao. *Liang Ch'i-ch'ao and Intellectual Transition in China, 1890–1907*. Cambridge: Harvard University Press, 1971.

Chen, Jocelyn. "Huang Tsun-hsien and Japanese Influence on the 1898 Reforms," *Journal of the Oriental Society of Australia* 6:16–32 (1968–1969).

Chen Ke. "Non-governmental Organizations and the Urban Control and Management System in Tianjin at the End of the Nineteenth Century," *Social Sciences in China* 4:54–77 (1990).

*Chengdu ribao* 成都日報 (Chengdu daily). Sichuan.

Ch'ü T'ung-tsu. *Local Government in China under the Ch'ing*. Cambridge: Harvard University Press, 1962.

Cohen, Paul A. and John E. Schrecker, eds. *Reform in Nineteenth-century China*. Cambridge: East Asian Research Center, Harvard University, 1976.

Collected Explications. See *Minzheng bu difang zizhi zhangcheng jieshi huichao.*

de Bary, Wm. Theodore. *The Liberal Tradition in China*. New York: Columbia University Press, 1983.

Dennerline, Jerry. *Qian Mu and the World of Seven Mansions*. New Haven: Yale University Press, 1988.

*Difang zizhi zhangcheng jieshi huichao*. See *Minzheng bu difang zizhi zhangcheng jieshi huichao.*

*Difang zizhi zhi gangyao* 地方自治制綱要 (An outline of systems of local self-government), ed. Qian Run 錢潤. 2 vols. Shanghai: Shangwu yinshuguan, 1907.

*Dongfang zazhi* 東方雜志 (Eastern miscellany). Shanghai.

*Donghua lu* 東華錄 (Records from within the Flowery Gate), comp. by Zhu Shoupeng 朱壽朋. Shanghai: Jicheng tushu, 1909.

Duanfang 端方. *Duan Zhongmin gong zougao* 端忠敏公奏稿 (Draft memorials of Duanfang). 1918. Reprint. Taibei: Wenhai chubanshe, 1967.

Duara, Prasenjit. *Culture, Power, and the State: Rural North China, 1900–1942*. Stanford: Stanford University Press, 1988.

Elvin, Mark. "The Gentry Democracy in Chinese Shanghai, 1905–1914," in Jack Gray, ed., *Modern China's Search for a Political Form*. London: Oxford University Press, 1969.

——— . "The Administration of Shanghai, 1905–1914," in Mark Elvin and G. William Skinner, eds., *The Chinese City between Two Worlds*. Stanford: Stanford University Press, 1974.

Esherick, Joseph W. *Reform and Revolution in China: The 1911 Revolution in Hunan and Hubei*. Berkeley: University of California Press, 1976.

——— and Mary Backus Rankin, eds. *Chinese Local Elites and Patterns of Dominance*. Berkeley: University of California Press, 1990.

Fairbank, John K., ed. *The Cambridge History of China*. Vol. 10. Cambridge: Cambridge University Press, 1978.

——— and Kwang-ching Liu, eds. *The Cambridge History of China*. Vol. 11. Cambridge: Cambridge University Press, 1980.

Fang Hanqi 方漢奇. *Zhongguo jindai baokan shi* 中國近代報刊史 (A history of modern Chinese journalism). Taiyuan: Shanxi renmin chubanshe, 1981.

Fang Zhaoying 房兆楹, comp. *Qingmo minchu yangxue xuesheng timinglu chuji* 清末民初洋學學生題名錄初輯 (First collection of namelists of students in foreign or new-style schools of the late Qing and early Republic). Taibei: Zhongguo jindaishi yanjiusuo, 1962.

*Fazheng guanhua bao* 法政官話報 (Law and administration gazette). Tianjin.

Feng Guifen 馮桂芬. "Fuxiang zhiyi" 復鄉職議 (A proposal to restore local rule), in Feng Guifen. *Jiaobinlu kangyi* 校邠廬抗議 (Essays of protest from Feng Guifen's studio). 1:12–14 (1884).

*Fengtian zizhi chouban fangfa* 奉天自治籌辦方法 (Methods for preparing for self-government in Fengtian). Shenyang: Fengtian zizhi choubanchu, 1910–1911.

Fincher, John H. *Chinese Democracy: The Self-government Movement in Local, Provincial, and National Politics, 1905–1914*. London: Croom Helm, 1981.

*Foreign Relations of the United States*. Washington, D.C.: U.S. State Department.

Fung, Edmund S. K. *The Military Dimension of the Chinese Revolution: The New Army and Its Role in the Revolution of 1911*. Vancouver: University of British Columbia Press, 1980.

Ge Gongzhen 戈公振. *Zhongguo baoxue shi* 中國報學史 (A history of journalism in China). 1927. Reprint. Taibei: Xuesheng shuju, 1976.

Gneist, Rudolph. *The History of the English Constitution*, tr. Philip A. Ashworth. 2 vols. New York: G. P. Putnam's Sons, 1886.

———. *Selfgovernment: Communalverfassung und Verwaltungsgerichte in England* (Self-government: The [old] constitution of local authority and the [new] jurisdictions of local government). Berlin: Verlag von Julius Springer, 1871.

*Guangdong difang zizhi yanjiulu* 廣東地方自治研究錄 (Guangdong Local Self-government Research [Society] Memoirs). Guangzhou: Guangdong difang zizhi yanjiushe.

*Guangdong xianzheng choubeichu baogaoshu* 廣東憲政籌備處報告書 (Guangdong Constitutional Government Preparation Office Reports).

*Guangxu zhengyao* 光緒政要 (Important political events for the Guangxu reign), comp. Shen Tongsheng 沈桐生. Shanghai: Chongyi tang, 1909.

Guo Tingyi 郭廷以. *Jindai Zhongguo shishi rizhi* 近代中國史事日誌 (A chronology of events in modern Chinese history). Taibei: Shangwu yinshuguan, 1963.

*Guofeng bao* 國風報 (Talk of the Nation). Shanghai.

Hayes, James. *The Hong Kong Region, 1850–1911: Institutions and Leadership in Town and Countryside*. Hamden, Conn.: Shoestring Press, 1977.

*Henan quansheng ziyiju choubanchu diyici baogaoshu* 河南全省諮議局籌辦處第一次報告書 (Henan Province Provincial Assembly Preparation Office Reports, No. 1).

Ho, Ping-ti. *Studies on the Population of China.* Cambridge: Harvard University Press, 1959.

*Hōrei zenshu: Meiji nenkan* 法令全書: 明治年間 (Compilation of laws and ordinances: Meiji period). Tokyo: Naikaku kampo kyoku.

Hsiao, Kung-ch'uan. *Rural China: Imperial Control in Nineteenth Century China.* Seattle: University of Washington Press, 1960.

———. *A Modern China and a New World: K'ang Yu-wei, Reformer and Utopian, 1858–1927.* Seattle: University of Washington Press, 1975.

Hu Sijing 胡思敬. *Tuilu shugao* 退廬疏稿 (Draft memorials from Tuilu), in *Tuilu quanji* 退廬全集 (Collected works from Tuilu). 1918. Reprint. Taibei: Wenhai chubanshe, 1970.

Hummel, Arthur W., ed. *Eminent Chinese of the Ch'ing Period (1644–1912).* 2 vols. Washington, D.C.: Government Printing Office, 1943.

Ichiko Chuzo. "Political and Institutional Reform, 1901–1911," in John K. Fairbank and Kwang-ching Liu, eds.

Ishii, Ryosuke, ed. *Japanese Legislation in the Meiji Era*, tr. William J. Chambliss. Vol. 10 of *Japanese Culture in the Meiji Era.* Tokyo: Centenary Culture Council, 1958.

Jansen, Marius. "Japan and the Chinese Revolution of 1911," in John K. Fairbank and Kwang-ching Liu, eds.

*Japan Weekly Mail.* Yokohama.

*Jiading xian xuzhi* 嘉定縣續誌 (Gazetteer for Jiading county, Jiangsu, continued). 1926.

*Jiangsu* 江蘇. Tokyo: Jiangsu tongxiang hui, 1903–1908.

*Jiangsu fazheng xuetang jiangyi* 江蘇法政學堂講議 (Lectures [given at] Jiangsu Law School).

*Jilin gongshu zhengshu* 吉林公署政書 (Official documents of the Jilin provincial government). Jilin: Jilin sheng zhengfu, 1908.

*Jilin guanbao* 吉林官報 (Jilin gazette).

*Jilin quansheng difang zizhi choubanchu diyici baogaoshu* 吉林全省地方自治籌辦處第一次報告書 (Jilin Province Local Self-government Preparation Office Reports, No. 1).

*Jilin xingsheng Binzhou fu zhengshu* 吉林行省賓州府政書 (Official documents from Binzhou prefecture, Jilin province). Jilin, 1910.

*Jilin ziyiju diyiniandu baogaoshu* 吉林諮議局第一年度報告書 (Jilin Provincial Assembly Reports, First year).

*Jingbao* 京報 (Beijing gazette).

[*Huangchao*] *Jingshi wenbian* 皇朝經世文編 (Collected writings on statecraft from the period of the reigning dynasty). 1826. Reprint. Taibei: Wenhai chubanshe, 1972.

*Jinian Xinhai geming qishi zhounian qingnian xueshu taolunhui lun wen xuan* 紀念辛亥革命七十週年青年學術討論會論文選 (Selected essays from the conference of young scholars on the seventieth anniversary of the 1911 Revolution). Beijing: Zhonghua shuju, 1983.

Kamachi, Noriko. *Reform in China: Huang Tsun-hsien and the Japan Model.* Cambridge: Council on East Asian Studies, Harvard University, 1981.

Kang Youwei 康有為. "Gongmin zizhi" 公民自治 (Citizen self-government), in Zhang Nan 張枬 and Wang Renzhi 王忍之, eds. *Xinhai geming qianshinianjian shilun xuanji* 辛亥革命前十年間時論選集. Vol. 1. 172–190. Beijing: Sanlian shudian, 1960.

Kojima Yoshio 小島淑男. "Shinchō makki no toshi to nōson: Kōnan chihō o chūshin ni" 清朝末期の都市と農村：江南地方を中心に (City and village in the Late Qing: The Jiangnan region), *Shichō* (Historical tide) n.s., no. 8:84–101 (1980).

Kuhn, Philip A. *Rebellion and Its Enemies in Late Imperial China: Militarization and Social Structure, 1796–1864.* Cambridge: Harvard University Press, 1970.

———. "Local Self-government under the Republic: Problems of Control, Autonomy, and Mobilization," in Frederic Wakeman, Jr., and Carolyn Grant, eds., *Conflict and Control in Late Imperial China.* Berkeley: University of California Press, 1975.

———. "Late Ch'ing Views of the Polity," in *Select Papers from the Center for Far Eastern Studies,* no. 4:1–18 (1979–1980).

Kwong, Luke S. K. *A Mosaic of the Hundred Days: Personalities, Politics, and Ideas of 1898.* Cambridge: Council on East Asian Studies, Harvard University, 1984.

Landauer, Carl. *Corporate State Ideologies: Historical Roots and Philosophical Origins.* Berkeley: Institute of International Studies, University of California, 1983.

Lee, Leo Ou-fan, and Andrew J. Nathan. "The Beginnings of Mass Culture: Journalism and Fiction in the Late Ch'ing and Beyond," in David Johnson, Andrew J. Nathan, and Evelyn S. Rawski, eds., *Popular Culture in Late Imperial China.* Berkeley: University of California Press, 1985.

Li Jiannong. *The Political History of China, 1840–1928,* tr. Ssu-yu Teng and Jeremy Ingalls. Stanford: Stanford University Press, 1967.

Li Kan 李侃 and Gong Shuduo 龔書鐸. "Wuxu bianfa shiqi dui 'Jiaobinlu kangyi' de yici pinglun" 戊戌變法時期對"校邠廬抗議"的一次評論 (A review of "Essays of Protest from Feng Guifen's Studio" during the 1898 reforms), *Wen wu* (Cultural Artifacts), no. 266:53–59 (July 1978).

Li Pengnian 李鵬年. "Zhao Erxun quanzong dang'an gaishu" 趙爾巽全宗

檔案概述 (A general explanation of the Zhao Erxun archives), *Qingdai dang'an shiliao congbian* (Collections of historical sources from the Qing Archives), no. 8:395–419 (1982).

Li Zongyi 李宗一. *Yuan Shikai zhuan* 袁世凱傳 (A biography of Yuan Shikai). Beijing: Zhonghua shuju, 1980.

Liu, Kwang-ching. "Nineteenth-Century China: The Disintegration of the Old Order and the Impact of the West," in Ho Ping-ti and Tang Tsou, eds., *China in Crisis*, vol. 1. Chicago: The University of Chicago Press, 1968.

Liu Ruxi 劉汝錫. "Xianzheng bianchaguan yanjiu" 憲政編查館研究 (A study of the Constitutional Commission). M.A. Thesis. National Taiwan Normal University, 1977.

Lojewski, Frank A. "Reform Within Tradition: Feng Kuei-fen's Proposals for Local Administration," *Tsing Hua Journal of Chinese Studies*, n.s., 11.1 and 2:147–159 (December 1975).

Ma, Amy Fei-man. "Local Self-government and the Local Populace in Ch'uan-sha, 1911," in *Select Papers from the Center for Far Eastern Studies*, no. 1:47–84 (1975–1976).

*Macheng xianzhi xubian* 麻城縣志讀編. (Continuation of gazetteer for Macheng county, Hubei). 1935.

MacKinnon, Stephen R. *Power and Politics in Late Imperial China: Yuan Shi-kai in Beijing and Tianjin, 1901–1908*. Berkeley: University of California Press, 1980.

McLaren, W. W., ed. "Japanese Government Documents, 1867–1889," *Transactions of the Asiatic Society of Japan* 42 (1914).

Maltbie, Milo Roy. *English Local Government of To-day: A Study of the Relations of Central and Local Government*. New York: Faculty of Political Science of Columbia University, 1897.

Mann, Susan. *Local Merchants and the Chinese Bureaucracy, 1750–1950*. Stanford: Stanford University Press, 1987.

Mao Zedong. *Report from Xunwu*, tr. Roger R. Thompson. Stanford: Stanford University Press, 1990.

Mayers, William Frederick. *The Chinese Government: A Manual of Chinese Titles, Categorically Arranged and Explained, with an Appendix*. 3rd. ed., rev. G. M. H. Playfair. 1897. Reprint. Taibei: Ch'eng-wen Publishing Co., 1970.

Meienberger, Norbert. *The Emergence of Constitutional Government in China (1905–1908): The Concept Sanctioned by the Empress Dowager*. Bern: Peter Land, 1980.

Min Tu-ki. *National Polity and Local Power: The Transformation of Late Imperial China*, eds. Philip A. Kuhn and Timothy Brook. Cambridge: Council on East Asian Studies and the Harvard-Yenching Institute, Harvard University, 1989.

*Minzheng bu difang zizhi zhangcheng jieshi huichao* 民政部地方自治章程解釋彙鈔 (Ministry of Interior's collected explications of local self-government regulations). Beijing: Minzheng bu, 1911.

Morrison, Esther. "The Modernization of the Confucian Bureaucracy: A Historical Study of Public Administration." Ph.D. dissertation, Radcliffe College, 1959.

Nai Xuan 耐軒. "Zizhi zhi shiyi" 自治制釋義 (An explanation of the system of self-government), *Jiangsu*, no. 4:1–8 (1903).

Nathan, Andrew J. "The Late Ch'ing Press: Role, Audience, and Impact," in *Proceedings of the International Conference on Sinology: Section on History and Archaeology*, III. Taibei, 1981.

*Nongan xian baogaoshu* 農安縣報告書 (Nongan county, Jilin, reports).

*North China Herald*. Shanghai.

Ocko, Jonathan K. "The British Museum's Peking Gazettes," *Ch'ing-shih wen-t'i* 2.9:35–49 (1973).

Pearson, Thomas S. *Russian Officialdom in Crisis: Autocracy and Local Self-government, 1861–1900*. Cambridge: Cambridge University Press, 1989.

Perdue, Peter C. *Exhausting the Earth: State and Peasant in Hunan, 1500–1850*. Cambridge: Council on East Asian Studies, Harvard University, 1987.

Playfair, G. M. H. *The Cities and Towns of China: A Geographical Dictionary*. 2nd ed. Shanghai: Kelly and Walsh, 1910.

Polachek, James. "Gentry Hegemony: Soochow in the T'ung-chih Restoration," in Frederic Wakeman, Jr., and Carolyn Grant, eds., *Conflict and Control in Late Imperial China*. Berkeley: University of California Press, 1975.

Prazniak, Roxann. "Community and Protest in Rural China: Tax Resistance and County-Village Politics on the Eve of the 1911 Revolution." Ph.D. dissertation, University of California, Davis, 1981.

*Qingmo choubei lixian dang'an shiliao* 清末籌備立憲檔案史料 (Historical archival documents on preparations for constitutional government in the late Qing). Beijing: Zhonghua shuju, 1979.

*Quanguo Zhongwen qikan lianhe mulu, 1833–1949* 全國中文期刊聯合目錄 (Union list of Chinese periodicals), comp. by Quanguo tushu lianhe mulu bianji zubian. Beijing: Shumu wenxian chubanshe, 1981.

Rankin, Mary Backus. *Early Chinese Revolutionaries: Radical Intellectuals in Shanghai and Chekiang, 1902–1911*. Cambridge: Harvard University Press, 1971.

————. *Elite Activism and Political Transformation in China: Zhejiang Province, 1865–1911*. Stanford: Stanford University Press, 1986.

————. "The Origins of a Chinese Public Sphere: Local Elites and Community Affairs in the Late Imperial Period," *Études chinoises* 9.2:13–60 (Autumn 1990).

Redlich, Josef. *Local Government in England*, ed. Francis W. Hirst. 2 vols. London: MacMillan, 1903.

Reynolds, Douglas R. "A Golden Decade Forgotten: Japan-China Relations, 1898–1907," *Transactions of the Asiatic Society of Japan*, 4th ser., 2:93–153 (1987).

Richard, Timothy. *Forty-five Years in China*. New York: Frederick A. Stokes, 1916.

*Rongan dizi ji* 容菴弟子記 (Biography of Yuan Shikai), comp. by Shen Zuxian 沈祖憲 and Wu Kaisheng 吳闓生. Taibei: Wenxing shudian, 1962.

Rowe, William T. *Hankow: Conflict and Community in a Chinese City, 1796–1895*. Stanford: Stanford University Press, 1989.

Sanetō, Keishū 實藤惠秀. *Chūgokujin Nihon ryūgaku shi* 中國人日本留學史 (A history of Chinese students in Japan), tr. Tan Ruqian 譚汝謙 and Lin Qiyan 林啟彥 under the title *Zhongguoren liuxue Riben shi* 中國人留學 日本史. Beijing: Sanlian shudian, 1983.

Schoppa, R. Keith. *Chinese Elites and Political Change: Zhejiang Province in the Early Twentieth Century*. Cambridge: Harvard University Press, 1982.

*Shandong quansheng difang zizhi choubanchu disanci baogaoshu* 山東全省 地方自治籌辦處第三次報告書 (Shandong Provincial Local Self-government Preparation Office Reports, No. 3).

Sheel, Kamal. *Peasant Society and Marxist Intellectuals in China: Fang Zhimin and the Origin of a Revolutionary Movement in the Xinjiang Region*. Princeton: Princeton University Press, 1989.

Shen, Huaiyu 沈懷玉. "Qingmo difang zizhi zhi mengya, 1898–1908" 清末 地方自治之萌芽: 1898–1908 (The sprouts of local self-government in the late Qing, 1898–1908), *Zhongyang yanjiuyuan jindaishi yanjiusuo jikan* (Bulletin of the Institute of Modern History, Academia Sinica), no. 9:291–320 (1980).

*Shinmatsu minsho Chūgoku kanshin jinmeiroku* 清末民初中國官紳人名錄 (Biographical dictionary of gentry and officials of the late Qing and early Republic), comp. Tahara Tennan 田原禎次. Beijing: chūgoku kenkyūka, 1918.

*Shuntian shibao* 順天時報 (Shuntian [Beijing] Times). Beijing.

*Sichuan ziyiju choubanchu diyici baogaoshu* 四川諮議局籌辦處第一次報告書 (Sichuan Provincial Assembly Preparation Office Reports, No. 1).

Skinner, G. William. "Cities and the Hierarchy of Local Systems," in G. William Skinner, ed., *The City in Late Imperial China*. Stanford: Stanford University Press, 1977.

Smith, J[oshua] Toulmin. *Government by Commissions Illegal and Perni-cious. The Nature and Effects of all Commissions of Inquiry and other Crown-appointed Commissions. The Constitutional Principles of Taxa-tion; and the Rights, Duties, and Importance of Local Self-government.* London: S. Sweet, 1849.

————. *Local Self-government and Centralization: The Characteristics of Each; and its Practical Tendencies, as affecting Social, Moral, and Politi-cal Welfare and Progress.* London: John Chapman, 1851.

————. *Local Self-government Un-mystified. A Vindication of Common Sense, Human Nature, and Practical Improvement, against the Mani-festo of Centralism Put Forth at the Social Science Association, 1857.* 2nd ed. London: Edward Stanford, 1857.

————. *The Parish. Its Powers and Obligations at Law, as regards the Wel-fare of every Neighbourhood, and in Relation to the State: Its Offices and Committees: and the Responsibility of every Parishioner. With Illustrations of the Practical Working of this Institution in all Secular Affairs; and of some Modern Attempts at Ecclesiastical Encroachments.* 2nd ed. London: H. Sweet, 1857.

Staubitz, Richard Louis. "The Establishment of the System of Local Self-government (1888–90) in Meiji Japan: Yamagata Aritomo and the Meaning of 'Jichi' (Self-government)." Ph.D. dissertation, Yale Univer-sity, 1973.

Steiner, Kurt. *Local Government in Japan.* Stanford: Stanford University Press, 1965.

Strand, David. *Rickshaw Beijing: City People and Politics in the 1920s.* Berkeley: University of California Press, 1989.

Su Yunfeng 蘇雲峯. "Qingmo Hubei shishen jieceng zhi tuibian" 清末湖北士紳階層之蛻變 (The transformation of the Hubei gentry in the late Qing). *Si yu yan* (Thought and speech) 17:327–342 (1979).

*Suishou dengji* 隨手登記 (Record book of documents handled by the Grand Council). Grand Council Archives, National Palace Museum, Taibei.

Sun E-tu Zen. "The Constitutional Missions of 1905–1906," *Journal of Modern History* 24:251–269 (1952).

Sun Yirang 孫詒讓. *Zhouli zhengyao* 周禮政要 (The political essentials of the Rites of Zhou). Ruian, Zhejiang, Pujin xuetang, 1902.

Sung Wook Shin. "Reform Through Study Societies in the Late Ch'ing Period, 1895–1900: The Nan hsueh-hui," in Paul A. Cohen and John E. Schrecker, eds.

Syed, Anwar Hussain. *The Political Theory of American Local Govern-ment.* New York: Random House, 1966.

Teraki Tokuko 寺木德子. "Shinmatsu minkoku shonen no chihō jichi" 清末民國初年の地方自治 (Local self-government in the late Qing and early Republic), *Ōchanomizu shigaku* (Ōchanomizu historical studies), no. 5:14–30 (1962).

*Tianjin zizhi ju wenjian luyao* 天津自治局文件錄要 (Important documents from the Tianjin Self-government Bureau). Tianjin.

Tocqueville, Alexis de. *The Old Régime and the French Revolution*, tr. Stuart Gilbert. Garden City, N.Y.: Doubleday, 1955.

United States, Department of State. General Records of the Department of State. Record Group 59. Numerical and Minor Files of the Department of State (1906–1910). Microfilm Series 862. National Archives, Washington, D.C.

————. Records of the Peking Legation of the Department of State. Record Group 84. *Despatches from Tientsin*. National Archives, Washington, D.C.

Walker, Mack. *German Home Towns: Community, State, and General Estate, 1648–1871*. Ithaca: Cornell University Press, 1971.

Wang Di 王笛. "Qingmo Sichuan liuRi xuesheng shugai" 清末四川留日學生述概 (A general sketch of Sichuanese in Japan in the late Qing), *Sichuan daxue xuebao* (Sichuan University Journal) 1987.3:80–92.

Wang Jiajian 王家儉. "Wan Qing difang xingzheng xiandaihua de tantao, 1838–1911" 晚清地方行政現代化的探討, 1838–1911 (Modernization of local administration during the later Qing period, 1838–1911), *Lishi xuebao* (History Journal), no. 8:181–235 (1980).

Wang Shuhuai 王樹槐. "Qingmo Jiangsu difang zizhi fengchao" 清末江蘇地方自治風潮 (Local self-government and disturbances in Jiangsu in the late Qing). *Zhongyang yanjiuyuan jindaishi yanjiusuo jikan* (Bulletin of the Institute of Modern History, Academia Sinica), no. 6:313–327 (1977).

Wang Xiaoqiu 王曉秋. "Huang Zunxian 'Riben guozhi' chutan" 黃遵憲《日本國誌》初探 (A preliminary inquiry into Huang Zunxian's *Riben guozhi*). *Jindai lishi yanjiu* (Studies on modern history) 1980.3:182–187.

Wang, Yeh-chien. *Land Taxation in Imperial China, 1750–1911*. Cambridge: Harvard University Press, 1973.

Wen Juntian 聞鈞天. *Zhongguo baojia zhidu kao* 中國保甲制度考 (An investigation into the baojia system in China). Shanghai: Shangwu yinshuguan, 1935.

[*Huangchao xu*] *Wenxian tongkao* 皇朝續文獻通考 (An overview through documents of the reigning dynasty, continued), comp. Liu Jinzao 劉錦藻. 1936. Reprint. Taibei: Xinxing shuju, 1965.

Wright, Mary Clabaugh, ed. *China in Revolution: The First Phase, 1900–1913*. New Haven: Yale University Press, 1968.

Wu Tingxie 伍廷燮. "Jingmu ziding nianpu" 景牧自訂年譜 (Wu Tingxie's chronological autobiography), *Guoshiguan guankan* (Bulletin of the Historiography Institute) 1.4:*zhuanzhu* 48–56.

Wu Xingrang 吳興讓. "Difang zizhi zhi yanjiu" 地方自治之研究 (A study of local self-government), *Beiyang fazheng xuebao*, no. 12 (January 1907).

[*Da Qing Guangxu*] *Xin faling* 大清光緒新法令 (New laws and ordinances of the Guangxu reign). Shanghai: Shangwu yinshuguan, 1909.

*Xinhai geming* 辛亥革命 (The 1911 Revolution), comp. Chai Degeng 柴德賡 et al. 8 vols. Shanghai: Renmin chubanshe, 1957.

*Xinhai geming qianshinianjian minbian dang'an shiliao* 辛亥革命前十年間民變檔案史料 (Historical documents on popular uprisings in the ten years before the 1911 Revolution), ed. Zhongguo diyi lishi dang'anguan and Beijing shifan daxue lishixi (No. 1 Historical Archives and Beijing Normal University, History Department). 2 vols. Beijing: Zhonghua shuju, 1985.

*Xinhai geming qianshinianjian shilun xuanji* 辛亥革命前十年間時論選集 (A selection of essays written in the ten years before the 1911 Revolution), ed. Zhang Nan 張枬 and Wang Renzhi 王忍之. 3 vols. Beijing: Sanlian shudian, 1960–1977.

*Xinhai geming shi* 辛亥革命史 (A history of the 1911 Revolution). Zhang Kaiyuan 章開源 and Lin Zengping 林增平 et al., eds. 3 vols. Beijing: Renmin chubanshe, 1981.

*Xinhai geming shiqi qikan jieshao* 辛亥革命時期期刊介紹 (An introduction to publications in the era of the 1911 Revolution). 5 vols. Beijing: Zhongguo shehui kexueyuan jindaishi yanjiusuo, 1982–1987.

Yang Shouqi 楊壽祺. "Difang zizhi chuyi" 地方自治芻議 (Simple thoughts on local self-government), in *Minguo jingshi wenbian* 民國經世文編 (Collected writings on statecraft from the Republican period) 15:17b–24b. 1914. Reprint. Taibei: Wenhai chubanshe, 1970.

Ye Longyan 葉龍彥. "Qingmo minchu zhi fazheng xuetang (1905–1919)" 清末民初之法政學堂 (1905–1919) (Law schools in the late Qing and early Republic). M.A. thesis, Zhongguo wenhua xueyuan, Shixue yanjiusuo, 1974.

[*GuangXuan*] *YiJing xuzhi* 光宣宜荊續誌 (Gazetteer for Yixing and Jingqi counties, Jiangsu, during the Guangxu and Xuantong reigns). 1921.

Young, Ernest P. *The Presidency of Yuan Shih-k'ai: Liberalism and Dictatorship in Early Republican China.* Ann Arbor: University of Michigan Press, 1976.

*Yuan Shikai zouyi* 袁世凱奏議 (Memorials of Yuan Shikai). Liao Yizhong 廖一中 and Luo Zhenrong 羅真容, eds. 3 vols. Tianjin: Tianjin guji chubanshe, 1987.

Zhang Jinglu 張靜廬. *Zhongguo xiandai chuban shi ziliao* 中國現代出版史資料 (Historical sources on contemporary publishing in China). Beijing: Zhonghua shuju, 1956.

Zhang Pengyuan 張朋園. *Lixian pai yu Xinhai geming* 立憲派與辛亥革命 (Constitutionalists and the 1911 Revolution). 2nd ed. Taibei: Zhongyang yanjiuyuan jindaishi yanjiusuo, 1983.

Zhang Yufa 張玉法. *Qingji de lixian tuanti* 清季的立憲團體 (Constitutional organizations of the Qing period). Taibei: Zhongyang yanjiuyuan jindaishi yanjiusuo, 1971.

———. "Qingmo minchu de Shandong difang zizhi" 清末民初的山東地方自治 (Local self-government in Shandong at the end of the Qing and the beginning of the Republic), *Zhongyang yanjiuyuan jindaishi yanjiusuo jikan* (Bulletin of the Institute of Modern History, Academica Sinica), no. 6:159–184 (1977).

Zhang Zhidong 張之洞. *Zhang wenxianggong quanji* 張文襄公全集 (Complete works of Zhang Zhidong), ed. Wang Shu'nan 王樹枏. 6 vols. 1937. Reprint. Taibei: Wenhai chubanshe, 1970.

Zhao Binglin 趙炳麟. "Guangxu dashi huijian" 光緒大事彙鑑 (A compilation of important events in the Guangxu reign), in *Zhao Boyan ji* 趙柏巖集 (Works of Zhao Binglin). 1922. Reprint. Taibei: Wenhai chubanshe, 1968.

Zhao Erxun 趙爾巽. Zhao Erxun dang'an 趙爾巽檔案 (Zhao Erxun papers). No. 1 Historical Archives, Beijing.

Zheng Li. 鄭里 "Qingdai zhongyang junzheng jiguan de dang'an" 清代中央軍政機關的檔案 (Archives of the Qing central government organizations), *Gugong bowuyuan yuankan* (Bulletin of the National Palace Museum) 1979.4:72–83.

*Zhengyi congshu* 政藝叢書 (Annual compilations of the "Art of Government [Journal]"). Shanghai.

*Zhengzhi guanbao* 政治官報 (Government administration gazette). Beijing.

*Zhongguo jindai qikan bianmu huilu* 中國近代期刊篇目彙錄 (Modern Chinese periodicals: a compilation of tables of contents), comp. Shanghai tushuguan. 3 vols. Shanghai: Shanghai renmin chubanshe, 1965–1984.

*Zhongguo jindaishi cidian* 中國近代史詞典 (A dictionary of modern Chinese history). Shanghai: Shanghai cishu chubanshe, 1982.

Zhu Xianhua 朱先華. "Qing Minzheng bu jianshu" 清民政部簡述 (An overview of the Qing Ministry of Interior), *Qingdai dang'an shiliao congbian* (Collections of historical sources from the Qing Archives), no. 9:275–288 (1983).

# Character List

Omitted from this list are proper names indexed in either Arthur W. Hummel, ed., *Eminent Chinese of the Ch'ing Period*, or Howard L. Boorman, *Biographical Dictionary of Republican China*; and subprovincial jurisdictions appearing in "Administrative Cities of China arranged alphabetically under their provinces," a set of lists appended to G. M. H. Playfair, *The Cities and Towns of China*. Names and titles appearing in the Bibliography are also omitted.

*Anhui guanbao* 安徽官報

bagong 拔貢
bai shi li 百十里
Baihu 白湖
baihua 白話
bao 堡
baojia 保甲
baosong 保送
*Beiyang fazheng xuebao* 北洋法政學報
"Bianfa pingyi" 變法評議
Bianzhi guan 編制館
bing 稟
bulin 補廩
bushi wenzi 不識文字
buzeng 補增

canyi ting 參義廳
canyu zhengzhi 參與政治
*Changsha ribao* 長沙日報
cheng (petition) 呈
cheng (administrative seat) 城
"Cheng zhen xiang difang zizhi zhangcheng" 城鎮鄉地方自治章程
"Chengzhai riji" 澄齋日記
chihō jichi 地方自治

"Chouban difang zizhi jianzhang" 籌辦地方自治簡章
choubanchu 籌辦處
chuoji 戳記
cun 村
cundong 村董

dianbao 電報
diaohan 刁悍
diaoshen liejian 刁紳劣監
*Dibao* 邸報
die 牒
difang 地方
difang shenshi 地方紳士
*Difang xingzheng zhidu* 地方行政制度
difang yihui 地方議會
difang zizhi 地方自治
difang zizhi jiangxi hui 地方自治講習會
Difang zizhi ke 地方自治科
*Difang zizhi qianshuo* 地方自治淺説
Difang zizhi xuanju ju 地方自治選舉局
Difang zizhi yanjiu hui 地方自治研究會
difang zizhi yanjiusuo 地方自治研究所
dong 董
*Dongsansheng ribao* 東三省日報
dongshi 董事
dongshihui 董事會

engong 恩貢

fansheng 繁盛
fazheng jiangxi suo 法政講習所
fazheng sucheng ke 法政速成科
fazheng xuetang 法政學堂
Fei Tinghuang 費廷璜
fengjian 封建
Fotan 佛曇
"Fu ting zhou xian difang zizhi zhang-
    cheng" 府廳州縣地方自治章程
*Fujian ribao* 福建日報
fusheng 附生

Gelao hui 哥老會
gong 公
gongju 公舉
*Gonglun xinbao* 公論新報
gongmiao 公廟
gongmin 公民
*Gongmin bidu* 公民必讀
gongmin yangcheng suo 公民養成所
"Gongmin zizhi" 公民自治
Gongmin zizhi yanjiu hui 公民自治研究會
gongsheng 貢生
gongsuo 公所
gongtui 公推
gongyi 公議
Gongyi jiyihui 公益集議會
gongzheng 公正
gongzheng shenqi 公正紳耆
gongzheng shenshi 公正紳士
gongzhi 公直
Gongzhong dang 宮中檔
Gu Yuan 顧瑗
guan (official; government) 官
guan (to manage) 管
guanbao 官報
guanbao ju 官報局
guandu shenban 官督紳辦
Guangdong difang zizhi yanjiushe 廣東地
    方自治研究社
*Guangdong difang zizhi yanjiushe chou-
    zhenchu baogaoshu* 廣東地方自治研究社
    籌賑處報告書
Guangdong xianzheng choubeichu 廣東憲
    政籌備處
*Guangxi guanbao* 廣西官報
guanzhi (official rule) 官治
guanzhi (administrative system) 官制
guohui 國會
guojia 國家
guomin 國民

*Heilongjiang guanbao* 黑龍江官報
Henan quansheng ziyiju choubanchu 河南
    全省諮議局籌辦處
Huang Shizuo 黃世祚
*Hubei guanbao* 湖北官報
hui 會
huidong 會董
huishou 會首
huiyuan 會員
*Hunan fazheng yanjiulu* 湖南法政研究錄
*Hunan guanbao* 湖南官報
*Hunan tongsu yanshuobao* 湖南通俗演説報

jiandu 監督
Jiang Bingzhang 蔣炳章
Jianghu hui 江湖會
*Jiangsu fazheng xuetang xuean* 江蘇法政學
    堂學案
Jiangsu jiaoyu zonghui 江蘇教育總會
*Jiangxi guanbao* 江西官報
jiangxi hui 講習會
jiangxi suo 講習所
jiansheng 監生
jiaolian suo 教練所
jiaoyu hui 教育會
jichi dantai 自治團體
jie 界
jiguan daihao 機關代號
Jilin difang zizhì yanjiu zonghui 吉林地方
    自治研究總會
Jin Bangping 金邦平
Jin Zhanlin 金湛霖
*Jinbao* 晉報
jingli 經理
jingshi 經世
jinshi 進士
Jiujiang shanghui 九江商會
ju 局
jumin 居民
Junjichu lufu zouzhe 軍機處錄副奏摺
junxian 君縣
juren 舉人
jushen 局紳

ke 課
kōmin 公民

li (measurement) 里
li (principle) 理
li (clerk) 吏
Li bu (Ministry of Ritual) 禮部
Li bu (Ministry of Personnel) 吏部

Li Jiaju 李家駒
Li Shuen 李澍恩
liang 兩
Liang Qinggui 梁慶桂
liangnuo 良懦
liangzhi 良知
lianzhuang hui 聯莊會
lianzong 練總
lijia 里甲
lijin 釐金
Lin Kunxiang 林鵾翔
Ling Fupeng 淩福彭
linsheng 廩生
linshi tuanlian 臨時團練
Liu Tieyun 劉鐵雲
Liulichang 琉璃廠
liuzhong 留中
lizheng 里正
Lu Bingzhang 陸炳章

mending 門丁
Meng Zhaochang 孟昭常
minju 民舉
minquan 民權
mintuan 民團
Minzheng bu 民政部
minzheng zhang 民政長
minzhi kaitong 民知開通
Minzhi si 民治司
minzhu 民主
mu 畝

*Nanfang ribao* 南方日報
Nantai 南台
Nanxue hui 南學會
*Neige guanbao* 內閣官報
Ning Shifu 甯世福

Pan Mingdian 潘明典
Peng Zijing 彭子經
pi 批
pian 片
pianpi 偏僻
pingdeng 平等

qi 氣
Qi Shukai 齊樹楷
qianze xiaoshuo 譴責小説
qicheng hui 期成會
qingdan 清單
*qingyi bao* 清議報
qu 區

quanxue suo 勸學所
qun 羣

Sanhe hui 三合會
shaju 沙局
*Shandong guanbao* 山東官報
"Shandong sheng Zhangqiu dengchu qishi zhou xian choushe yishihui canshihui chengji biao" 山東省章邱等處七十州縣籌設議事會參事會成績表
*Shangbao* 商報
Shanghai shangwu zonghui 上海商務總會
Shangwu fenhui 商務分會
*Shangwu guanbao* 商務官報
shangyu 上諭
Shantou 汕頭
*Shanxi baihua yanshuobao* 山西白話演説報
Shao Congen 邵從恩
she 社
shen 紳
Shen Rongzhao 沈蓉照
*Shenbao* 申報
shendong 紳董
shendong gongsuo 紳董公所
shendong ju 紳董局
shengjian 生監
shengyuan 生員
Shengze 盛澤
shenmin 紳民
shenqi 紳耆
shenshang 紳商
shenshi 紳士
shenshi hui 紳士會
sheshou 社首
shezhang 社長
shi 士
Shi Fujin 史履晉
"Shiban Tianjin xian difang zizhi zhang-cheng" 試辦天津地方自治章程
*Shibao* 時報
shimin 士民
shishen 士紳
shiyong 試用
Shizheng gongyi hui 市政公議會
Shizheng gongyi hui 市政公益會
Shuanglin 雙林
*Shubao* 蜀報
*Shunde gongbao* 順德公報
shuotie 説帖
si 私
*Sichuan guanbao* 四川官報
*Sichuan sheng zougao* 四川省奏稿
"Sichuan Suiding fu Taiping xian cheng

zhen xiang difang zizhi quyu biao" 四
川綏定府太平縣城鎮鄉地方自治區域表
[Sichuan] tongsheng zizhi yanjiusuo 〔四
川〕通省自治研究所
sijia zhi bao 私家之報
sixuan yuan 司選員
Song Yuren 宋育仁
Songyu 松毓
*Subao* 蘇報
sui 歲
suigong 歲貢
Sun Pei 孫培
Sun Songling 孫松齡
suo 所
Susheng difang zizhi diaocha yanjiu hui
蘇省地方自治調查研究會
Susheng fazheng xuetang 蘇省法政學堂
Suzhou 蘇州

tangpi 堂批
*Tianjin riri xinwen* 天津日日新聞
ting 廳
tingcheng 廳丞
tingji 廷寄
tiqian 提前
tiyao 提要
tongsheng 童生
tuanlian 團練
tuanti 團體
tuanzong 團總
tun 屯

Ume Kenjirō 梅謙次郎

Wang Bing'en 王秉恩
Wang Sijing 汪思敬
Wang Tongyu 王同愈
Wang Xianbin 王賢賓
Wang Zutong 王祖同
weiyuan 委員
weizhang 圩長
wen 文
wenshe 文社
Wu Xingrang 吳興讓
wuduan 武斷
*Wuxu zhengbian ji* 戊戌政變記

xia yiyuan 下議院
xian 縣
xiang 鄉
xiang shendong 鄉紳董
xiangbao 鄉保

*Xiangbao* 湘報
xiangcun 鄉村
xiangcun shendong 鄉村紳董
xiangguan 鄉官
xiangli 鄉里
xiangqi 鄉耆
xiangshe 鄉社
"Xiangting zhizhi" 鄉亭之職
xiangyue 鄉約
xiangzhang 鄉長
xiangzheng 鄉正
Xianzheng bianchaguan 憲政編查館
Xianzheng yanjiu hui 憲政研究會
Xianzheng zhuanti 憲政專體
xianzhi difang guan 縣之地方官
xiezhu yuan 協助員
Ximen 西門
*Xinglun ribao* 興論日報
*Xinmin congbao* 新民叢報
xinzheng 新政
Xiong Zhaowei 熊兆渭
xu 序
Xu Chengjin 徐丞錦
xuanjiang suo 宣講所
xuanju 選舉
xuanmin 選民
xuansong 選送
xue qu 學區
*Xuebu guanbao* 學部官報
xunfu 巡撫
Xunjing bu 巡警部
Xunwu 尋烏

Yan Fengge 閻鳳閣
Yang Shipeng 楊士鵬
Yang Xiangeng 楊先庚
yanjiusuo 研究所
yi 移
Yin Mingze 殷銘澤
yishen 邑紳
yishi ting 議事廳
yishihui 議事會
you gongzhong tuiju 由公眾推舉
youzhong gongju 由眾公舉
yu 諭
yuan 元
Yubei lixian gonghui 預備立憲公會
Yun Yuding 惲毓鼎

Zeng Qingbang 曾慶榜
zha 扎
zhaizhang 寨長

Zhang Luxiang 張履祥
Zhang Shutang 張樹棠
zhangcheng 章程
*Zhejiang chao* 浙江潮
*Zhejiang guanbao* 浙江官報
zhen 鎮
zhendong 鎮董
Zhengwu chu 政務處
*Zhengyi tongbao* 政藝通報
zhengzhi 政治
zhi 旨
zhihui 知會
zhili ting 直隸廳
zhili zhou 直隸州
zhong 眾
zhongdeng 中等
*Zhongwai ribao* 中外日報
zhou 州
Zhou Xuyi 周敘彝
zhuanxi suo 傳習所
zi 自
zishou 自守

ziyiju 諮議局
ziyiju choubanchu 諮議局籌辦處
zizhi 自治
zizhi choubanchu 自治籌辦處
zizhi hui 自治會
zizhi ju 自治局
zizhi qishen 自治其身
zizhi qu 自治區
*Zizhi ribao* 自治日報
zizhi tuanti 自治團體
Zizhi xiangtuan ju 自治鄉團局
zizhi yanjiu ban 自治研究班
zizhi yanjiu hui 自治研究會
zizhi yanjiu ju 自治研究局
zizhi yanjiusuo 自治研究所
zizhi zhi 自治制
zizhu 自主
Zong xuehui 總學會
zongdu 總督
Zongli yamen 總理衙門
zouzhe 奏摺

# Index

Administration, county, 31–32, 56, 77, 90, 129, 185n34, 222n55

Administration, local, 144–146; descriptions of, 18–19, 85, 95, 103, 188n31, 191n49; assessments of, 25–26, 219n22; calls for reform of, 26–31, 33–35, 84, 90, 156–157, 211n2; and gentry bureaus, 62, 84, 95–96, 103, 105, 145, 230n23. *See also* Election districts; Elites, local; Reform model

Administration, metropolitan, 90. *See also individual ministries and commissions*

Administration, provincial, 32, 77, 90–91, 94, 190n47. *See also individual provinces*

Administration, theories of, 11–12, 19, 26–27, 74. *See also* "Local self-government"; Reform model; *Xiangguan*

Administrative seat *(cheng), see* Election districts: defined in regulations

Anhui, 59, 97, 114–115, 118

Assemblies, provincial, 83, 94, 97, 109, 110, 114, 140; electorate for, 68, 139, 140, 231n30. *See also* Bureaus, consultative

Baojia, *see* Security, local

Bastid, Marianne, 213n22

*Beiyang guanbao*, 41–42, 97

Bell, Lynda, 231n43

Bianzhi guan, *see* Compilation Commission

Bland, J. O. P., 117, 141

Boards *(dongshihui):* prototypes of and proposals for, 39, 79; imperial calls for (pre-1909), 77, 80, 96; imperial regulations for, 86; membership of, 120–121, 123

Bucher, Lothar, 15, 160

Bureau of Government Affairs, 32, 33, 34, 35, 38, 81, 230n28

Bureaucracy, 27, 45, 93–94, 101, 186n12, 189n34, 211n2

Bureaus, consultative, 68, 96–97, 101, 110, 140–141, 204n68. *See also* Assemblies, provincial

Cameralism, 73–74

Cameron, Meribeth, 84–85, 207n25

Cao Rulin, 136, 208n42

Cen Chunxuan, 24, 42

Centralization, 71, 74–75, 94–95, 104, 155, 211n11

Chamber of Commerce, 58, 64, 148–149

Chang, Chung-li, 139, 185n35

Chen Baozhen, 7

Chen Kuilong, 60, 102

Chen Tianhua, 98

*Cheng* (administrative seat), *see* Election districts: defined in regulations

Chengdu City Council, 131–133

Citation conventions, 171, 183n16, 198n7

Civil-service examination system, *see* Examination system

*Collected Explications*, 126–130, 142, 150

Communication, official, 32, 40, 41–42, 49–50, 131–132, 150, 183n16, 195n22; between administrative levels, 24–25, 40, 60, 92, 126, 234n58; and reporting on constitutional reform, 115–125

Communities, local, 25–26, 29–33, 79, 188n31, 217n53

*Index*

# Harvard East Asian Monographs